Heta Aali, Anna-Leena Perämäki, Cathleen Sarti (eds.)
Memory Boxes

(in collaboration with Jörg Rogge and Hannu Salmi)

Mainz Historical Cultural Sciences | Volume 22

Editorial

The **Mainzer Historische Kulturwissenschaften** [Mainz Historical Cultural Sciences] series publishes the results of research that develops methods and theories of cultural sciences in connection with empirical research. The central approach is a historical perspective on cultural sciences, whereby both epochs and regions can differ widely and be treated in an all-embracing manner from time to time. Amongst other, the series brings together research approaches in archaeology, art history, visual studies, literary studies, philosophy, and history, and is open for contributions on the history of knowledge, political culture, the history of perceptions, experiences and life-worlds, as well as other fields of research with a historical cultural scientific orientation.
The objective of the **Mainzer Historische Kulturwissenschaften** series is to become a platform for pioneering works and current discussions in the field of historical cultural sciences.

The series is edited by the Co-ordinating Committee of the Research Unit Historical Cultural Sciences (HKW) at the Johannes Gutenberg University Mainz.

HETA AALI, ANNA-LEENA PERÄMÄKI, CATHLEEN SARTI (EDS.)

Memory Boxes

An Experimental Approach to Cultural Transfer in History, 1500-2000

(in collaboration with JÖRG ROGGE and HANNU SALMI)

[transcript]

Bibliographic information published by the Deutsche Nationalbibliothek
The Deutsche Nationalbibliothek lists this publication in the Deutsche Nationalbibliografie; detailed bibliographic data are available in the Internet at http://dnb.d-nb.de

Cover: Kordula Röckenhaus, Bielefeld
Print: Majuskel Medienproduktion GmbH, Wetzlar
Print-ISBN 978-3-8376-2786-2
PDF-ISBN 978-3-8394-2786-6

Content

Preface

This book is the result of a cultural and scientific exchange between the members of the Department of Cultural History at the University of Turku (Finland) and the members of the Special Research Unit "Historical Cultural Sciences" at the Johannes Gutenberg University in Mainz (Germany).

This binational project started in 2011 and was funded by the Academy of Finland and the German Academic Exchange Service (DAAD) in 2012 and 2013. The funding enabled us to organise two meetings of the project group in Turku and in Mainz each year.

We like to thank DAAD and the Academy of Finland for their financial support. We also thank the Special Research Unit at Mainz University and the Cultural History Department of the University of Turku for providing additional resources during the project and the publishing of this volume.

On behalf of the project group
Jörg Rogge (Mainz) and Hannu Salmi (Turku)

Memory Boxes

An Experimental Approach to Cultural Transfer in History, 1500–2000

JÖRG ROGGE AND HANNU SALMI

A memory box, or a keepsake box, is associated with romantic fiction and childhood culture. It has often been a wooden chest, made for storing mementos. As cultural artefacts memory boxes have their own long history; they can be interpreted as artefactual expressions of the self, as vehicles of memory as well as transmitters of material reminiscences of the past to the future.

In her book *Cultural Memory and Western Civilization* (2011, originally published as *Erinnerungsräume*, 1999) Aleida Assmann points out that the Latin word for box is *arca*, the ark, which, as in the case of Noah's Ark, can be interpreted as a safe refuge. The Israelites, in turn, took the Ark of the Covenant with them into the desert in order to be able to preserve the Ten Commandments.[1] The ark, like a memory box, is a portable container that can be used to transmit memories.

It seems that, towards the end of the nineteenth century, the term memory box also gained allegorical layers and the human mind was often described as a box. In 1890, *The Leeds Mercury* reported on a strange recovery of memory. The editor wrote:

1 ASSMANN, 2011, pp. 101f.

> Physicians are, I believe, able to adduce many cases in which people whose minds have, owing to some sudden shock, become, so to speak, a total blank as regards events which happened before the blow fell which upset the balance on their memory box, have had their recollections all at once restored by some old familiar sight or sound supplying the key-note, as it were, of the long-forgotten tune.[2]

Here, the human brain is like a box of memories, a fragile chest that can be emptied by a sudden shock.

Despite the fact that the history of keepsake boxes would be fascinating in its own right, this book is based on the metaphorical use of the term. The major motive for this book is the fact that a memory box offers ample possibilities for experimentation. As already the concrete use of the word refers to something (memory) being isolated from its surroundings (box) in order to make it portable, it seems possible to apply the idea of memory box in the analysis of cultural transfer. Since a memory box is a container of memories, or includes material references to memory, it can be a means for cultural transfer not only between borders in a social and geographical sense but also for temporal shifts from the past to the present and from the present to the future. Cultural transfer is often viewed from the perspective of synchronic displacements, but the notion of a memory box would also set this synchronic movement into the context of diachronic transfer.

Aleida Assmann points out, that places of memory should not be studied merely on a temporal, vertical axis, as something that derive from the past and prove to be meaningful for the future: memories also have horizontal ramifications. It is important to question the kind of spatial and material manifestations memories have. Assmann considers memory boxes to be "objects in which important documents are preserved".[3] In the book *Cultural Exchange in Early Modern Europe* (2007), the German historian Bernd Roeck also refers to these materialisations in arguing that "there are instances of *Erinnerungsschachteln* (packets or boxes of memories): every artefact was a container which already contained legacies from the past when it was being made".[4]

2 The Leeds Mercury, 12 April 1890.
3 Assmann, 2011, p. 101.
4 Roeck, 2006, p. 11.

Before going further, it is important to relate these thoughts to recent debates on cultural interaction. It seems that there has been a gradual change in the key concepts employed by researchers of the field. Notions such as cultural diffusion, assimilation and acculturation have been replaced to a large extent by more interactive concepts, like cultural transfer, cultural translation, cultural interaction and cultural exchange.[5] The movements between cultures are, more often than not, seen as cases of two-way traffic than unidirectional influences. The historian Peter Burke has emphasised the notion of *transculturation,* which was originally coined by the Cuban sociologist and folklorist Fernando Ortiz. Burke stresses reciprocal interaction between cultures, intercultural traffic where influences transgress borders in a two-way manner.[6] The emphasis on trans*cultural* seems to be more flexible than the concept of trans*national* that has become increasingly popular during the last decades. As the historian of technology, Erik van der Vleuten, has pointed out there are different uses of the concept transnational, stressing such features as fluidity, circulation and flow as well as connections and relationships.[7] Still, transnationalism is obviously bound together by the notions of nation and nationality and therefore cannot be applied to older history without problems. Thus, the book at hand focuses on the transcultural rather than the transnational.

Burke further supported the idea of cultural hybridity in history, the fact that there have always been flows over borders. There are manifold examples of cultural artefacts that cannot be considered as products of one single culture: they are hybrids.[8] On other hand, in order to be able to argue that there can be such things as cultural hybrids in the first place, there has to be an assumption that cultures are entities with boundaries that can be deciphered. And, further, if there are boundaries, there must be various transfer processes between cultures.

Bernd Roeck made an effort to conceptualise transfer processes in cultural interactions. As Roeck defines, cultural transfer refers to "something that has been 'transferred' from one culture to another – a process with an active giver and a completely passive receiver", while cultural exchange implies a "more dynamic process involving an interaction between 'giver' and 'receiver'".[9] To

5 WENDLAND, 2012, pp. 51-55.
6 BURKE, 1997, p. 158.
7 VAN DER VLEUTEN, 2008, p. 978.
8 BURKE, 2009.
9 ROECK, 2007, pp. 3f.

be sure, the concept of cultural transfer can be separated from the notion of cultural exchange which covers the wide array of material and immaterial flows over borders. The essential feature is not the traffic itself but the fact that cultures are transformed, and continuously transform themselves, by and with these interactions.

There are, however, two remarks to be made. In contrast to Roeck's view, cultural transfer does not necessarily imply an "active sender" or a "passive recipient". Transfer can be seen as a general concept that refers to any kind of cultural displacement: something may be transferred without active impetus, but on the other hand it may entail two-way or perhaps even multi-centred flows. This is important from the perspective of memory box as a theoretical and methodological tool: in our view, the box is an agent of cultural displacement. Again, the very notions of cultural transfer and cultural exchange seem to suggest that cultures are not open by definition but entities with borders to be transgressed.

Usually, cultural exchange and transfer have been studied as synchronic processes on a horizontal level by concentrating on those cultural entities that exist simultaneously. Here, cultural negotiation can happen on multiple levels, as suggested by the recent discussion on *histoire croisée*.[10] The aim of this collection is, however, to expand the notion of cultural transfer so that it applies also to the traffic between past and present cultures or different layers of temporality in the past. If cultural transfer is seen as an event that has its spatial ramifications in history, it also has to have an itinerary and thus a dimension in time. It is crucial to acknowledge that exchange has always a temporal perspective and, thus, can be interpreted as diachronic, vertical transfer.

In the case of past and present cultures it may of course be argued that the traffic has to be unilateral by nature, the past being able to transfer things to the future, while the present phenomena cannot be transferred to the past. Still, it is intriguing to consider those situations when, through historical writing and historical imagination, the present transfers its own cultural features into the past where they are etched into the image of the past to such an extent that these cultural representations again are seen to influence what later came into being.

In order to be able to combine the analysis of both horizontal and vertical transfers, this book covers different geographical areas in Europe and North

10 WERNER/ZIMMERMANN, 2006, pp. 30-50.

America, from Scotland to Italy and Germany and from Finland and France to the transatlantic colonies. The time span of the book runs from the Early Modern Europe to the present day. The scope of the book is however not defined by its geographical and historical focus, but by the particular notion it attempts to emphasise: the *memory* box. To be able to elaborate the concept further, it is important to consider the topical discussions on the nature of memory, especially cultural memory, in greater detail. What are memories that ultimately become boxes? In popular imagination, memory boxes are linked with the intimate aspects of memory, while the debate on history and memory has often emphasised the collective side of remembering. Obviously, memory boxes are also used to trigger memory.

During recent decades, cultural historians have focused on the pre-requisites, manifestations, functions and effects of different forms of social memory and memories within particular social groups. They have been particularly interested in the part that texts, media and artefacts play and have played, in the construction of collective memory as well as the storage and circulation of their components of knowledge.[11]

The researchers of memory and remembrance have especially focused on the functions of memory for individuals, current social groups and societies. In this respect it is important to consider the difference between collective memory and cultural memory. The term collective memory was coined by the French sociologist Maurice Halbwachs in his book *La mémoire collective* (1950). Halbwachs argued that all memory is collective memory because memory depends on social environment. Individual recollections do not just combine and thus create something that can be called collective memory. It is the social environment that shapes individual memories into a coherent collective memory. Therefore, the individual and the social memories of groups determine each other. Halbwachs' idea was that individual memory emerges from the communication of social groups, because the individual can only remember what is jointly discussed in the communication between the members of a social formation. He applied this model of collective memory to enduring, cohesive communities such as families and social classes. An individual could, therefore, contribute and subscribe to multiple collective memories, each shaped by the groups to which he or she belonged.[12]

11 LANDWEHR, 2009, p. 52.
12 GREEN, 2008, pp. 104f.

Halbwachs' notion of the collective memory was later picked up by Jan Assmann who developed the notion of communicative memory which encompasses a variety of collective memories based on everyday communication. This form of memory is similar to the exchanges in oral culture or memories collected (and made collective) through oral history methods. This form of memory needs the active participation of the members of a generation or contemporaries. Therefore this form of collective memory ranges back a mere 80 or 100 years at the most.

Instead of communicative memory, Jan Assmann is interested in, what he calls cultural memory. He applies this form of memory to the stock of knowledge responsible for the internal cohesion of societies. Cultural memory works like a filter and determines which kind of knowledge is retained through the times. This cultural memory works in a synchronic way at a specific point in history as well as in diachronic way over a longer period.[13]

Cultural memory has a particular relevance for cultures as every culture develops a connective structure which unites its members. The connective structure manages the bond within a culture by providing its members with mutual rules and values on one hand and the remembrance of a shared past – invented or not – on the other.

One important question is how cultures manage to remember over long periods of time and in which way they do so. Important means are external memories (*Speicher*) which function as carriers of cultural sense, values and traditions and can be used by contemporaries if needed. Of course, the most important of these carriers is scripture, but rituals, pictures, music, narratives and artefacts are also important because they too preserve everything that is fundamental for the identity and orientation of a community independent of its individual members.

The cultural memory is the storage location (*Speicherort*) which helps – by the use of diverse media – to produce meaning and sense from a shared history, in order to enable social action on the principle of overlapping experiences and expectations.[14]

Communicative memory and cultural memory are the two main concepts of collective memory, which are used by historians and other researchers interested in how the past was or is used by individuals, social groups, political parties, societies and so forth. In both concepts memory is a social issue, which

13 ASSMANN, 1992; ASSMANN, 2008, pp. 111-118.

14 LANDWEHR, 2009, p. 54.

helps to create meaning or interpret the world people live in. Every member of a given social group or society takes part in the communicative memory of his/her generation or family, and they use the storage locations of cultural memory which are transferred to them over the centuries.

It is obvious that cultural memory is not a unified entity controlled only by a few powerful interpreters. In principle all members of a society can take part in the dynamic process which does not refer to a simple and known past, but creates different memory cultures. There is no one dominating memory but a heterogeneity of cultural memories; they "are sites of conflicts in which the mnemonic interests of different cultural groups and their interpretations of the past are publicly negotiated and discussed in regard to their legitimate validity."[15]

Storage locations have played and are still playing a crucial role in this dynamic process and the disputes between different cultural groups about the interpretations of the past. However, in the last decade the focus on the artefacts has shifted from the cultural artefact as a product to an interest in the way those artefacts circulate and influence their environment. Ann Rigney has stressed that the dynamics of cultural memory, the process how this kind of memory has been and is created, is now more important than the products of memory.[16]

***

In this book, we understand memory boxes as cultural constructions that are involved in the process of making and disputing memory but which, simultaneously, are important agents for cultural transfer over space and time. This book emphasises memory box as an idea that allows us to study the cultural processes of transfer in conjunction with cultural memory.

In our view, a memory box is based on the idea of isolation: it is applicable with cultural processes that isolate specific objects from their original context and, thus, give them a mobile nature. It is important to note that the question of isolation is something that is seen in the past, that happens as a cultural practice or through random changes in circumstances but our approach as cultural historians is strongly contextualising by nature. The question of

15 NEUMANN/ZIEROLD, 2012, pp. 225-248, quote 237.
16 RIGNEY, 2008, pp. 345-353.

isolation also involves the idea that there are breaks and ruptures in the history of remembering. Here, we see a difference to reception history or *Wirkungsgeschichte*. Instead of focussing on the layered, cumulative receptions of the particular object, the emphasis on memory boxes, or memory-box-ness, is on the ruptures of reception and concentrates on, for example, a particular moment in history when the memories about the past are revitalised or reinterpreted.

A memory box is a carrier or a container of cultural meanings, symbols, emotions and memories. It involves a particular kind of inertia in a sense that the social construction of a memory box can be seen as a set of practices that separate a group of objects from their surroundings and give them a different temporal rhythm. Memory box encapsulates cultural features for later, potential activation. In our use of the term, a memory box needs to be perceived and opened in order to be conceived as a chest of memories from the past. Its very nature as a container of "important documents", to draw on Assmann, or symbols and meanings is actualised only when it has moved forward in time and become an effective transmitter between the past and the present.

The aim of this book is to study those cultural practices that produce those isolated, accumulated and layered receptions about the past that can be called memory boxes. This aim has two edges: on one hand, we can study those practices in the past that produce memory boxes by isolating and layering memories, but on the other hand we have to first identify those memory boxes from the flow of history. How people of the past constructed memory boxes to make sense of their past and to move their interpretations and representations over to the next generations? What features do we have to find from the past in order to identify a memory box?

In the subsequent part of the book, the articles can be seen as experiments that have different focal points. It contains articles on the intentional creation (Anna-Leena Perämäki, Juhana Saarelainen, Matthias Schnettger) and the accidental creation (Hannu Salmi) of memory boxes. The book also includes cases where a particular moment in reception creates the memory-box-ness by giving a strong interpretation of its contents (Heta Aali, Kristina Müller-Bongard, Asko Nivala, Cathleen Sarti, Alexandra Schäfer). There are also articles that concentrate on the material, on the carrier of memories (Jörg Rogge, Hannu Salmi).

In our approach, memory boxes are cultural constructions of intersubjective quality. They are not personal inventions but culturally shared. This book aims to be an experiment in history, and we have tested the fruitfulness of the concept of memory box in three different settings; naturally, several other approaches may also have been possible. We aim at interpreting *topoi*, material artefacts and representations of historical figures, personalities as memory boxes. Thus, the book is divided into three sections, and each section has a separate introduction on how to approach *topoi*, artefacts and personalities as agents of diachronic and synchronic cultural transfer.

List of References

ASSMANN, ALEIDA, Cultural Memory and Western Civilization: Functions, Media, Archives, Cambridge 2011.

ASSMANN, JAN, Communicative and Cultural Memory, in: Cultural Memory Studies. An international and interdisciplinary Handbook, ed. by ASTRID ERLL/ANSGAR NÜNNING, Berlin 2008, pp. 109-118.

ID., Das kulturelle Gedächtnis. Schrift, Erinnerung und politische Identität in frühen Hochkulturen, München 1992,

BURKE, PETER, Cultural Hybridity, Cambridge 2009.

ID., Varieties of Cultural History, Cambridge 1997.

GREEN, ANNA, Cultural History, New York 2008.

LANDWEHR, ACHIM, Kulturgeschichte, Stuttgart 2009.

NEUMANN, BIRGIT/ZIEROLD, MARTIN, Cultural Memory and Memory Cultures, in: Travelling Concepts for the Study of Culture, ed. by BIRGIT NEUMANN/ANSGAR NÜNNING, Berlin 2012, pp. 225-248.

RIGNEY, ANN, The Dynamics of Remembrance: tests between monumentality and morphing, in: Cultural Memory Studies An international and interdisciplinary Handbook, ed. by ASTRID ERLL/ANSGAR NÜNNING, Berlin 2008, pp. 345-353.

ROECK, BERND, Introduction, in: Cultural Exchange in Early Modern Europe. Vol. IV: Forging European Identities, 1400–1700, ed. by HERMAN ROODENBURG, Cambridge 2006, pp. 1-30.

VAN DER VLEUTEN, ERIK, Toward a Transnational History of Technology: Meanings, Promises, Pitfalls, in: Technology and Culture 49, 4 (2008), pp. 974-994.

WENDLAND, ANNA VERONIKA, Cultural Transfer, in: Travelling Concepts for the Study of Culture, ed. by BIRGIT NEUMANN/ANSGAR NÜNNING, Berlin 2012, pp. 45-66

WERNER, MICHAEL/ZIMMERMANN, BÉNEDICTE, Beyond Comparison: Histoire croisée and the Challenge of Reflexivity, in History and Theory 45 (2006), pp. 30-50.

Topoi as a Memory Box

KRISTINA MÜLLER-BONGARD, ASKO NIVALA, CATHLEEN SARTI, ALEXANDRA SCHÄFER

Topoi are collections of stereotypical textual and visual images pertaining to a place or time, or an idea. Referring to *topoi* can be a powerful rhetorical tool, especially because they unconsciously evoke emotions, connotations and preset images and ideas in the audience,[1] and are thus able to legitimate things without having to rely on elaborate arguments. A *topos* is a non-material, metaphorical place, often used as a rhetorical means to structure an argument through categorisation and classification.[2] For instance, the *topoi* discussed in the following articles – massacre, martyrdom, Golden Age and providence – already evoke certain expectations and ideas. Applying a familiar line of argument enables one to persuade the audience by using ideas and connotations associated with the *topos* without explicitly naming them. However, it can also transfer inherent implicit meanings without the speaker's intention. Relying on common knowledge in a specific community, *topoi* belong to culturally shared hermeneutic preconceptions – including prejudices – that guide and regulate the interpretation of texts or images in a specific culture.

Applying the general definition of memory box as elaborated in the introduction of this book, all *topoi* can be approached as memory boxes.

1 See e.g. KOSELLECK, 1972, p. XVI.

2 The Greek word τόπος (*topos*, pl. *topoi*) means literally a place. The term *topos* is variously translated in English as commonplace, topic or line of argument. In classical rhetoric, *topos koinos* referred to commonplaces, which were used as a base for standardised arguments, see ARISTOTLE, *Rh.* 1358a. The Latin word for *topos* was *locus communis*. See further CICERO, 1983. See also CURTIUS, 1993 (1948), p. 79.

Compared with previous research on *topoi*, the methodological approach related to the concept of a memory box offers the possibility to approach *topoi* from a new angle. The concept of a memory box enables the often very abstract *topos* to be connected with concrete historical events and communities. Moreover, this approach allows to analyse the changes of meaning, respectively layers of meaning, of a certain *topos* by opening the memory box in a particular historical situation. It therefore focuses rather on a diachronic than a synchronic perspective. Nevertheless, *topoi* can also be transferred through space; however, they require shared cultural knowledge to be recognised as memory boxes.

Looking at *topos* as a memory box highlights two characteristics of *topoi*: inertia and movement. The history of *topoi* is typically studied by focusing on long-durational time levels, where meanings change relatively slowly. In contrast to this, *topos* as a memory box is always disclosed in a particular historical setting. In other words, all following four articles are going to study memory boxes as closed *packets* from the past that are opened in several past moments as well as in the present. Concentrating on certain carefully selected past moments instead of the development of long processes enables the historian to grasp the multiplicity of the past situation with an open future without a pre-determined end or some anachronistic *telos* projected to the past.

Concentrating on the moment(s) of opening the existing memory box, i.e. uses of the *topos* in certain historical situations, demands special attention to the interaction between the various agents and other factors in the communication process (e.g. author, speaker or painter; the chosen media; and the receiving audience). The aim, the function and the reception related to the public opening of the memory box can differ significantly. For instance, the speaker wants to imply a certain meaning with the usage of a specific *topos*, yet his audience may associate different things with this *topos*. *Topoi* may also have some media-specific traits or follow conventions of a specific (literary) genre. The person opening the memory box may aim to emphasise some aspects of the *topos*, but is not able to control completely the associated interpretative process.

Topoi as research objects are often approached by the principles taken from the *Begriffsgeschichte* (conceptual history),[3] i.e. concentrating on the change of meaning over time and the relevance of *topoi* for the study of society and structures. Compared to this, the concept of memory box concentrates on

3 See KOSELLECK, 1972, especially pp. XXIf.

selected moments of openings and their contexts, demanding a broader selection of sources than mere *Höhenkammliteratur*. The sources used in the following articles include images, material sources, not-so-well known texts or broadly circulated texts, which are almost forgotten today. The concept concentrates on very brief moments in time instead of developments of a *topos* from its beginning to the present. A more profound understanding is also reached by contextualising the moment of opening and making it thus comparable to other openings.

The separation of form (memory box) and content (assigned meanings) – or *signifié* and *significant* following Ferdinand de Saussure – relate the concept of *topoi* as a memory box also to semiotics.[4] As the sign is the unchangeable container, the denotations consist of a fixed core, but are mutable. While this belongs to the field of semantics, the relation between signs and agents using these is the subject of pragmatics. The receiving audience is part of a cultural system who shares a certain knowledge how those signs have to be understood which, however, does not prevent misunderstandings. Therefore, in both concepts the usage, its understanding and the actors are central aspects. Often, those signs are regarded as symptoms of something else, i.e. as indicators of the cultural context to which they belong. Therefore the local and temporal setting of the sign (or box) and how this influences the (change of assigned) meanings and connotations is part of this field of research, especially when the signs are read as indexes, instead of symbols or icons[5].

***

The following articles all look at certain *topoi* as memory boxes that are opened at various moments in the past.

Alexandra Schäfer focuses on the use of topical elements in the representation of massacres in the French Wars of Religion. What makes a massacre recognisable as such? She therefore closely examines the different layers of argumentation in the painting of the *St. Bartholomew's Day Massacre* by François Dubois, a French Reformed refugee in Geneva.

Kristina Müller-Bongard refers to martyrdom as a memory box and the martyr as its agent (of mediation) by using the characteristic practices of a memory box – conserving, collecting, transferring, producing – to test the

4 See KJØRUP, 2009, p. 14; also SAUSSURE, 1998.

5 See KJØRUP, 2009, pp. 7-9, 46; also PEIRCE, 2000.

concept by way of an iconic case study. Therefore, she looks closer at the sixteenth-century martyrdom cycle in the English Jesuit College in Rome and its different use of martyrdom to build religious, social and symbolic capital to shape a collective memory.

The article by Asko Nivala analyses Friedrich Schlegel's reception and usage of the *topos* of Golden Age (*goldenes Zeitalter*). Nivala studies this *topos* by focusing on four relevant moments during which this very famous memory box of Western civilisation was disclosed: Hesiod in ancient Greece, Roman Virgil, eighteenth-century neoclassicism and finally early nineteenth-century German Romanticism. This article researches Schlegel as a literary agent who both received many past features of this literary figure, but simultaneously revised this *topos* according to the needs of his time.

Cathleen Sarti concentrates on various openings of the memory box of providence from the sixteenth century until the twenty-first. She particularly focuses on the changes of meaning from a theological to a mostly political concept and the deeply intertwined mixture of religious, cultural and political meaning. The article shows the multiple re-fillings of this memory box and their consequences for later opening moments of this box.

The common denominator of all four articles in this section is their focus on the reception of *topos* rather than its production. Typically, the first creation of a *topos* is lost in a mythical past; nonetheless, almost all sharing the same cultural tradition understand its usage at least roughly. When studying the act of reception, the articles will analyse the displacements of the memory box in a diachronic perspective. Hence, the cognitive surplus of the concept of memory box is its provision of a tool to understand the simultaneous process of renewing old as well as adding new meanings based on a unique historical situation of disclosing a memory box.

List of References

ARISTOTLE, Aristotle in 23 Volumes, Volume 22, Cambridge/London 1926, http://www.perseus.tufts.edu, 07.11.2013.

CICERO, MARCUS TULLIUS, Topik, (Philosophische Bibliothek 356), Hamburg 1983.

CURTIUS, ERNST ROBERT, Europäische Literatur und lateinisches Mittelalter, 11th ed., Tübingen/Basel 1993.

KJØRUP, SØREN, Semiotik, Paderborn 2009.

KOSELLECK, REINHART, Einleitung, in: Geschichtliche Grundbegriffe. Historisches Lexikon zur politisch-sozialen Sprache in Deutschland. Band 1, ed. by OTTO BRUNNER et al., Stuttgart 1972.

PEIRCE, CHARLES SANDERS, Semiotische Schriften, 3 vol., Frankfurt a.M. 2000.

SAUSSURE, FERDINAND DE, Cours de Linguistique générale, Paris 1998.

How to Visualise an Event that is not Representable?

The *Topos* of Massacre in François Dubois' *St. Bartholomew's Day Massacre*

ALEXANDRA SCHÄFER

> Situated as it was at the centre of such swirling emotions, revolutionary implications, festering resentments and indeterminate intellectual repercussions, the Massacre of St. Bartholomew became a legend almost before it happened, and it grew with the telling and with the passage of time.[1]

The *topos* of massacre as a memory box and the French Wars of Religion

The French Wars of Religion (1562-1598) were some of the most brutal, important and captivating confessional conflicts in the sixteenth century.[2] On the night of the 24th August 1572, one of the most crucial violent events took

1 KELLEY, 1972, p. 1342.

2 The confessional conflict was entangled with many other domains, among them the preservation of the Valois dynasty, the concurrence between noble houses, the recovering from recent war, financial problems, failed reforms and the fight about hegemony in Europe against Habsburg Spain.

place and soon became labelled St. Bartholomew's Day Massacre by contemporaries.[3]

This article[4] examines how the *topos* of massacre, seen as a memory box, became pressing in the representation of this event. Therefore, one of the best known but rarely examined visual representations of St. Bartholomew's Day Massacre, the sole known contemporary Huguenot painting, was chosen: François Dubois' *St. Bartholomew's Day Massacre*[5]. Dubois opened the memory box of massacre when composing his depiction of the historical massacre on St. Bartholomew's Day, using layers from this box and adding new aspects hitherto not linked with it.

Of course, phenomena of extreme cruelty and mass killing and terms such as carnage or murder were known since Antiquity (Greek *phonos*).[6] The French term *massacre* – meaning "the killing of a great number of defenceless people, mostly civilians" by another group who can "undertake the killing without physical danger to themselves" – became widely used during the period of the French Wars of Religion.[7] However, only in the 1560s, *massacre* was used for a specific type of mass violence which had occurred lately to create a judgmental and emotional short-cut picture of actors and events from the recent past, pressing for a certain way of memorising it. At first, the analogy to slaughtering animals was a central motif, used as a drastic image by Protestants to condemn the Catholic violence, acting so fiercely as if they were not facing humans. Soon further emotions, stereotypical interpretations, were added together with newly experienced ways of how to represent those layers. This was the creation of the memory box as it is understood in this article.

3 Confer for example: CAPILUPI, [1572].

4 This article is based on the research for my master thesis at the Johannes Gutenberg-University in Mainz in 2009 on the painting of François Dubois.

5 DUBOIS, between 1572 and 1584. The painting is mentioned in many works, short biographical articles and catalogue entries with basic data, but only few research literature exists: the Monograph in the nineteenth century by Henri Bordier; the articles on some aspects by Waldemar Deonna, René Gilbert, Jean Ehrmann, Cornette Joël, Godehard Janzing, Ralf Beil and Dominique Radrizzani as well as most recently David El Kenz. The article "Die göttliche Ordnung der Geschichte. Massaker und Martyrium im Gemälde ‚La Saint-Barthélemy' von François Dubois" by MARTIN SCHIEDER (in: Bilder machen Geschichte. Historische Ereignisse im Gedächtnis der Kunst, ed. by UWE FLECKNER) was not yet published when this chapter was completed.

6 Confer EL KENZ, 2007a, p. 2.

7 EL KENZ, 2007a, p. 2 (first quotation); confer as well: BURUCÚA/KWIATKOWSKI, 2012, p. 1; LEVENE, 1999, p. 5 (second quotation).

In the lampoon HISTOIRE || MEMORABLE || DE || LA PERSECVTION || & saccagement du peuple de Merindol & || Cabrieres & autres circonuoisins, appelez || VAVDOIS. || [...][8] from 1555, shortly before the French Wars of Religion started, massacre was used as a politico-confessional accuse against the excessive Catholic killings of the Vaudois in Provence in 1545.[9] While the French verb massacre used in the lampoon meant the brutal mass killing of people who could not defend themselves, the noun functioned as a synonym for murder, carnage and slaughter (French: assassinat, boucherie, carnage, héctacombe, tuerie).[10]

Then, and especially after the beginning of the wars in 1562, the *topos* of massacre was frequently used by French Protestants during the Wars of Religion to qualify massive Catholic violence.[11] To make sense of those experiences in their recent past, massacres were inscribed into the tradition of narrating the suffering of the Reformed persecuted community, fitting the Protestant self-perception. In the competition over the interpretation of the recent events (i.e. what was remembered and how), the *topos* of massacre was used by French Protestants as a means of persuasion. Protestant representations relied on pre-set images such as the idealised victims and emotions such as hatred or a feeling of moral superiority, for example, instead of logical

8 Confer French vernacular Books online: USTC 4879.

9 Confer GREENGRASS, 1999, p. 69; EL KENZ, 2007a, p. 2; BURUCÚA/KWIATKOWSKI, 2012, p. 10.

10 Following the French Vernacular Books online, it was Jean Crespin, the Genevan printer and publisher of Calvinist literature, who printed two editions of this lampoon. The *HISTOIRE || MEMORABLE* was not only reprinted in France, but also translated into German (by Johann Anton Tillier and edited by Samuel Apiarius in Bern). Here kill, murder, destroy and devastate (e.g. "vernüttet" and "vmbbracht" in the preface) served as equivalents to the French *massacre* (Confer Verzeichnis der im deutschen Sprachbereich erschienenen Drucke des 16. Jahrhunderts (VD 16): VD16 ZV 8010 and VD16 ZV 8011). In Germany *Massaker*, derived from the French term, can be proved for the first time in 1664 in the context of the Ottoman Wars, whereas in England the term massacre was adopted shortly after St. Bartholomew's Day Massacre (confer EL KENZ, 2007a, p. 2; EL KENZ, 2006, p. 3; GREENGRASS, 1999, p. 69).

11 Confer BEIL, 2003, p. 9; VOGEL, 2006, p. 10; MEDICK, 2005, p. 16; GREENGRASS, 1999, p. 69. While both tried to clean their communities from pollution and act in accordance with God, Catholics tended to eradicate persons with *false belief*, whereas Protestants rather destroyed symbols of Catholic belief such as liturgical objects (confer DAVIS, 1974, p. 228; EL KENZ, 2007b, pp. 4, 6; BURUCÚA/KWIATKOWSKI, 2012, p. 5). On some factors forwarding the outbreak of massive violence: EL KENZ, 2007b, p. 4; GREENGRASS, 1999, p. 70.

arguments. However, using the *topos* of massacre could also serve to make the extreme, shocking violence – which was sometimes seen as non-representable, a unique event without comparison[12] – manageable by providing patterns apt to organise the perception as well as representation.

The memory box was filled with new layers by the experiences of the wars. Novel iconographic ways to represent the recent events were experienced, taking up pre-set images from the Bible, the Antiquity and recent French history which were highly emotionally charged (e.g. Massacre of the Innocents).[13] While only few Calvinist iconographic productions existed, a certain representational type for massacre was established by depictions such as in the *Quarante Tableaux* of Tortorel and Perrissin, to cite one famous example,[14] instituting how to visualise a massacre. The perhaps best known sheet from the *Quarante Tableaux* showed the massacre of Vassy in 1562.

To be perceivable, the *topos* (idea of the type of event; patterns, stereotypes, pre-set images, emotional connotations; memories of earlier massacres) had to be addressed – or in other words: the memory box had to be opened by someone. The label of massacre was employed to make an emotional judgement, consciously evoke certain layers, while others emerged without intentional use. Or, in visual representations, different traits which made those layers perceivable were shown and the *topos* of massacre was thereby unveiled indirectly. Thus, also iconographic traits were attached to the memory box and patterns for narrating were provided as parts of the *topos*.[15]

After the St. Bartholomew's Day Massacre (1572) there was a wave of media representations, above all pamphlets, but some broadsheets as well, which used the *topos* of massacre to address the concrete historical massacre in

12 El Kenz: "In fact, massacres constitute such terrifying acts that they elicit ideological, scholarly and memorial narratives to try to make sense of them and, sometimes, a refusal to put forward any discourse, a sort of silent text. Furthermore, the slaughter mostly remained inexplicable, because its protagonists suppressed it." (EL KENZ, 2007b, p. 3; confer as well: BURUCÚA/KWIATKOWSKI, 2012, p. 6).

13 The Bible (especially the massacre of the Innocents), the Antique (the triumvirate and the proscription) and recent French history (the persecution of the Waldensians; parallels with the crusade of the Albigenses) served as an argumentative pool (confer BABEL, 2006, pp. 109-112; EL KENZ, 2007a, p. 2; EL KENZ, 2006, p. 8).

14 Confer BENEDICT, 2007; EL KENZ, 2006.

15 Confer KELLEY, 1972, p. 1324; GREENGRASS, 1999, pp. 70, 74; BURUCÚA/KWIATKOWSKI, 2012, p. 23.

their depictions. It was all the more important which reading succeeded in developing from a communicative memory to a cultural memory (an interpretation of the event which lasted), because St. Bartholomew's Day Massacre soon turned into the prototype of a massacre in early modern time.

François Dubois opened the memory box by composing *St. Bartholomew's Day Massacre*. This article examines how Dubois made use of the *topos* of massacre in his painting, which pre-existing layers of the *topos* of massacre or rather iconographic traits to visualise those layers he included, which layers and ways of depicting he added and at which points he did not resort to the already existing *topos*. As Dubois' depiction was the unique painting of a contemporary Huguenot of St. Bartholomew's Day Massacre, it seems apt to also study how his painting was received and which role it played in memorising the central founding event for French Reformed: St. Bartholomew's Day Massacre.[16]

The St. Bartholomew's Day Massacre

In August 1572, the marriage of the king's sister with the Protestant prince Henri of Navarra took place in Paris as a royal act of conciliation. But the assassination attempt against the Huguenot military leader Admiral Coligny fuelled the already explosive atmosphere in Paris, where many Huguenots were present because of the wedding. In his council, the Catholic King Charles IX decided to kill the Huguenot leaders. However, these royal measures were extended against the king's will and the mass killing by the population of Paris started in the night of the 24th August 1572. It lasted several days and resulted in 3000 dead, most of whom were Huguenots. Thereafter several other mass killings took place in various cities of the French realm until October.[17]

While, on one hand, the events of August were assigned a unique character, they were, on the other, seen in one line with other massacres of the Wars of Religion.[18] Following Donald R. Kelley, "the witnesses, participants and

16 Confer EL KENZ, 2007b, p. 3.

17 There is a vast amount of literature on St. Bartholomew's Day Massacre, confer among the more recent studies esp. CROUZET, 1994; BOURGEON, 1995; JOUANNA, 2007; for a short literature survey, confer SABEAN, 2006.

18 Confer BURUCÚA/KWIATKOWSKI, 2012, pp. 6f.; the massacre was extraordinary in this respect that it happened in peacetime, initiated by the government, and had exceptionally vast dimensions. Furthermore, it was assigned an extraordinary

interpreters of the events of late Summer 1572 knew what the phenomenon was practically before it happened: [...] it was a massacre, by no means unexpected and not even the first in that generation. And they knew which part they might ultimately have to play".[19] This comment suggests that the massacre was acted out following the example of earlier massacres and following the type of event of massacre, which was generally – but not exclusively – known through depictions in media. The stereotypical, repetitive character was true even more for the representations of massacre.[20] How these elements were set together, how known motifs were interwoven into an account of the event and which elements were newly attached to representing a massacre, all formed part of the struggle for dominance over the interpretation of the event immediately after the St. Bartholomew's Day Massacre ("une compétition mémorielle"[21]). This provided the setting for Dubois' opening of the memory box.

The topic aspects in François Dubois' *St. Bartholomew's Day Massacre*

Between 1572 and 1584, François Dubois painted his picture *St. Bartholomew's Day Massacre*, one of today's best known interpretations of

meaning by contemporaries (Confer EL KENZ, 2007b, pp. 3-5). Natalie Zemon Davis however judged: "St. Bartholomew was certainly a bigger affair [...]. But on the whole, it still fits into a whole pattern of sixteenth-century religious disturbance." (DAVIS, 1974, p. 241, see also p. 226).

19 KELLEY, 1972, p. 1324.

20 Confer KELLEY, 1972; GREENGRASS, 1999, p. 83. Mark Greengrass speaks of "copycat incidents", especially for the St. Bartholomew's Day Massacre in the provincial cities throughout France (Confer GREENGRASS, 1999, p. 70). There was however a "relative absence of coherent explanations": Many victims felt unable to address what they had witnessed, local authorities responsible for keeping order during the massacre willingly destroyed the relevant passages in the registers (in accordance with the King's edicts) and the perpetrators risked revenge and possibly legal consequences when they revealed their participation (confer GREENGRASS, 1999, pp. 82f).

21 JOUANNA, 2007, p. 244. This was a struggle on different levels: Catholic versus Protestant, head of communities versus basis, centre versus provinces, realm versus international, etc. On competing massacre representations in media, confer as well: LEVENE, 1999, p. 3; GREENGRASS, 1999, p. 84.

the event, in Geneva.[22] So, the memory box was displaced – though its spatial and temporal transfer is rather cut short – and opened up again in Geneva. Dubois was a French painter born in Amiens (*1529), who possibly lived and worked – influenced by the School of Fontainebleau – in Paris.[23] He presumably left France for Geneva after August 1572.[24] Little is known about him, since the only sources left are an entry in the city records upon his cause of death[25] and a testament.[26] But this testament confirms that Dubois was a Reformed and that the painter was integrated into French refugee society in Geneva, as he was funded by the wealthy French Pournas family.[27]

22 The painting is shown on several book covers of scientific research, as an illustration in school books, as the centre of various recent exhibitions, and in the majority of Wikipedia-articles on St. Bartholomew's Day Massacre. Poster reproductions of the painting are available, as well. But either it is used without the necessary remarks on the context, the painter or a problematisation of the painting itself, or it has been interpreted as a reliable source for the course of events. Most studies have adopted the Dictum of Border: "François Dubois s'est attaché à ne rien inventer et qu'il a voulu que chacun de ses groupes fût exactement vrai." (BORDIER, 1879, p. 26). In my opinion, Dubois' painting provides an insight into an individual handling of various contemporary discourses in the context of negotiation processes on the Reformed communal identity after St. Bartholomew's Day Massacre.

23 Confer RADRIZZANI, 1998, p. 1.

24 Confer BORDIER, 1879, p. 4; BEIL, 2003, pp. 8, 18, note 5; RADRIZZANI, 1998, p. 1. The city registers that only reach up to 1572/1573 do not contain Dubois' name (confer BORDIER, 1878, p. 28/8; BORDIER, 1879, p. 6).

25 Dubois died "d´une defluxions de cerveaux avec fièvre continue, âgé d'environ 55 ans, ce 24 aoust 1584" (Dubois, François, in: Registre des décès genevois, cited by: BORDIER, 1878, p. 31/11; BORDIER, 1879, p. 9).

26 Testament, pp. 44f.

27 Testament, p. 44.

Figure 1 : Dubois, François, Le Massacre de la Saint-Barthélemy, between 1572 and 1584, oil on wood, 94 cm x 154 cm, Lausanne: Musée Cantonal des Beaux-Arts. Photo: Nora Rupp, Musée cantonal des Beaux-Arts, Lausanne; Don de la Municipalité de Lausanne, 1862

Explicit evidence is lacking, but the painting was possibly a remittance work and the Pournas family the contractor for the painting.[28] If this was the case, they might have been an influential factor for the representation chosen and they would have been the crucial audience of Dubois' depiction of the St. Bartholomew's Day Massacre as well as the gatekeepers to promote and constrain the publicity of the painting.

Dubois had to provide a persuasive account as he was competing with other readings of the massacre, even though few visual representations existed and only one Catholic painting.[29] One possibility was to cite core facts of the events on the 24th August 1572 – persons involved, key events and important places – to prove he was well-informed and to serve the expectations of his audience who surely had heard about the defenestration of Admiral Coligny, for example. Dubois included important historical persons such as King Charles IX, his mother Catherine of Medici and the Huguenot leader Admiral Coligny, well-known scenes (especially the sufferings of Coligny) and architectural quotations, among them the Louvre and the Hôtel de Ponthieu in the Rue de Béthisy.[30] All these concrete, non-topical quotations directly addressed the St. Bartholomew's Day Massacre and allowed to identify the depicted event easily. Apart from these quotations, unallocated, stereotypical scenes of a massacre dominated: mass violence which defenceless victims had to endure from superior perpetrators who acted with extraordinary cruelty.

28 Since the Jean Pournas family can be related to Dubois whom they had given some money (which the testament proves) and since they were a Reformed French family that had fled to Geneva immediately after the massacre in Lyon, it is quite probable that they were interested in the subject, especially when the painter was a French exiled as well – as the French historian Henri Bordier has suggested. But Bordier could not provide evidence for this thesis as well as there was none for his idea of how the picture was transferred: If the picture belonged to the Pournas family, which we cannot be certain of, Marie de Gabiano might have taken it with her from Geneva to Lausanne when fleeing from a suit of adultery which her husband, Pournas, filed in 1597. As the next reference to the picture in the late seventeenth century placed it in the Lausanne town hall, Bordier speculated that Marie de Gabiano might have given it as a present to the town (confer BORDIER, 1879, pp. 9-11; BORDIER, 1878, p. 56/36).

29 Vasari's depiction of St. Bartholomew's Day Massacre in Rome which will be treated below.

30 Topographical aspects: BORDIER, 1878, pp. 24/4, 50f. as well as 48/28; BORDIER, 1879, pp. 2, 25, 36, 38-38A; EHRMANN, 1972, p. 452; RADRIZZANI, 2003, p. 21. Other elements pointed to the constructed character of the painting, such as the construction as an overview picture with simultaneous scenes and parallels to the coulisse of the tragedy (Sebastiano Serlio).

This was presented with an overwhelmingly large amount of details in an accurate, eyewitness-like style.[31]

Dubois expressly developed the polarity of perpetrators and victims, one core element of the *topos* of massacre, as his guiding theme: While the committers were presented as uncivilised barbarians[32], stocky, dark skinned, heavily built, some armed with cudgels, all with some headgear, their victims were unarmed, bare headed and mostly of a light skin tone. The male perpetrators,[33] reaching from youth to mid-aged, dressed like civilians and militia, attacked men and women regardless of age or rank, new-born babies as well as old men, nobles as well as simple people. They acted with extreme cruelty when dragging corpses through the streets with ropes around their neck and fired with archebuse at people drowning in the river. Masses of dead people lying in the streets, accumulations of naked bodies and blood spread on the ground, dead corpses floating in the Seine which was red with blood and fleeing people who were hunted down underlined the vast dimensions of this massacre.[34] These were depictions of the course of St. Bartholomew's Day Massacre as it might have happened, seeming to be realistic especially because

---

31 Recently it has been suggested that Dubois – instead of being an eyewitness as it was hitherto assumed – used Simon Goulart's vast work *Mémoires de l' Estat de France sous Charles Neufiesme* as a basis for his picture (confer RADRIZZANI, 2003, pp. 25-27, esp. p. 25). A detailed analysis of the picture and Goulart's *Mémoires* has shown that the only superficial parallels are not forcing this interpretation. Nevertheless, a loose relation of Dubois to the work of Goulart remains possible (confer BORDIER, 1878, pp. 26/6, 29/9; BORDIER, 1879, p. 4; BENEDICT, 2007, p. 189, note 57).

32 On the use of the concept of the barbarian in the representations of the Religious Wars, confer: CROUZET, 1982, pp. 103-126.

33 Cruelties against female victims were committed mostly by other women. But women were not more likely to become victims of a massacre, although they were far more often represented, especially pregnant women (Confer EL KENZ, 2006, p. 8; DAVIS, 1974, pp. 229, 237). Dubois, however, did not include female offenders. The *massacreurs* were a cross-section of the local society, usually led by priests or militia, sometimes artists or lawyers, as well. The lowest classes who were not well-integrated into the parishes only participated in pillaging. Apart from those exercising violence, many were present to watch (confer DAVIS, 1974, pp. 218, 236-240; in addition: DIEFENDORF, 1991, esp. pp. 104f.).

34 The impression of the vast dimension of the massacre and the impossibility to escape it was supported by various details: Hunting of fleeing people, a carriage with corpses, closed town gates, the useless attempts to seek protection inside the houses. There was no safety zone left as especially the defenestration proved (confer JANZING, 2005, pp. 81f.).

they looked like typical elements of massacre depictions and therefore fulfilled the expectations of the viewers.

As Dubois placed his audience at the spot of a direct, immediate observer, he reduced the (emotional) distance between the spectator and the image. He achieved this effect, as several of the buildings and actors, intersected by the image borders, seemed to extend beyond the visible space and in the foreground the trail of blood reached out beyond the panel. It was as if the spectator was standing at the centre (core) of the event.

Apart from the (seemingly) authentic elements, Dubois interlaced biblical and antique motifs. Of course, the river stained with blood associated with apocalyptic imagery (Rev 16,4-16,7) and eschatological expectations.[35] The Massacre of the Innocents (Matt 2,16-18) had already been used in the context of mass violence judged to be unjustly committed during confessional struggles before Dubois' *St. Bartholomew's Day Massacre*. The perhaps most prominent parallel between the Massacre of the Innocents and contemporary Catholic misconduct of soldiers against unarmed Protestants was drawn by Pieter Brueghel the Older in his painting *The Massacre of the Innocents* (ca. 1565).[36] Dubois included a motif which had already proved to be apt, raising pity and compassion with the defenceless naked babies and women treated unjustly with extraordinary cruelty, as especially the scene where a woman's womb had been opened and the baby left lying amidst her bowels emphasised. In addition, there was a deeper-reaching implication: The parallel with the Massacre of the Innocents suggested a righteous, pious behaviour on the side of the victims (while the offenders opposed God) which evoked the image of God's chosen ones which was at the core of the Protestant self-perception.[37]

As a representation already paralleled to the massive violence in the confessional struggle of sixteenth-century France well before *St. Bartholomew's Day Massacre*, Dubois employed elements taken from representations of the Antique Roman proscriptions and the Second Roman Triumvirate: Showing a beheading, financial motivations (bounty for beheading; pillage) as well as displaying prominently a group of three

35 On the importance of the end of the world-perception for Catholic violence, confer: CROUZET, 1990.

36 Confer BEIL, 2003, pp. 11-13; BURUCÚA/KWIATKOWSKI, 2012, esp. p. 21; EL KENZ, 2006, p. 8; EL KENZ, 1998, p. 228; BURSCHEL, 2004, pp. 341-343.

37 On this Protestant image confer: JOUANNA, 2007, pp. 232-236; CROUZET, 1994, pp. 50, 158.

negatively connoted nobles in one scene[38], Dubois alluded to this popular contemporary motif prominently linked to the complex of persecution, suppression and mass violence in the contemporary discourse, though not exclusively known as representational traits of massacres. About twenty pictures from the mid-sixteenth century had treated the triumvirate as well as the mass killings of Sulla's proscriptions (from 82 BC and 43 BC) parallel to the recent French events, especially the aspect of civil war; among them Antoine Caron's famous *Massacres du Triumvirat* (ca. 1566) and with very different characteristics the many copies and adoptions of the painting by Hans Vredeman de Vries.[39] Those pictures developed the representation of predominant offenders, asymmetrical violence and masses of victims: they showed a mass of dead bodies, chaos, stacked corpses, sometimes naked, anonymous victims without individual features, beheaded, impaled, strangled and mutilated, not treated like humans, sometimes like trophies. Furthermore, defenestration, civilians and militia acting jointly and perpetrators looting the corpses were shown.[40] The great similarities with the massacre depiction by Dubois shows that those images of the triumvirate must have served as a model. Dubois even went one step further foiling the Catholics' justification: When they seized the opportunity to carry away clothes, bags and chests, they revealed low, profane motives such as acquisitiveness, instead of the self-assigned piety and purity in faith.[41] This argumentation of *self-revelation* was

38 These three Catholic nobles maybe represented the duke of Guise, the chevalier of Angoulême and the duke of Aumale (confer BORDIER, 1878, p. 34/14; BORDIER, 1879, p. 26; BEIL, 2003, p. 14; RADRIZZANI, 2003, p. 20; DEONNA, 1943, p. 118; EL KENZ, 2006, p. 17). Bordier had named the three men, but when comparing them with contemporary portraits only vague similarities can be observed, because they rather represented types than individuals.

39 Confer EHRMANN, 1972, pp. 448-451; EHRMANN, 1945, pp. 195-199; CROUZET, 1994, pp. 252f.; EL KENZ, 2006, pp. 13-16; RADRIZZANI, 1998, p. 1; BORDIER, 1879, pp. 12-14. Burucúa and Kwiatowski suggested that Dubois' whole painting was based on the motif of the Triumvirate and Radrizzani insisted that the series following Vredemann de Vries was the main model for Dubois (confer BURUCÚA/KWIATKOWSKI, 2012, p. 11; RADRIZZANI, 1998, p. 1).

40 Confer EL KENZ, 1998, pp. 226-228; EHRMANN, 1972, pp. 448-451; BORDIER, 1879, pp. 12-14. *Massacre* was used as a metonym for a hunting trophy in the sixteenth century as well (confer EL KENZ, 2007a, p. 2).

41 On the Catholic self-assigned image and the motivation to act: DIEFENDORF, 1991, pp. 37f., 150, 153; JOUANNA, 2007, p. 232; CROUZET, 1994, pp. 18f.; DAVIS, 1974, p. 211. Protestant presentations of Catholic motivations as profane: GREENGRASS, 1999, p. 72. There is another strategy Dubois has taken up as well: In order to legitimate their actions, the perpetrators imitated the legal system when using the

persuasive because the (above-mentioned) markers of authenticity supported the effect of an eyewitness-like report.

So far, Dubois employed quite established visualisations of mass violence illustrating the *topos* of massacre, developing above all polar images of victims and perpetrators as the core element of the *topos*. To heighten and further develop the main characteristics, Dubois included two quite different discourses of his time: firstly, the hunting, and secondly, the Turks.[42] In both cases, the actors were described as unusually cruel, even barbaric and denying the value of their counterparts. Therefore, these allusions served Dubois to evoke prejudices and to induce an emotional negative attitude in his audience against the committers.

In the foreground, Dubois painted a scene arousing associations of a noble hunting party on their horses, accompanied by some dogs and a beater dressed in black. Other perpetrators bore a spike for a pig hunt. With the hunting-motif Dubois added a new element to his painting that had been discussed in the contemporary discourse on excessive violence in close connection with the massacre of St. Bartholomew's Day and was quite a new motif to illustrate the topical character of a massacre. To that date the Turks had not been used widely to characterise the perpetrators in a massacre, although they appeared in different contexts to defame the actors paralleled with them. Dubois painted some of the perpetrators with an unusually dark complexion, a hooknose, black hair, cavernous eyes, a morion and scimitars, so that they alluded to the stereotyped image of the Turks. Thus, he linked the hereditary enemies of Christendom with the Catholic perpetrators in his depiction of St. Bartholomew's Day Massacre, as a double condemnation.[43] Here, Dubois

official proceedings, instruments and places of execution, e.g. the execution place of Montfaucon, which Dubois represented on the hill on the left outside Paris (For this practice to imitate officials when acting out violence, confer: DAVIS, 1974, pp. 213-217, 234).

42 Confer BURUCÚA/KWIATKOWSKI, 2012, pp. 9, 13. Probably, Michel de Montaigne was the most prominent figure in this discussion apart from François Hotman ("chasse des huguenots"; anagram of King Charles IX: "chasseur déloyal"): Montaigne criticised the uncivilised cruelty of the hunt, the lack of pity and the cynic-playful handling of life, which was transferred to the context of the Wars of Religion to condemn the excessive violence (confer EL KENZ, 2007b, p. 7; KELLEY, 1972, p. 1338).

43 Confer MALETTKE, 2000, pp. 392-394; CROUZET, 1982, pp. 122f. Besides the destructive religious attack, the equalising with the Ottomans included a moral denunciation as well: Greed, disloyalty, a tyrannical and cruel nature were only some of the stereotypical characteristics assigned to the Turks (confer MALETTKE, 2000, p. 394). Protestant publications widely spread the polemic identification of

developed a new motif to represent a massacre which was then attached to the memory box.

Dubois organised his painting following the polarity of victims and perpetrators, as mentioned already. So far, we have seen allusions to the *topos* of massacre on different levels: Firstly, realistic depictions showed typical elements of a massacre as it might have happened. Secondly, older incidents of massive violence – be it biblical or antique – had previously served as references in the Wars of Religion and were linked to the *topos* of massacre. Thirdly, rather new motifs to further develop stereotypical judgments on perpetrators and victims appeared and were attached to the memory box.

In other parts of the painting, Dubois did not resort to the *topos*, but rather used a unique way of expressing his interpretation – however, once again aiming at the characterisation of the two polar groups of actors: François Dubois' visualisation reflected that the conviction of the heretic's deviance from the godly order was a Catholic construction. In Catholic conviction a heretic, by turning away from God, ceased to be a human being and his internal dehumanisation became apparent in his physical appearance.[44] One contemporary example for this belief is the famous triptych on the St. Bartholomew's Day Massacre by Giorgio Vasari in the Sala Regia in the Vatican: the inhuman appearance of the Reformed was programmatically presented and contrasted with the idealised Catholics who fought heroically[45] –

the pope with the antichrist only after St. Bartholomew's Day Massacre (confer BABEL, 2006, p. 111).

44 Confer CROUZET, 1994, pp. 18f.; EL KENZ, 2007b, p. 6; BURUCÚA/KWIATKOWSKI, 2012, pp. 4f. The ritual killing was meant to lay open the presence of the devil in the body of the Reformed, the mutilation of the body until it appeared non-human marked the departure of the Reformed from the Creation, the animalisation (e.g. execution on the swine market) highlighted the monstrosity of the Reformed body and the ordeal anticipated the agony in hell that awaited the Reformed (confer DIEFENDORF, 1991, p. 102; EL KENZ, 2006, p. 11; EL KENZ, 2007b, pp. 5f.). In their self-perception the Catholic community acted in priest-like function, as an instrument of God, in legal respect taking over magistrates' functions (confer CROUZET, 1994, p. 18; DIEFENDORF, 1991, pp. 6, 177; GREENGRASS, 1999, p. 72; DAVIS, 1974, esp. pp. 216f.).

45 Vasari's fresco was the only contemporary painting on St. Bartholomew's Day Massacre apart from Dubois' *St. Bartholomew's Day Massacre*. His triptych was part of a cycle of thirteen frescos in the pope's audience chamber, the Sala Regia in the Vatican, where it was placed prominently next to the papal chair. These frescoes were often regarded to form a unit with those showing the battle of Lepanto (1571), because they represented two Catholic victories against the unfaithful of some ideological, strategic importance to the pope. Apart from the

a stereotypical interpretation drawing on pre-set images of the same two groups of actors as in Dubois' depiction, but from the Catholic perspective. In contrast to Vasari, Dubois presented the dehumanisation of the Reformed body as a product of the violent acts of the Catholics: It was them who transformed human beings into masses of fragmented bones, of distorted parts of the body covered with unnaturally grey skin, the faces pale and distorted in horror.[46] By reversing the Catholic interpretation (of the Protestant being inhuman to the Catholic acting inhuman), Dubois turned the Catholic justification based on self-assigned piety into a revelation of deceitfulness.[47]

Being a Reformed refugee himself, Dubois naturally did not portray degenerated, nonhuman fellow-believers. This is why the complex reversal of the Catholic argument seems to be rather a by-product in the painting. But, be it intentional or not, this line of reasoning was present in *St. Bartholomew's Day Massacre* and one possible interpretation that exceeded the hitherto typical representations of massacres.

Based on the arguments so far it seems obvious that most parts of the picture depicted a whole spectre of devaluating aspects about the Catholic perpetrators in an offensive, aggressive way, whereas the victims were much less in the focus,[48] even though the polarity – as a typical element of all massacre depictions – naturally only became obvious in relating perpetrators and victims. Even the depiction of a mass of weak, defenceless, dehumanised victims served first of all to characterise the offenders as cruel, barbarian and acting inhuman, as explained above.

The focus on accusing the Catholic opponent might be better understood when the moment of opening of the memory box by Dubois as he painted the massacre of St. Bartholomew's Day is further contextualised by the Protestant struggle for identity. St. Bartholomew's Day Massacre marked a turning point for the Huguenot self-perception: there was a shift towards a more active,

---

fresco, the pope commissioned a commemorative coin for St. Bartholomew's Day Massacre with his portrait and an angel with a cross (confer RÖTTGEN, 1975, pp. 89, 97f.; HERZ, 1986, esp. pp. 41, 46f.; BURSCHEL, 2004, pp. 347-349; KINGDON, 1974, p. 26).

46 Many individual scenes associated with models such as the scene of the men hanged which might evoke the representation of the execution of Anne Du Bourg in the *Quarante Tableaux*, for example.

47 Similar argumentation in: BURUCÚA/KWIATKOWSKI, 2012, p. 11.

48 This seems to be a general tendency as El Kenz has pointed out (EL KENZ, 2006, p. 10).

belligerent, military-orientated self-perception.[49] To create a shared, collective memory of St. Bartholomew's Day Massacre was crucial to the Huguenot community in order to secure the continuation of a communal, if (slightly) changed identity despite or rather because of this massacre, which has been called a founding event.[50] The memory work was initially aimed at the present Reformed community to create a collective memory, but in a longer perspective also at the future, enforcing their interpretation of the events in competition with Catholic interpretation.

In representations, a balance had to be found between complying with expectations of what a massacre was like, the possibilities to use the *topos* as a means to persuade and the necessity to develop the concrete St. Bartholomew's Day Massacre – even as a unique event. So far, Dubois' painting mirrored a Reformed reading of the massacre which had become predominant: Catholic opponents appeared in stereotypical depictions as an antitype of the Protestant self-perception, which was visualised using different motifs attached to layers from the memory box. Few elements in the picture had alluded to the concrete historical events in August 1572, but there were more: The new aggressive self-assured air of the Protestants was clearly expressed in the concrete assignments of responsibility to the Royal family.

Catherine of Medici was illustrated as the antitype of the Virgin of Mercy, spreading her black veil over a mass of dead bodies and thus perverting the highly emotionally loaded symbol of comfort and protection into its opposite.[51] This negative characterisation was a general attack on Catherine reaching

49 After the massacre, the community still perceived itself as the chosen people and aimed at a coalescence with God, but as the St. Bartholomew's Day Massacre was seen as a serious threat to their existence, the French Protestants chose to focus harder on their temporal survival (confer EL KENZ, 2007b, p. 2; JOUANNA, 2007 pp. 237f., 251; DIEFENDORF, 1991, p. 144; BURUCÚA/KWIATKOWSKI, 2012, p. 17).

50 Confer EL KENZ, 2007b, p. 3.

51 Confer CORNETTE, 1995, p. 117; EL KENZ, 2006, pp. 17f. There are various engravings for this representation type of Catherine de Medici dressed completely in black, examining the piles of bodies during St. Bartholomew's Day Massacre (confer JOUANNA, 1998, p. 203). More often Catherine of Medici appeared as the new Jezabel, the Old Testament Queen who sold out the Israel people out of lust for power, unscrupulousness and her misbelief in Baal. She was claimed to be the incarnation of the bad and godless government, handing over France to the devil (confer EL KENZ, 2006, p. 3; JOUANNA, 1998, p. 108; CROUZET, 1999, p. 1[illegible]3; KINGDON, 1988, p. 73).

beyond her concrete comportment during the events in August 1572.[52] The inversion of expectations and viewing habits in regard to the Queen mother as an antitype of the Virgin of Mercy was a personalised and specific interpretation developed by Dubois that was not apt to be generalised and included into the representations of the *topos* of massacre.

Concerning the representation of the king, Dubois provided a reading linked more closely to the general representation of the perpetrators in a massacre than the very individual depiction of Catherine of Medici. King Charles IX ("le Roy chasseur") was painted shooting out of the window of his palace at those subjects who were trying to escape the massacre.[53] This resumed the motif of the hunt,[54] which served, as shown above, to further develop the characterisation of brutal, scrupulous mass killing and the tendency to deny to the victims being human, linked to the *topos* of massacre. King Charles IX was degraded to being one fierce committer among others, although the portrayal of the king as a hunter of his subjects was an accusation on a different level. Hardly any other visual Protestant representation, neither the earlier on massacres nor those on St. Bartholomew's Day Massacre, went as far as Dubois when painting the King's active participation in mass violence. This image of the king highlighted his failure to act kingly and fulfil the demands of his office (protect his subjects, guarantee peace and order). As a result, the painting questioned Charles' integrity and status as king, tending to desacralize him.[55] As Denis Crouzet has put it, the moral destruction functioned as a political iconoclasm, which can be classified as kind of a

52 Catherine of Medici was assigned the primary responsibility for St. Bartholomew's Day Massacre, but she had already been blamed and attacked before for her widespread Italian network, her merchant background, her ambitions and reputed Machiavellian style of politics as well as her influence on the King, among others (confer CROUZET, 1982, p. 117; JOUANNA, 2007, pp. 15f., 255f.; KELLEY, 1972, p. 1336).

53 The focus on the royal family was intensified by the image's formation because the alignments in the picture all led to the palace of the Louvre.

54 Confer EL KENZ, 2007b, p. 7; CROUZET, 1994, p. 296.

55 Charles was shown using brutal violence instead of the legitimate power of the king's authority, which he applied to harm or even murder those subjects he should protect (confer CROUZET, 1994, pp. 24f., 184-205; JOUANNA, 1998, p. 31). Other attempts to desacralize the king had preceded St. Bartholomew's Day Massacre: Charles was compared to Achab, the husband of Jezabel, and thereby his ability and the competence to fight false belief were questioned (confer DIEFENDORF, 1991, pp. 151-153, 156f.; CROUZET, 1994, pp. 24, 124-141; RACAUT, 2002, p. 39).

substitutional regicide or rather tyrannicide.[56] Connections to early modern discourses of a legal right of resistance (especially the Monarchomachs), which were led with new verve after St. Bartholomew's Day Massacre, can easily be drawn.[57] Obviously, Dubois here connected different contemporary discourses in an individual manner, thus deviating clearly from the hitherto experienced way of depicting a massacre.

Up to this point, the focus was placed on the dominating complex accusation of Catholic perpetrators on various levels – topical traits and concrete aspects of the massacre on St. Bartholomew's Day. The weak, dehumanised victims had served above all to mirror the character of the perpetrators and picture the vast dimension of the massacre. This accusative interpretation of the massacre, meant to mobilise Protestants, tended to interpret the events on St. Bartholomew's Day as unique, without comparison and surpassing earlier massacres. The St. Bartholomew's Day Massacre was remembered as a watershed.

In addition, Dubois included another interpretation of the St. Bartholomew's Day Massacre, embedding the recent massacre in a continuous narration of Protestant suffering: Several Protestants in Dubois' painting appeared glorified, following certain traits of the iconography of martyrs.[58] They were presented with a certain dignity in their long black coats or dresses, kneeling on the ground, their hands folded, their faces turned upwards towards heaven or their eyes fixed at a point of blankness as if they had their gaze turned inwards. Their white, pure skin contrasted with the red or brown complexion of the perpetrators. While those glorified were depicted with a certain dignity and individualised without representing a concrete historical person, the offenders' faces disappeared in the shadows under a hat or helmet so that they stayed anonymous. This depiction of Catholic committers invoked the association of depersonalised instruments of martyrdom, which only served as attributes to the martyr.

For his portrayal of the faithful men and women who were superior to their offenders, characterising the massacre victims as martyrs,[59] Dubois took up

56 Confer CROUZET, 1999, p. 111.

57 Confer EL KENZ, 2006, pp. 17f.; JOUANNA, 2007, p. 259; CROUZET, 1999, pp. 99f.; KINGDON, 1988, p. 75; KINGDON, 1974, p. 29. On the monarchomaques confer: MELLET, 2006, pp. 79-99.

58 On the *topos* of martyrdom confer the article by Kristina Müller-Bongard in this book.

59 Confer EL KENZ, 2007b, p. 3.

well-established layer of the memory box: the idealisation of the victims visualised in the motif of the faithful men and women with martyr-like traits. This image of the martyrs loaded heavily with emotion had already been used in earlier massacre representations such as in the *Quarante Tableaux*[60] and was therefore already attached to the memory box. But while those depictions took up traits of martyr iconography, victims of a massacre were in contemporary discourse distinguished from martyrs being only persecuted believers.[61]

Dubois inscribed himself into a narration of continued Protestant suffering which formed the core of Reformed communal memory; to invoke the hagiographical roots at the base of the reformed self-image functioned as an offer for the identification with the victims and integration into Protestant memory work. This allowed him to draw on established representational types,[62] evoking assigned meanings and positive emotional associations: Those who suffered for their belief and thus proved themselves worthy were attested to be God's own people and provided an example for the believer and served as a fix point for integrative communal self-perception.[63] This interpretation of St. Bartholomew's Day encased the recent events in a continuous narration of Protestant suffering. Understanding the massacre as one among others allowed to accept patterns as to how to handle and represent the extreme violence by repeating motifs, taking up experienced representations, drawing on layers

60 Confer EL KENZ, 2006, p. 9; BURUCÚA/KWIATKOWSKI, 2012, pp. 13, 21. Generally, Dubois orientated himself on the *Quarante Tableaux* by Jean Perrissin and Jacques Tortorel (confer BENEDICT, 2007, p. 189, note 57; EHRMANN, 1945, p. 195).

61 In the *History of Martyrs* (*Histoire des martyrs persecutez et mis a mort pour la verité de l'Évangile*) by JEAN CRESPIN the victims of massacres were labelled "fidèles persecutés", but not martyrs. The representation of their sufferings was summarized and often depersonalized (EL KENZ, 2006, p. 10; EL KENZ, 1998, p. 225; JOUANNA, 2007, p. 239). Only when Goulart took over the *Histoire des Martyrs*, the witness to the faith in a massacre started to converge the representational status of the martyr (confer VOGEL, 2006, p. 158; EL KENZ, 2006, pp. 9f.; RACAUT, 2002, p. 120).

62 Among the many Protestant martyrologies (John Foxe, Ludwig Rabe as well as Heinrich Pantaleone, Johann Sleidan, Flacius Illyricus) the one by Jean Crespin, *History of Martyrs*, was extraordinarily influential for France (KELLEY, 1972, pp. 1324f.; BURUCÚA/KWIATKOWSKI, 2012, pp. 15, 22). Simon Goulart continued the *History of Martyrs* after the death of Jean Crespin in April 1572 and used large parts of the scenes described on St. Bartholomew's Day Massacre in his *Mémoires* as well (confer RADRIZZANI, 2003, pp. 23f.; JOUANNA, 2007, pp. 238f.; BENEDICT, 2007, p. 125; RACAUT, 2002, p. 80).

63 Confer VOGEL, 2006, pp. 156f.; CROUZET, 1994, among others: pp. 40, 47, 125, 155, 158-179; JOUANNA, 2007, pp. 244, 247, 252; LESTRINGANT, 2003, pp. 113f.

from the memory box and giving examples of model behaviour or by just realising that the community had gone through this before and survived – even though the vast dimension of St. Bartholomew's Day Massacre provoked a Protestant crisis.[64] In this respect, the *topos* provided orientation.

The function of a model and fix point for identification was personified in the Reformed Admiral Gaspard de Coligny[65], to whom Dubois assigned a unique role, being the sole person depicted various times in his painting, neither as a hero nor a martyr.[66] While Coligny shared the fate of his coreligionists in being brutally killed, dehumanised and mocked, his portrayal did not draw on stereotypical elements, but was unique and personal. This singularity made the admiral and his fate memorable, apt to become an integrative figure of positive Protestant self-perception in regard to the St. Bartholomew's Day Massacre.

Dubois' interpretation of the St. Bartholomew's Day Massacre has received wide publicity today and become quite influential as part of cultural memory with respect to the Wars of Religion. Thanks to exhibitions, illustrations of school books and research monographs, even Wikipedia-articles on this massacre, Dubois' interpretation seems omnipresent. However, it has been widely ignored that Dubois had interwoven layers from the *topos* of massacre into his painting instead of giving an account of the event. Examining the painting *St. Bartholomew's Day Massacre* might provoke new openings of the memory box when emotional connotations and pre-set images linked to the *topos* of massacre are evoked, possibly in the persuasive sense in which Dubois made use of the *topos*, possibly in a different manner, taking into account that new layers have been added when this box was displaced and opened over the past centuries (e.g. colonial context; massacre of the Armenians).

However, whether the painter's interpretation was influential in adding new layers to the memory box and attaching new types of representation of the *topos* of massacre which then were used when the box was displaced and

64 Confer DIEFENDORF, 1991, pp. 142-144; JOUANNA, 2007, pp. 231-252, esp. pp. 244, 247; RACAUT, 2002, p. 79.

65 Among others: JOUANNA, 2007, p. 241; JANZING, 2005, p. 97; KINGDON, 1988, p. 32; KINGDON, 1974, p. 27; BURUCÚA/KWIATKOWSKI, 2012, p. 15.

66 He is the sole historical person represented simultaneously in the painting, accompanied on his imitation of the Stations of the Cross (confer JANZING, 2005, pp. 80f.): the militia threw his body out of the window, one man cut of the admiral's head, hands and genitals, observed by three nobles, and two civilians dragged the deformed body in the direction of the town gate. However, neither of the scenes was placed in the centre of the picture.

opened again, is uncertain. Dubois' importance for establishing a certain reading of St. Bartholomew's Day Massacre in the Protestant community and thereby help to create a collective memory at his time, is even more doubtful. Because of the lack of sources it is impossible to decide how contemporaries understood *St. Bartholomew's Day Massacre* at the moment when Dubois opened the memory box. Clear allusions to the painting in scripture or visual depictions are not known with one exception: More than one hundred years after the creation of the painting, two travelling Swiss briefly mentioned having seen it in the Lausanne town hall – but without further commenting it.[67] Apparently, Dubois' interpretation did not receive much attention. At the beginning of the nineteenth century it was even put in an attic, completely forgotten but rediscovered a few years later (1841).[68] Only since the end of the nineteenth century, when the painting was reproduced and a first broader examination was conducted, Dubois' reading of St. Bartholomew's Day Massacre started to gain more and more attention.[69]

67 Concerning later understandings of the image there are some sources left, even if only a few: In 1686, the painting is known to have hung in the Lausanne town hall. Labrune and Reboulet, two French Reformed, who visited the Reformed parishes in the Swiss Confederation, saw it there, as reported in their *Voyage de Suisse*. Their description shows that the picture was seen above all as a representative object which was accessible at least for a limited public; however, it did not provoke the two Frenchmen to reflect on the depicted event or even to discuss the interpretation Dubois had given. Apart from some very short remarks on the state of the painting, neither scriptural references nor any interpretation of the picture in other visual sources is known (Confer GRANDJEAN, 1965, p. 411).

68 Confer BORDIER, 1878, p. 31/11; BORDIER, 1879, p. 9; BEIL, 2003, p. 19, note 51. In 1862 the painting was made available for permanent exhibition in the Musée cantonal des Beaux-Arts where it is still today.

69 Only at the end of the nineteenth century did a more intense examination of this picture begin: Alexandre Duruy produced the lithographic print *La Saint-Barthélemy à Paris (24 août 1572)* after Dubois' picture in 1878 (confer BORDIER, 1878, p. 56/36 and image 1/appendix; BORDIER, 1879, p. 24, image 5), and, in the same year, the French historian Henri Bordier published the first scholarly reflections on the painting.

Visualising a non-representable event? – Dubois' usage of the *topos* of massacre

Without doubt, in the aftermath of St. Bartholomew's Day Massacre many competing interpretations of the recent events circulated. The categorisation as a massacre helped to make the event – difficult to determine, even seen as non-representable – manageable. Thus, patterns and pre-set images as well as a whole array of layers to draw on were provided to overcome the overwhelming character of the events by organising the perception as well as representation. Therefore, traits of the concrete event and topical aspects were interwoven in depictions.

In the context of the ongoing negotiation processes about the Reformed communal identity after St. Bartholomew's Day Massacre, closely linked to the question how to memorise the event, François Dubois opened the memory box when he painted *St. Bartholomew's Day Massacre* in Geneva between 1572 and 1584. To present a persuasive account, Dubois cited core facts from the historical massacre as markers of authenticity and credibility which directly alluded to St. Bartholomew's Day Massacre (e.g. the Louvre, the defenestration of Admiral Coligny) and immediacy placing the audience in the position of an on-site observer. In addition, he integrated unallocated, stereotypical elements from the general type of event of massacre, such as the omnipresence of blood and corpses and the extreme brutality of the perpetrators.

His guiding theme was the simplifying polarity of victims and perpetrators and most representational traits evoked layers from the memory box linked with the characterisation of these two groups, namely victims and committers. Dubois was able to draw on pre-set images to evoke prejudices and already existing emotional judgements, citing biblical and antique motifs which had already served as references in the Wars of Religion and were linked to the *topos* of massacre: While the motif of the massacre of the Innocents evoked the parallel to pure, righteous, pious victims (God's chosen), the allusion to Sulla's proscriptions and the Second Roman Triumvirate revealed low profane, financial motives, for example. *St. Bartholomew's Day Massacre* included rather new motifs, hitherto not closely linked to the *topos* of massacre, taken from contemporary discourses, in which the actors were described as unusually cruel and denying the value of their counterparts (the Turks, the hunt). This emphasis on a devastating characterisation of the Catholic committers was driven even further: Catholic justifications (using the dehumanised Protestant bodies as a marker) were turned into their opposite, declassing the Catholics themselves through their inhuman behaviour, cruelness and deceitfulness. Dubois developed ways to further highlight the condemnation of the perpetrators exceeding the hitherto known depictions of a massacre, departing from the concrete events in august 1572.

A rather aggressive self-assurance of the Protestant community – connected to the interpretation of the St. Bartholomew's Day Massacre as a unique event without comparison – was expressed in the concrete assignments of responsibility to the Royal family, questioning King Charles IX integrity and status as king, tending to desacralise him (substitutional regicide). As counterpart of the perpetrators, Dubois used the established representational type of the martyr-like victim, already attached to the memory box well before. Thus, Dubois embedded his interpretation of the St. Bartholomew's Day Massacre – then understood as one massacre among others – into the continuous narration of Protestant suffering. Invoking the hagiographical roots on which the Reformed self-image was based, Dubois provided an anchor for identification and a collective memory. Coligny was singled out as the integrative figure, a symbol of a communal Huguenot memory.

Dubois gave a complex interpretation of the St. Bartholomew's Day Massacre, drawing on the memory box on various levels. As there was apparently not much publicity for Dubois' opening of the memory box at his time, his interpretation had then little impact, whereas today the painting has become the best known visual depiction of the St. Bartholomew's Day Massacre. The painting therefore provides an access point to the handling of the *topos* of massacre by Dubois when enforcing his interpretation of the St. Bartholomew's Day Massacre.

List of References

Sources

CAPILUPI, CAMILLO, Le stratagème de Charles IX, roi de France, contre les Huguenots, rebelles à Dieu et à lui, ou relation du massacre de la Saint-Barthélemi; [1572]; 8°, 294 p. (= USTC 61448).

CRESPIN, JEAN, HISTOIRE || DES MARTYRS || PERSECVTEZ ET MIS A || mort pour la verité de l'Euangile, depuis le temps || des Apostres iusques à l'an 1574. [...] || M. D. LXXXII.; [Geneva, heirs of Eustace Vignon]; 2°, [8], 732, [6] fol. (= USTC 2949).

DUBOIS, FRANÇOIS, Le Massacre de la Saint-Barthélemy, between 1572 and 1584, oil on wood, 94 cm x 154 cm, Lausanne: Musée Cantonal des Beaux-Arts.

HISTOIRE || MEMORABLE || DE || LA PERSECVTION || & saccagement du peuple de Merindol & || Cabrieres & autres circonuoisins, appelez || VAVDOIS. || PSEAV. LXXIX. || Seigneur! Que la vengeance du sang de tes seruiteurs || respandu soit cogneue parmi les gens, en nostre pre- || sence. || ACTES IX. || Saul, Saul, pourquoy me persecutes-tu? || L'AN M. D. LV.; [Geneva, Jean Crespin]; 8°, [8], 135, [1] p. (= USTC 4879).

Testament du feu maistre Françoys du Boys dict Silvius, paintre, natif de la ville d'Amyens, en son vivant habitant à Genève, in: Le Monde selon François Dubois. Peintre de la Saint-Barthélemy (Les Cahiers du Musée des Beaux-Arts de Lausanne 13), ed. by RALF BEIL, Lausanne 2003, pp. 44f.

Secondary Literature

BABEL, RAINER, Kreuzzug, Martyrium, Bürgerkrieg. Kriegserfahrungen in den Französischen Religionskriegen, in: Religionskriege im Alten Reich und in Alteuropa, ed. by FRANZ BRENDLE/ANTON SCHINDLING, Münster 2006, pp. 107-117.

BEIL, RALF, Le Monde selon François Dubois, in: Le Monde selon François Dubois. Peintre de la Saint-Barthélemy (Les Cahiers du Musée des Beaux-Arts de Lausanne 13), ed. by RALF BEIL, Lausanne 2003, pp. 6-19.

BENEDICT, PHILIP, Graphic History. The Wars, Massacres and Troubles of Tortorel and Perrissin (Travaux d'Humanisme et Renaissance 431), Geneva 2007.

BORDIER, HENRI, La Saint-Barthélemy et la Critique moderne, Geneva/Paris 1879.

ID., Peinture de la Saint-Barthélemy par un Artiste contemporain. Comparé avec les Documents historiques (Mémoires et Documents publiés par la Société d'Histoire et d'Archéologie de Genève 1, Series 4), Geneva 1878, pp. 23/3-56/36.

BOURGEON, JEAN-LOUIS, Charles IX devant la Saint-Barthélemy (Travaux d'histoire éthico-politique 55), Geneva 1995.

BURSCHEL, PETER, Das Heilige und die Gewalt. Zur frühneuzeitlichen Deutung von Massakern, in: Archiv für Kulturgeschichte 86 (2004), pp. 341-368.

BURUCÚA, JOSÉ EMILIO/KWIATKOWSKI, NICOLÁS, Martirio individual y colectivo como fórmula para la representación de masacres históricas [manuscript, from 2nd Forum of Sociology, Buenos Aires, August 2012, p. 1-27; going to be published in: 'Cómo sucedieron estas cosas'. Representar masacres y genocidios, ed. by JOSÉ EMILIO BURUCÚA/NICOLÁS KWIATKOWSKI].

CORNETTE, JOËL, Maria die Tröstende, Katharina die Mordende, in: Geschichte der Frauen im Bild, ed. by GEORGES DUBY/MICHELLE PERROT, Frankfurt a.M. 1995, pp. 116-117.

CROUZET, DENIS, Calvinism and the Uses of the Political and the Religious (France, ca. 1560-ca. 1572), in: Verhandelingen, Afd. Letterkunde, Neue Reihe 176 (1999), pp. 99-114.

ID., La Nuit de la Saint-Barthélemy. Un Rêve perdu de la Renaissance (Chroniques), [Paris] 1994.

ID., Les Guerriers de Dieu. La Violence au Temps des Troubles de Religion (vers 1525-vers 1610), 2 vol., Seyssel 1990.

ID., Sur le Concept de Barbarie au XVIe Siècle, in: La Conscience Européenne au XVe et au XVIe Siècle (Collection de l'École Normale Supérieure de Jeunes Filles 22), Paris 1982, pp. 103-126.

DAVIS, NATALIE ZEMON, The Rites of Violence. Religious Riot in sixteenth Century France, in: The Massacre of St. Bartholomew. Reappraisals and Documents, ed. by ALFRED SOMAN, Den Haag 1974, pp. 203-242.

DEONNA, WALDEMAR, Une Peinture genevoise de la Saint-Barthélemy, in: Genava 21 (1943), pp. 116-120 and Images VII, VIII.

DIEFENDORF, BARBARA B., Beneath the Cross. Catholics and Huguenots in Sixteenth-Century Paris, New York/Oxford 1991.

EHRMANN, JEAN, Tableaux de Massacre au XVIe siècle, in: Société de l'Histoire du Protestantisme Français. Bulletin. Études, Documents, Chronique littéraire 118 (Jul.-Sep. 1972), pp. 445-455.

ID., Massacre and Persecution Pictures in Sixteenth Century France, in: Journal of the Warburg and Courtauld Institutes 8 (1945), pp. 195-199.

EL KENZ, DAVID, Massacre, in: Online Encyclopedia of Mass Violence (Nov. 2007a), http://www.massviolence.org/Massacre, 13.08.2013.

ID., Massacres during the French Wars of Religion, in: Online Encyclopedia of Mass Violence (Nov. 2007b), http://www.massviolence.org/Article?id_article=6, 13.08.2013.

ID., La Mise en Scène médiatique du Massacre des Huguenots au Temps des Guerres de Religion. Théologie ou Politique?, in: Sens public (2006), p. 1-19, http://www.sens-public.org/spip.php?article333, 13.08.2013.

ID., La Sacralisation par l'Image, au Temps des Guerres de Religion. Études Comparée des Massacres d'un Livret Calviniste et d'un Livret Catholique, in: Histoire, Images, Imaginaires. Fin XVe Siècle – Début XXe Siècle, ed. by MICHÈLE MÉNARD/ANNIE DUPRAT, Maine 1998, pp. 223-235.

GRANDJEAN, MARCEL, Les Monuments d'Art et d'Histoire du Canton de Vaud, vol. 1: La Ville de Lausanne (Les Monuments d'Art et d'Histoire de la Suisse [51]), Basle 1965.

GREENGRASS, MARK, Hidden Transcripts. Secret Histories and Personal Testimonies of Religious Violence in the French Wars of Religion, in: The Massacre in History, ed. by MARK LEVENE/PENNY ROBERTS, New York/Oxford 1999, pp. 69-87.

HERZ, ALEXANDRA, Vasari's 'Massacre' Series in the Sala Regia. The Political, Juristic, and Religious Background, in: Zeitschrift für Kunstgeschichte 49 (1986), pp. 41-54.

JANZING, GODEHARD, Fenstersturz als Fanal. Zur Bildlogik von Gewaltexzessen, in: Bürgerkrieg. Erfahrung und Repräsentation (Potsdamer Beiträge zur Kultur- und Sozialgeschichte 4: Kollektive Gewalt – Krieg – Kultur 1, Sonderdruck), ed. by ISABELLA VON TRESKOW, Berlin 2005, pp. 73-101.

JOUANNA, ARLETTE, 24 août 1572. La Saint-Barthélemy. Les Mystères d'un Crime d'État (Les Journées qui ont fait la France), [Paris] 2007.

ID. et al., Histoire et Dictionnaire des Guerres de Religion (Bouquins Collection), [Paris] 1998.

KELLEY, DONALD R., Martyrs, Myths, and the Massacre. The Background of St. Bartholomew, in: The American Historical Review 77, 5 (Dec. 1972), pp. 1323-1342.

KINGDON, ROBERT M., Myths about the St. Bartholomew's Day Massacres. 1572-1576, London 1988.

ID., Reactions to the St. Bartholomew Massacre in Geneva and Rome, in: The Massacre of St. Bartholomew. Reappraisals and Documents, ed. by ALFRED SOMAN, Den Haag 1974, pp. 25-49.

LESTRINGANT, FRANK, Témoignage et Martyre. Donner à voir, donner à croire (XVIe-XVIIIe siècle), in: Martyrs et Martyrologes (Revue des Sciences Humaines 269, 1), ed. by FRANK LESTRINGANT/PIERRE-FRANÇOIS MOREAU, Lille 2003, pp. 111-134.

LEVENE, MARK, Introduction, in: The Massacre in History, ed. by MARK LEVENE/PENNY ROBERTS, New York/Oxford 1999, pp. 1-37.

MALETTKE, KLAUS, Die Vorstöße der Osmanen im 16. Jahrhundert aus französischer Sicht, in: Europa und die Türken in der Renaissance (Frühe Neuzeit. Studien und Dokumente zur deutschen Literatur und Kultur im europäischen Kontext 54), ed. by BODO GUTHMÜLLER/WILHELM KÜHLMANN, Tübingen 2000, pp. 373-394.

MEDICK, HANS, Massaker der Frühen Neuzeit, in: Gewalt in der Frühen Neuzeit (Historische Forschungen 81), ed. by CLAUDIA ULBRICH et al., Berlin 2005, pp. 15-19.

MELLET, PAUL-ALEXIS, Nouveaux espaces et autres temps. Le problème de la Saint-Barthélemy et l'horizon européen des Monarchomaques, in: "Et de sa bouche sortait un glaive." Les Monarchomaques au XVIème siècle, ed. by PAUL ALEXIS MELLET, Geneva 2006, pp. 79-99.

RACAUT, LUC, Hartred in Print. Catholic Propaganda and Protestant Identity during the French Wars of Religion, Aldershot 2002.

RADRIZZANI, DOMINIQUE, Les Protestants et les Coiffeurs. De Simon Goulart à Christian Boltanski, in: Le Monde selon François Dubois. Peintre de la Saint-Barthélemy (Les Cahiers du Musée des Beaux-Arts de Lausanne 13), ed. by RALF BEIL, Lausanne 2003, pp. 20-29.

ID., Dubois, François, [1998], in: SIKART. Lexikon und Datenbank zur Kunst in der Schweiz, http://www.sikart.ch/KuenstlerInnen.aspx?id=4023026&lng=de, 13.08.2013.

RÖTTGEN, HERWARTH, Zeitgeschichtliche Bildprogramme der Katholischen Restauration unter Gregor XIII., 1572-1585, in: Münchner Jahrbuch der Bildenden Kunst. Dritte Folge 26 (1975), pp. 89-122.

SABEAN, DAVID WARREN, Reading sixteenth Century religious Violence. The Historiography of St. Bartholomew's Day Massacre, in: Religion und Gewalt. Konflikte – Rituale – Deutungen (1500-1800) (Veröffentlichungen des Max-Planck-Instituts für Geschichte 215), ed. by KASPAR VON GREYERZ/KIM SIEBENHÜNER, Göttingen 2006, pp. 109-123.

VOGEL, CHRISTINE, Einleitung, in: Bilder des Schreckens. Die mediale Inszenierung von Massakern seit dem 16. Jahrhundert, ed. by CHRISTINE VOGEL, Frankfurt/New York 2006, pp. 7-14.

The *Topos* of Martyrdom as a Memory Box

The Book of Martyrs by John Foxe and the Fresco Cycle at San Tomaso di Canterbury

KRISTINA MÜLLER-BONGARD

This article deals with the *topos* of martyrdom as a memory box. The term martyrdom comes from the original language of the court, where the Greek word *martyrs* means witness. It was then used in the New Testament for the apostles and in the course of the second century as a loan word taken over into Latin (martyrs) and transferred to tortured and executed Christians, the so-called "blood-witnesses".[1] Thus, the semantics have changed to a more militant connotation and, until today, emphasise less the witnessing than suffering, pain and cruelly dying.

To see the *topos* of martyrdom as a memory box allows focusing on one special moment of "opening": the chosen moment in this article is the second half of the sixteenth century, since the *topos* of martyrdom became an important instrument for confessional legitimation and in the politics of conversion.[2]

After the Council of Trent (1541-1563) various factors helped to renew the consciousness as well as the appreciation of martyrdom in Catholic Europe.[3] The reminiscence of the Early Christian Church brought martyrdom that was in theological tradition an argument for the divine Origin of Christianity in the

1 FRANK, 2007, pp. 209f.
2 Confer BAUMGARTEN, 2007, p. 465.
3 See BURSCHEL, 2001 and 2004.

centre to legitimate the Catholic doctrine. In addition, the apostles as the first martyrs served as models for an ideal Christian way of life.[4] To suffer martyrdom became the most aspired way of death, because that was the highest form of an "imitatio Christi".[5] In that sense, especially the reform-orders cultivated a martyrological sensibility, but no order did it more consciously than the Society of Jesus.[6] The meaning of martyrdom as an imitation and renewal of Christ's Passion was tightly integrated in the Jesuit spiritual doctrine and fixed in the *Exercitia Spiritualia* by Ignatius of Loyola, who was one of the main cofounders of the order in 1534.[7] This is why the Jesuits were particularly eager in restoring the old and re-enacting the recent martyrs, as it can be exemplarily seen by the monumental martyrdom cycles at the Jesuit College Churches in Rome. During the pontificate of Gregory XIII (1572-1585), three Roman Jesuit College Churches were decorated with a martyrdom cycle: the German College San Apollinare (1580), the Hungarian Santo Stefano Rotondo (1581-1582) and the Venerable English College San Tomaso di Canterbury (1582-1583).

But not only the Catholic Church operated with the *topos* of martyrdom; also Protestants needed a legitimation strategy especially since the 1550s, when the Reformation itself became an increasingly fading memory.[8] However, to keep that memory alive it was important to raise a Protestant publicity, through which a collective identity could be formed. The representation of martyrs proved to be particularly qualified to catch the public's attention. This is not an invention of sixteenth century; the "symbolic capital"[9] of martyrdom has been maintained since early Christian times. The Christian community made use of it to shape a collective memory through material cultures such as memorials, artefacts, texts, songs, etc. and emerged again in the mid of sixteenth century. On both sides – Catholic and Protestant – the new appreciation of Early Christianity and the cult of martyrdom became obvious in producing Martyrologies[10] as well as in martyrdom pictures.

4 Confer BURKE, 1987, pp. 54-66 and ANGENENDT, 1994.

5 ANGENENDT, 1994, p. 35.

6 To this aspect see HERZ, 1988.

7 The Society of Jesus was officially confirmed by Pope Paul III in 1540. For Ignatius and his Exercitia spiritualia see MEISSNER, 1997.

8 FUCHS, 1998, pp. 592f.

9 ROECK, 2007, p. 13.

10 E.g. Protestant ones by Ludwig Rabus "Historien der Heyligen Auserwölten Gottes Zeügen, Bekennern und Martyrern" (first published in 1552) and Jean Crespin's "Le livre de Martirs" 1564, or the revision of the Martyrologium Romanum by

Due to the new opportunities of the printing press, many religious-propagandistic pamphlets were produced. Thereby, particularly the images played an important role and turned out to be a very successful medium to highlight all the attributes of the *topos* of martyrdom carried in the memory box. Thus, there exists a special interrelation between the concept of memory box and images.

A memory box has special practical characteristics: it conserves, collects, transfers, and produces; it implies memories, meanings, and codes – but it needs publicity to be recognised as a memory box. Herein lays a main accordance of the memory box to the function of images.

Useful synergy effects could be produced by interrelating the memory box concept and images. The attributes of the *topos* collected in the memory box and set free at the moment of its opening could be well conserved and intensively unveiled within a picture, an engraving or a woodcut. Through the media representation of the memory box it became possible to transfer the convincing features of martyrdom to the public. Here, the purposes of using the memory box were similar with the role of images. Images are documents of cultural processes and thereby one of the most important information carriers in human communication. Like a memory box, also pictures can carry symbolic references, which make them capable of connecting different layers of awareness, e.g. spatial and temporal categories, individual and collective experiences. Within an image, cultural information is not only projected but also structured, and especially the structuring feature supports the converting and representation of complex cultural developments.[11] Thereby, images can function as a screen of the memory box, whereby publicity for the different layers of the box is achieved. This symbolises the main synergy-effect: a memory box needs publicity and images bring it into public.

This article introduces two examples, firstly the Protestant Martyrologium "Acts and monuments" by John Foxe, published in London 1563, and popularly known as the Book of Martyrs; secondly a Catholic fresco cycle, executed between the years 1582 and 1583 at the English Jesuit College Church *San Tomaso di Canterbury* in Rome. These two examples were chosen because both are dealing with the same "topographia" England, where many

Cesare Baronio in 1582, which is based on the martyrologium of Usuard of St. Germain in 875. For the Protestant Martyrologies, see GREGORY, 1999, pp. 165-196.

11 BISANZ, 2010, p. 13.

Catholics and Protestants were executed because of their religious faith during the Reformation process. In addition, both artefacts are interconnected because of their similar content: each narrates the history of the English Church from its beginnings to the present past – the Book of Martyrs in a textual manner including pictures of martyrdom and the fresco cycle in a visual representation. Thereby, the Protestant Martyrologium "Acts and monuments" by John Foxe, who initially opens the memory box for his purposes, can be seen as a model for the frescoes at the English College Church, where the same memory box was opened again and used as a direct reaction to the Protestant prototype.

The Book of Martyrs

The English Reformation began due to personal interests of King Henry VIII, who wanted a divorce from his wife Catherine of Aragon to marry Anne Boleyn, but Pope Clement VII refused the annulment and excommunicated Henry VIII. Accordingly, in 1534 Henry VIII decided to separate the English Catholic Church from Rome and to declare himself spiritual head of the Church of England by the Act of Supremacy. But this was no religious denomination to Protestantism; Protestantism was officially introduced for the first time as late as under the reign of Edward VI (1547-1553), but it took until the long reigns of Elizabeth I from 1558 to 1603 and her successor Protestant King James I (1603-1625) for the reformed confession to firmly settle. In between, Queen Mary I (1553-1558) tried to restore Catholicism which resulted in many Protestant martyrs who refused to return to the Roman Catholic Church. During this period John Foxe opened the memory box of martyrdom by starting his book project "Acts and Monuments".

The author John Foxe was born 1517 in Boston, Lincolnshire and settled in London in 1547, where he died in 1587. In 1550 he was ordained as deacon by Nicholas Ridley, Bishop of London and sympathiser of the Reformed Anglican Church. During the reign of Mary I (1553-1558) Foxe went into exile to Strasbourg, where he published a first version of his "Acts and Monuments", which already contained the martyrdoms of Englishmen in the fifteenth century. In a second version, published in 1559 in Basel, the martyrs under Mary's reign were added. Both exemplars were written in Latin.[12] After

12 HALLER, 1963, p. 13.

Elizabeth's accession to the throne and the acceptance of Protestantism[13], Foxe returned to England in 1559, where he published the first English edition of his "Acts and Monuments" in London 1563. The entire title simultaneously provides a survey of its content:

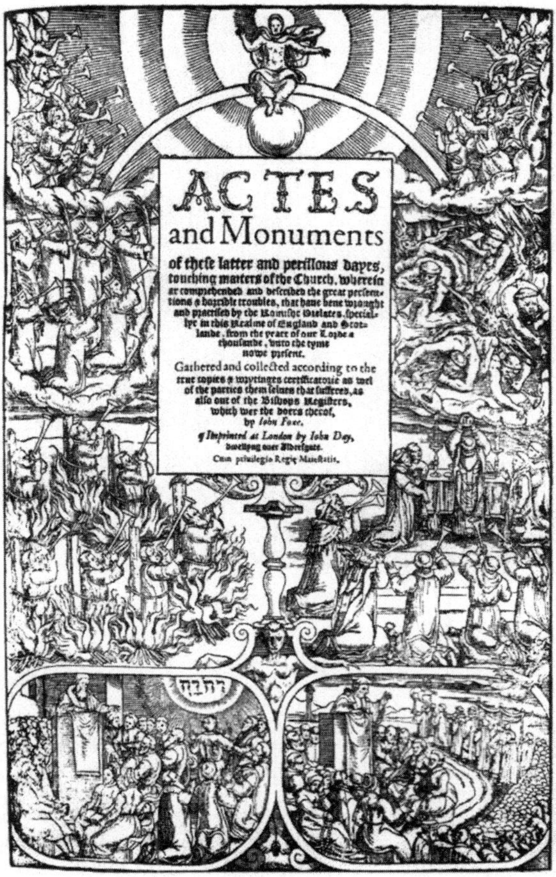

ACTES
and Monuments
of these latter and perillous dayes, touching matters of the Church, wherein ar comprehended and described the great persecutions & horrible troubles, that have bene wrought and practised by the Romishe Prelates, speciallye in this Realme of England and Scotlande, from the yeare of our Lorde a thousande, unto the tyme nowe present.
Gathered and collected according to the true copies & wrytinges certificatorie as wel of the parties them selves that suffered, as also out of the Bishops Registers, which wer the doers therof, by *John Foxe*.
¶ *Imprinted at London by John Day*, dwellyng over Aldersgate.
Cum privilegio Regiæ Maiestatis.

TITLE-PAGE *Actes and Monuments* 1563

Fig. 1: John Foxe, Acts and Monuments, London 1563, from: King 2006, p. 4, fig.2.

13 POLLEN, 1920, p. 17.

> Acts and Monuments of these latter and perillous dayes, touching matters of the Church, wherein ar comprehended and described the great persecutions & and horrible troubles, that have bene wrought and practised by the Romishe Prelates, speciallye in this Realme of England and Scotlande, from the yeare of oure Lorde a thousande, unto the tyme nowe present. Gathered and collected according to the true copies & wrytings certificatorie as wel of the parties them selves that suffered, as also out of the Bishops Registers, which wer the doers thereof, by John Foxe.[14]

That first version illustrates the English Church History from its beginning to the present on over 1400 pages, but concentrates on the faith, sufferings and martyrdoms of recent Protestant victims. Thus, most of the 56 woodcuts are illustrating the new Protestant martyrs who were executed during the reign of Queen Mary I. The second edition, published in 1570, already counts over 2300 pages and more than 150 woodcuts and was often bound together with the Bible to allow reading it in common places.[15]

The Book of Martyrs became one of the most influential books in sixteenth-century England. It was constantly printed over more than 120 years – apart from the Bible – more often than any other book.[16]

It starts with a calendar of Protestant martyrs, similar to Catholic calendars of saints[17], and a dedication to Queen Elizabeth I[18], wherein Foxe compared her to Emperor Constantine, who ended the persecutions of Christians and founded the Christian empire. Foxe associated himself with Bishop Eusebios (265-339), the author of the *Historiae Ecclesiasticae*, a calendar of early Christian martyrs, and that is exactly what Foxe was subsequently intending to do in his book.

In the first chapters Foxe narrated the English Church history. Thereby, he referred to the legends of early Christian martyrs under the Roman occupation

14 The title is framed by an image of the Last Judgement, picturing and caricaturing the Protestant religion at the left and Catholic religion at the right. Thereby Christ welcomes the souls of the Protestant martyrs, who are burning at stake and condemns the Catholic priests and "false" martyrs.

15 HALLER, 1963, p. 13.

16 HALLER, 1963, pp. 13f. At the end of the seventeenth century more than 10,000 copies were circulated.

17 Confer BAILEY, 2003, p. 155.

18 In the second edition 1570 Foxe began the dedication with begging Christ to crown Elizabeth and even naming her "our peaceable Salome". In detail see KING, 2006, p. 246.

such as St. Lucius, the first Christian king, and St. Alban, the English proto-martyr, as well as to medieval martyrs like St. Thomas Becket[19] – all accepted and canonised by the Roman Church –, and up to the dissociation of the English Church from the papacy through Henry VIII.

But his focus lay on the persecutions of Reformers and Protestants caused by the Catholic Queen Mary Tudor. Foxe reported on nearly 800 pages "what happened in the horrible and bloody time of Queen Mary".[20] Thereby, he relied on different sources such as first-person narratives, manuscripts written by eyewitnesses and oral testimony.[21] The most prominent martyrdoms are not only narrated, but also illustrated by woodcuts, such as those of Thomas Cranmer, Archbishop of Canterbury, and Nicholas Ridley, Bishop of London, together with Hugh Latimer, Bishop of Worchester, who were all burnt at the stake in Oxford.

19 FOXE, 1570, vol. 1, p. 55 (St. Lucius), p. 62 (St. Alban) and p. 263 (St. Thomas).
20 Quotation after HALLER, 1963, p. 122.
21 KING, 2009, p. xxvii.

The picture of the martyrdom of Latimer and Ridley on 16 October 1555 (fig. 2) shows the two reformers at the stake surrounded by a large crowd and Thomas Cranmer at the upper right, atop Bocardo prison, looking down to them and praying "O Lord strengthen them". The last words of the martyrs are also written on banderols which are coming out of their mouths: "Father of heaven receive my soul" and "Father, into thy hands I commit my spirit" as were Jesus' last words on the Cross (Luke 23, 46). Thereby Foxe stressed the notion of an imitation of Christ, of Latimer and Ridley in being innocently murdered.

Fig. 2: John Foxe, Acts and Monuments, London 1970: Martyrdom of Thomas Cranmer, woodcut, 13 cm x 17,5 cm, vol. 2, p. 2067 (Institutsbibliothek Evangelische Theologie, Johannes Gutenberg-Universität Mainz)

The memory box implied the same meaning of the martyrdom of Thomas Cranmer (fig. 3). He was following them at the stake six months later, on 21 March 1556, as Foxe wrote "for the confession of Christ's true doctrine"[22].

Fig. 3: John Foxe, Acts and Monuments, London 1970: Martyrdom of Nicholas Ridley und Hugh Latimer, woodcut, 18,5 cm x 25,5 cm, vol. 2, p. 1938 (Institutsbibliothek Evangelische Theologie, Johannes Gutenberg-Universität Mainz)

The reminiscence of Early Christianity and its first martyrs was one of the most effective attributes of the memory box, which was inserted by Foxe to highlight the tradition of being martyred and murdered for the "true faith" in England from his days back to the roots in early Christian times. The memory box implies the arguments for the legitimation of Protestant faith by comparing the victims with Christ and his followers, which were all officially accepted, meaning canonised, by the Catholic Church as being true martyrs. Thereby,

22 KING, 2009, p. 182.

Foxe referred to the use of the memory box not only to depict the recent martyrs but also their media representation in publicity:

> I see no reason why the martyrs of our time deserve not as great commendation as the others in primitive church, which assuredly are inferior unto them in no point of praise, whether we look upon the number of them that suffered or the greatness of their torments or their constancy in dying. […] we have found so many martyrs in this our age, let not fail them in publishing and setting forth their doings.[23]

Of course, copies of Foxe's "Acts and Monuments" also circulated in the Catholic community and, together with religious refugees, the book with its pictures of modern Protestant martyrs found its way to the English College at Rome. Its influence was known there, which became obvious by the statement of Robert Parsons, Rector of the English College in Rome in 1598: "[The Book] hath done more hurt alone to simple souls in our country by infecting and poisoning them unawares under the bait of pleasant histories, fair pictures and painted pageant, than many other of the most pestilent books together."[24]

To antagonise the propagandistic power of Foxe's Book of Martyrs and to open up the confessional controversy in the printing press, the same memory box was opened by English Catholics at Rome. The martyrdom cycle in the English College Church was commissioned and graphically reproduced as a series of engravings immediately after the frescoes were finished.

The martyrdom cycle in the Venerable English College Church

The illustrated pendant of Foxe's Book of Martyrs can be found in the Roman Jesuit College Church San Tomaso di Canterbury. It was the third College Church decorated with a martyrdom cycle in Rome but, among all the others, has the most interesting and really unusual pictorial program because it concentrates on English martyrs and those who had not yet been canonised or beatified. The fresco cycle consisted of 34 panels which were executed by the

23 FOXE, 1570, vol. 1, p. 522.
24 MOZLEY, 1940, p. 177.

painter Niccolo Circignani between the years 1582-1583 around the entire nave.[25] He also painted the other martyrdom cycles at San Apollinare and at Santo Stefano Rotondo[26], where he was assisted by Matteo da Siena. Niccolò Circignani, born around 1520 in Pomarance near Volterra, was one of the best employed fresco painters under Gregory XIII.[27] Unfortunately, the original fresco cycle was destroyed, but survived in a series of engravings entitled "Ecclesiae Anglicanae Trophaea" by Giovanni Battista Cavalieri. He reproduced all panels and published the series in 1584, only one year after the frescoes were finished.

As the engravings show today, it provided nearly the same pictorial program in drawing up the English Church History and the roots of Catholic faith as that of Foxe in his book 20 years earlier: The frescoes represented an almost chronological series of saints and martyrs of the English Church, both prominent and unknown, from the first century and the Middle Age until the contemporary present. As in case of John Foxe, here again the same famous martyrs such as St. Lucius, St. Alban and St. Thomas of Canterbury, to whom the College Church is dedicated[28], are used to depict the roots of the Christian faith in England. Afterwards – at which time Foxe concentrated on the victims under Queen Mary I –, the San Tomaso cycle illustrated recent Catholic victims under the reigns of Henry VIII and Elizabeth I on the last ten frescoes; the most famous being John Fisher, Bishop of Rochester and Thomas More, the former Lord Chancellor of King Henry (fig. 4). Both were accused of high treason because they refused to take the oath of Supremacy, established in 1534, whereby Henry declared himself head of the Church of England and separated his new founded Anglican Church from Rome. Next to their beheading in London 1535, the print also shows Margaret Pole, countess of Salisbury. The illustration does not capture a historical moment as in the martyrdom of Protestant Hugh Latimer and Nicholas Ridley, because More died some two weeks after Fisher and Margaret Pole even six years later. But the layers transferred into the memory box intended exactly the same meaning, namely to show them as direct followers of Christ and the early Christian and medieval martyrs which were pictured in the frescoes before. In addition, the enemy himself, King Henry, can be easily identified on the scaffold at the

25 Confer BAILEY, 2003, p. 158.
26 In particular for the cycle at Santo Stefano Rotondo see MONSSEN, 1981 and 1983.
27 Confer RÖTTGEN, 1975, p. 108 and MÂLE, 1932, p. 111.
28 Pope Gregory XIII donated a piece of Thomas' forearm to the College Church in 1580. See BAILEY, 2003, p. 156.

right. Henry is dressed in a contemporary costume, as are his soldiers, whose uniforms are equipped with the Tudor emblem.

Fig. 4: Giovanni Battista Cavalieri after Niccolò Circignani: Martyrdom of John Fisher and Thomas More, engraving, 26,5 cm x 20,5 cm, Ecclesiae anglicanae trophaea, Rome 1584 (Stadtbibliothek Trier)

Fig. 5: Giovanni Battista Cavalieri after Niccolò Circignani: Martyrdom of Edmund Campion, Ralph Sherwin and Alexander Briant, engraving, 26,5 cm x 20,5 cm, Ecclesiae anglicanae trophaea, Rome 1584 (Stadtbibliothek Trier)

The most famous Jesuit missionaries among the martyrs during the reign of Elizabeth I were Edmund Campion, Ralph Sherwin and Alexander Briant (fig.5). After their capture and torture in London Tower, they were hanged, disembowelled and quartered. Thereafter, their dismembered bodies were seethed. The persecutions of Jesuit missionaries usually ended in mass-executions by the same procedure, as is shown in the image illustrating the cruel martyrdom of thirteen students from the College, all executed between 1582 and 1583. The last, Richard Thirkeld, was killed in May 1583, shortly before the cycle was finished. Their bodies are draped in disorder and can only be identified because their names are written in the inscription beneath (fig. 6).

Fig. 6: Giovanni Battista Cavalieri after Niccolò Circignani: Martyrdom of Jesuit Priests, engraving, 26,5 cm x 20,5 cm, Ecclesiae anglicanae trophaea, Rome 1584 (Stadtbibliothek Trier)

In the case of this martyrdom cycle, the memory box was opened by the English refugee George Gilbert, who donated 700 *scudi* to the College for church decoration.[29] The Jesuit College churches and their decorations were closely bound to the function of the Colleges hosting foreign (Catholic European) students, from which three existed in Rome: San Apollinare was founded by Ignatius himself, who had intended to create an institution to house German students for education purposes under the leadership of Jesuit supervisors. The College was authorised by Pope Julius III in 1552, whose Bull of Foundation indicated that the intention was primarily to fight Protestantism.[30] For the same purpose, the Hungarian College was established in 1573 by Pope Gregory XIII, who was one of the greatest supporters of the Society of Jesus.[31] Later, in 1580, the German seminary was merged with the Hungarian and was from now on called the German-Hungarian College.[32] Furthermore, in 1579 Pope Gregory also founded the Venerable English College, which he assigned to the Society of Jesus. The English College is an English pilgrim's hospice and was established as a seminary by the English Catholic Cardinal William Allen as early as in 1577.

As mentioned above, the College's purpose was to train English priests for the dangerous pastoral work they would face in their home country. An interesting aspect is that all students were compelled to take a missionary oath before they entered the Jesuit Seminary, promising to return to England for missionary purposes and to serve persecuted Catholics.[33]

Before he went into exile, Gilbert himself was involved in the English mission by supporting the arriving missionaries; he therefore knew that many of them were captured and executed. Thus, in opening the memory box, he was fully aware of its purpose and impact, as is documented in a letter by Alfonso Agazzari, the rector of the College, to Claudio Acquaviva in June 1583:

---

29 BAILEY, 2003, p. 160.

30 Thus it was formulated in the Bull of Foundation "Dum Solicita" of the German College *San Apollinare* in 1552 by Pope Julius III, see CESAREO, 1993, p. 831.

31 In detail about Pope Gregory XIII and his relationship to the Society of Jesus see PASTOR, 1958, vol. 9, pp. 170-188.

32 For the history of the German-Hungarian College and its Churches San Apollinare and Santo Stefano Rotondo see SCHMIDT, 1984, BRANDENBURG/PÁL, 2000; for the frescoes see BAILEY, 2003, pp. 128-133.

33 For the history of the English College see GASQUET, 1920, p. 77, 118 and PASTOR, 1958, vol. 9, p. 177.

> Hence the holy man [Gilbert] took great pains to note down all the English martyrs, both ancient and modern, and to have their martyrdoms painted on panels, with which he adorned the entire church of this college [...] He used to say that he did this not only for the honour of these most glorious martyrs, and to show the glory and splendour of the English church, but also so that when the students in this college should see the example of these predecessors of theirs they might also be stirred toward martyrdom. And, moreover, that with the images of our new martyrdoms the miserable state of his fatherland would be placed before the eyes of Rome and of all the world, and thus move the people to pray to God on its behalf.[34]

The educational role of the pictures becomes obvious in this statement and is supported by their didactic layout, which is similar to that of pamphlets.[35] Mostly, each illustration depicts several martyrs or diverse scenes of their life. The prominent ones are placed in the foreground, the less known in the background. Letters placed near the protagonists correspond to Latin inscriptions under each illustration. These provide some short information about the depicted saint, making the identification much easier.[36]

This layout also served a meditative function. In Jesuit context, every student is held to bear his own cross, his own martyrdom, by which the greatest Imitation of Christ could be achieved.[37] In accordance with the Exercitia spiritualia by the order's founder Ignatius of Loyola, this could also be achieved by meditation. That is why the paintings illustrated emotionless, non-individual figures in anonymous landscapes without divine attributes such as the crown or the martyr's palm. They should provide the viewer with the utmost liberty for their individual imagination.

But the didactic function goes far beyond individual imagination. The frescoes were determined for the direct education in missions, by inspiring students to follow the illustrated martyrs. The final fresco showed Pope Gregory XIII, who encourages the students and sends them out to save Protestant souls by leading them back to Catholicism (fig. 7).

---

34 [Archivum Romanum Societatis Iesu (Angl. 7, 44a-b)], translated by and quoted after BAILEY, 2003, p. 160.

35 For the presentation principles of pamphlets see SCHILLING, 1990.

36 About this typical didactic layout in Jesuit education and its prototype "Evangelicae historiae imagines" by Jerome Nadal see BUSER, 1976, BAILEY, 2003, p. 36 and STEINEMANN, 2006, pp. 404-406.

37 Confer MEISSNER, 1997, p. 122 and KORRICK, 1999, p. 172.

Fig. 7: Giovanni Battista Cavalieri after Niccolò Circignani: Pope Gregory XIII., engraving, 26,5 cm x 20,5 cm, Ecclesiae anglicanae trophaea, Rome 1584 (Stadtbibliothek Trier)

The fact that an active and publically suffered martyrdom was able to be a tool of conversion is even mentioned in the inscription beneath the martyrdom of Edmund Campion, with "aliquot millia hominum ad Romanum Ecclesiam conversa sunt". Indeed, an execution was an event, which attracted many people[38], and the execution of Campion, together with his companions Alexander Briant and Ralph Sherwin, caused a sensation not only within the Catholic community; it is said that even John Foxe wrote a letter to Queen Elizabeth in which he asked for mercy and begged her pardon.[39]

In fact, the students concretely were prepared to achieve a similar fate, which actually meant to suffer a gruesome death. On account of the 41 College students who suffered for the faith in the following years, the crucial pictures did encourage them.[40]

For propagandistic issues the modern Protestant and Catholic martyrs – especially the seminary priests and Jesuit missionaries from the Roman College who were martyred in the 1580s, just before the cycle was finished – turned out to be very striking. But to exploit the executed College students in the religious controversy, they firstly had to be officially accepted as martyrs. To this effect, the pope made a number of concessions around 1580: including that the relics of present-day martyrs, who had studied within the college walls, could be used in the consecration of altars, that the "Te Deum" should be sung upon hearing news of one's martyrdom and that pictures from these martyrs might be painted on the church walls.[41] That suggested that even living students were treated as walking relics and greeted with "Salvete Flores Martyrum" – Hail, flowers of martyrdom.[42]

In general, the concessions made by Pope Gregory are similar to Foxe's written argumentation of praising the contemporary martyrs. Because the memory box transfers culturally shared knowledge (in both religious communities), it guaranteed the effective use of the *topos* of martyrdom depending on the religious point of view for the legitimacy or the falseness of the particular confession.

38 DAVIS, 1987, p. 181 and GREGORY, 1999.

39 Encyclopaedia Britannica 1963, vol. 9, p. 573.

40 WALSH, 1979, p. 4.

41 GASQUET, 1920, p. 122. The Fresco cycle was commissioned by George Gilbert an English refugee in the Roman College. For details see BAILEY, 2003, p. 157.

42 GASQUET, 1920, p. 118; Greeting of Filippo Neri when he met the College's students.

In fact, the propagandistic use becomes more than obvious in the anti-Catholic, respectively anti-Protestant, program. Foxe, as well as the Jesuits from San Tomaso, was eager to use the antagonisms produced by martyrdom respectively the martyr, as good and evil, suffered and executed violence, peaceful and aggressive faith, victim and offender, etc., to draw a clear concept of the enemy. In this way, the collective memory of the old martyrs became a distinctive memory when the new martyrs were shown and thereby formed a religious identity. This was one of the reasons for the reproduction of the frescoes into a medium: a fresco is limited to a pin point because it is painted upon the freshly laid plastering and therefore bound to the wall. Accordingly, by using engravings it was possible to displace the memory box in a wider publicity and publish the anti-Protestant message in England and all over the world, as it is written in the Annals of the College:

> But with the view of throwing light on the wretched state of that kingdom and the miserable plight of its Catholic inhabitants, a book of the English persecution has been re-published at the expense of this College […]. We have spread copies of this work far and wide, even to the Indies, that the infamy of this most disastrous persecution, the phrenzied [sic] rage of the heretics, the unconquerable firmness of the Catholics, may be known everywhere.[43]

Conclusion

Since the sixteenth century particularly images – primarily engravings and woodcuts – were used for the public mediation and commemoration of confessional martyrs since they were easy to reproduce. Thus, the pictured Protestant Martyrologium and the frescoes – respectively the engravings of the Jesuit College – served as screens for the modern martyrs. By their media representation, the transformation of meaning became visible: victims were transformed to heroes, the defeat was transformed to a spiritual and religious victory, suffering martyrdom meant eternal life and getting a direct ticket into heaven. That, again, plays an important role in producing publicity – there

43 FOLEY, 1880, vol. 6, p. 83; confer NOREEN, 1998, p. 698.

couldn't be any martyrs without – as well as for their commemoration and ritual veneration (the martyrs' bodies become relics).[44]

An advantage of images over written media was particularly the easier control of the receivers (=Rezipientensteuerung) as is suggested by the Italian art and media theorist Cardinal Gabriele Paleotti in his "Discorso".[45] In his book, Paleotti theorised what the Catholic Church had already recognised and practiced under the pressure of the confessional conflict, namely the efficiency of images as an instrument of/in mass communication[46] as can be seen in Roman church decorations under Pope Gregory XIII and their immediate graphical reproduction. In sixteenth and seventeenth-century Rome, both in painting and graphics, the representations of martyrdoms became very popular, which demonstrates the papal authorities' awareness of the sensational and convincing power of these mostly very gruesome illustrations.

At the same time, Paleotti provided the argumentation for the "verita istorica", the validity of the images by using the rhetorical device of "docere" that allowed seeing the image as perception medium (=Erkenntnismedium) and which is able to mediate the truth and knowledge.[47] This was previously argued by Giovanni Andrea Giglio da Fabriano in 1564 by comparing the historical painter with a translator of the text/literary source.[48] Indeed, the validity of the sources is a central problem, but by the visual translation of the martyrdoms, which were already proved to be true and accepted in Protestant as well as in Catholic faith, also the pictures of them and those who followed became valid as (mediators of) historical truth.

As in the Book of Martyrs, through using the memory box of martyrdom the San Tomaso cycle pointed out the long-lasting tradition of the Catholic Church in England and its legitimacy in claiming to be the historical "true" confession up to the contemporary past that is proved by the modern martyrs.

---

44 See HORSCH/TREML, 2011, p. 13. For the publicity-aspect of martyrs see also FRANK, 2007, pp. 220f., and for especially Protestant concerns MENSING, 2002, pp. 117-146.

45 "Discorso intorno alle imagine sacre e profane", Bologna 1582.

46 For a comprehensive analysis of Paleotti's Discorso see STEINEMANN, 2006, here p. 38.

47 STEINEMANN, 2006, p. 122. Next to Paleotti many others referred to the validity o images as Roberto Bellarmino, Antonio Possevino and Cesare Baronio. For th "verita historica"-concept see also HECHT, 1997, pp.185f.

48 Dialogo nel quale si ragiona degli errori e degli abusi de' pittori circa l'istori Camerino 1564, in: BAROCCHI, 1961, pp. 1-115, here pp. 35,55.

List of References

Sources

CAVALIERI, GIOVANNI BATTISTA, Ecclesiae anglicanea trophaea [...], Rom: Bartolomeo Grassi 1584.

FOXE, JOHN, Acts and Monuments of these latter and perillous dayes [...], London: John Day 1570.

PALEOTTI, GABRIELE, Discorso intorno alle imagine sacre e profane, Bologna 1582.

Secondary Literature

ANGENENDT, ARNOLD, Grundformen der Frömmigkeit im Mittelalter, Munich 1994.

BAILEY, GAUVIN ALEXANDER, Between Renaissance and Baroque. Jesuit Art in Rome 1565-1610, Toronto 2003.

BAROCCHI, PAOLA, Trattati d'arte del Cinquecento, Bari 1961.

BAUMGARTEN, JENS, Bekehrung durch Kunst? Jesuitische „Überwältigungsästhetik" und das Problem der Konversion, in: Konversion und Konfession in der Frühen Neuzeit, ed. by UTE LOTZ-HEUMANN et al., Heidelberg 2007, pp. 463-490.

BISANZ, ELIZE, Die Überwindung des Ikonischen. Kulturwissenschaftliche Perspektiven der Bildwissenschaft, Bielefeld 2010.

BRANDENBURG, HUGO/PÁL, JÓZEF (eds.), Santo Stefano Rotondo in Roma. Archeologia, storia dell'arte, restauro, Wiesbaden 2000.

BURKE, PETER, Wie wird man Heiliger der Gegenreformation?, in: Städtische Kultur in Italien zwischen Hochrenaissance und Barock. Eine historische Anthropologie, ed. by PETER BURKE , Berlin 1987, pp. 54-66.

BURSCHEL, PETER, Sterben und Unsterblichkeit. Zur Kultur des Martyriums in der frühen Neuzeit, Munich 2004.

ID., Paradiese der Gewalt. Martyrium, Imagination und die Metamorphosen des nachtridentinischen Heiligenhimmels, in: Jahrbuch des Historischen Kollegs 2001, pp. 139-181.

BUSER, THOMAS, Jerome Nadal and Early Jesuit Art in Rome, in: The Art Bulletin, 58, 1976, pp. 424-433.

CESAREO, FRANCESCO C., The Collegium Germanicum and the Ignatian Vision of Education, in: Sixteenth Century Journal XXIV/4, 1993, pp. 829-841.

DAVIS, NATALIE ZEMON, Die Riten der Gewalt, in: Humanismus, Narrenherrschaft und die Riten der Gewalt. Gesellschaft und Kultur im frühzeitlichen Frankreich, ed. by NATALIE ZEMON DAVIS , Frankfurt a.M. 1987, pp. 171-209.

ENCYCLOPAEDIA BRITANNICA: A new survey of universal knowledge, 23 vols., here vol. 9, Chicago et al. 1963.

FOLEY, HENRY, Records of the English Province of the Society of Jesus; 6 (suppl. vol.). The diary of the English College, Rome, from 1579 to 1773, with biographical and historical notes; the pilgrim-book of the ancient English hospice attached to the college from 1580 to 1656, London 1880.

FRANK, THOMAS, Zur Figur des christlichen Märtyrers, in: Nachleben der Religionen. Kulturwissenschaftliche Untersuchungen zur Dialektik der Säkularisierung, ed. by MARTIN TREML/DANIEL WEIDNER, Munich 2007, pp. 209-224.

FUCHS, THOMAS, Protestantische Heiligen-memoria im 16. Jahrhundert, in: Historische Zeitschrift, vol. 267 (1998), pp. 587-614.

GASQUET, KARDINAL A., A History of the Venerable English College, Rome. An Account of its Origins and Work from the erliest Times to the present Day, London 1920.

GREGORY, BRAD STEPHAN, Salvation at Stake. Christian Martyrdom in Early Modern Europe, London 1999.

HALLER, WILLIAM, Foxe's Book of Martyrs and the Elect Nation, London 1963.

HECHT, CHRISTIAN, Katholische Bildertheologie der frühen Neuzeit : Studien zu Traktaten von Johannes Molanus, Gabriele Paleotti und anderen Autoren, Berlin 1997.

HERZ, ALEXANDRA, Imitators of Christ: The Martyr-Cycles of Late Sixteenth Century Rome Seen in Context, in: Storia dell'arte, 62, 1988, pp. 53-70.

HORSCH, SILVIA/TREML, MARTIN, Grenzgänger der Religionskulturen. Kulturwissenschaftliche Beiträge zu Gegenwart und Geschichte der Märtyrer, Munich 2011.

KING, JOHN, Introduction, in: Foxe's Book of Martyrs. Select Narratives, Oxford/New York 2009, pp. xi-xl.

ID., Foxe's Book of Martyrs and Early modern print culture, Cambridge University Press 2006.

KORRICK, LESLIE, On the meaning of style: Nicolò Circignani in Counter-Reformation Rome, in: Word and Image, 15, 1999, pp. 170-189.

MÂLE, ÉMILE, L'art religieux après le Concile de Trente. Étude sur l'iconographie de la fin du XVIe siècle, du XVIIe, du XVIIIe siècle. Italie – France – Espagne – Flandres, Paris 1932.

MEISSNER, WILLIAM W, Ignatius von Loyola: Psychogramm eines Heiligen, Freiburg i. Br. et al. 1997.

MENSING, BJÖRN, Martyrien und ihre Rezeptionsgeschichte im deutschen Protestantismus. Erinnerungskultur und Geschichtspolitik, in: Widerstehen. Wirkungsgeschichte und aktuelle Bedeutung christlicher Märtyrer, ed. by MENSING, BJÖRN/RATHKE, HEINRICH, Leipzig 2002, pp. 117-146.

MONSSEN, LEIF HOLM, The Martyrdom Cycle in Santo Stefano Rotondo. Part Two, in: Acta ad Archaeologiam et Artium Historiam Pertinentia (Institutum Romanum Norvegiae. Series Altera), vol. 3, Rome 1983, pp. 11-106.

ID., Rex Gloriose Martyrum: A Contribution to Jesuit Iconography, in: The Art Bulletin, 63, 1981, pp. 130-137.

MOZLEY, JAMES FREDERIC, John Foxe and his Book, London/New York 1940.

NOREEN, KIRSTIN, Ecclesiae militantis triumphis. Jesuit Iconography and the Counter-Reformation, in: Sixteenth Century Journal, 29, 1998, pp. 689-715.

PASTOR, LUDWIG FREIHERR VON, Geschichte der Päpste im Zeitalter der katholischen Reformation und Restauration. Gregor XIII. (1572-1585) (Geschichte der Päpste seit dem Ausgang des Mittelalters, vol. 9), Freiburg i. Br. 1958.

POLLEN, JOHN HUNGERFORD, The English Catholics in the Reign of Queen Elizabeth. A Study of their politics, civil life and government, New York 1920.

ROECK, BERND, Introduction, in: Cultural Exchange in Early Modern Europe. Forging European Identities1400-1700, ed. by HERMAN ROODENBURG, vol. 4, New York 2007, pp. 1-29.

RÖTTGEN, HERWARTH, Zeitgeschichtliche Bildprogramme der katholischen Restauration unter Gregor XIII 1572-1585, in: Münchner Jahrbuch der bildenden Kunst, 26, 1975, pp. 89-122.

SCHILLING, MICHAEL, Bildpublizistik der frühen Neuzeit. Aufgaben und Leistungen des illustrierten Flugblattes in Deutschland um 1700 (Studien und Texte zur Sozialgeschichte der Literatur, vol. 29), Tübingen 1990.

SCHMIDT, PETER, Das Collegium Germanicum in Rom und die Germaniker. Zur Funktion eines römischen Ausländerseminars (1552-1914), Tübingen 1984.

STEINEMANN, HOLGER, Eine Bildtheorie zwischen Repräsentation und Wirkung. Kardinal Gabriele Paleottis "Discorso intorno alle imagini sacre e profane" (1582), Hildesheim et al. 2006.

WALSH, JAMES, The Catholic Martyrs of England and Wales, 1535-1680. A Chronological List, London 1979.

The *Topos* of Golden Age in Friedrich Schlegel's Notion of Cultural Transfer from Antiquity to Early Nineteenth-Century Germany

ASKO NIVALA

Golden Age *topos* as a memory box

In Western tradition, the *topos* of Golden Age is among the oldest myths survived to us. We can find its first written transcription in Hesiod's *Works and Days* (*Erga kai Hēmérai*, 700 BC). It is a farmer's almanac in which the author gives a reason for the present human condition of Iron Age that is characterised by hard agricultural labour. Humankind originated in Chronus' rule, during which lived a Golden Race and where there was no need for work. People were morally righteous and they could simply take what they needed for nourishment from the surrounding nature.[1] Originally, the myth of the Golden Age was used to explain and justify the burden of farming to people who had to work on fields.[2]

The cultural function of a myth was to legitimate a cultural institution by telling its story of origin.[3] The mode of argumentation used in mythological

1 HESIOD, XI.109-201. See also LOVEJOY/BOAS, 1997 (1935), pp. 24-31.

2 As Hans Blumenberg has emphasised, the ancient mythology was not simply irrational superstition, but it had necessary cultural and social function. BLUMENBERG, 1985 (1975), 3, 34f., 59, 63; FRANK, 1982, pp. 59-65.

3 Manfred Frank defines myth as *Beglaubigung* (legitimation or reinforcement) of social and cultural practices. FRANK, 1982, pp. 80f.

poetry was not logical inference, to be sure, but rhetorical persuasion. In the ancient art of rhetoric, *koinoì tópoi* (common places) referred to an entire warehouse of literary images.[4] The collection of *topoi* included arguments, motives and background settings that authors could utilise in order to convince their audience.This huge collection of rhetorical *topoi* was used to aid human memory when a *rhapsode* delivered an oral performance for audience, to give an example.

This classical collection of common places had a major impact on the formation of European culture. Golden Age has been an influential *topos* applied by countless Western authors in various historical situations from antiquity to the Middle Ages and modernity.[5] I suggest that this chain of tradition forms an instance of diachronic cultural transfer from antiquity to modernity. However, the function of the *topos* of Golden Age has changed as well during this process. For example, the introduction of Christianity triggered a complicated process of cultural transfer during which the Greek representation of Golden Age was fused and mixed with the *topos* of paradise from the Hebrew Genesis.

In this article I shall focus on Friedrich Schlegel's (1772-1829) analysis of the Roman way to use the *topos* of Golden Age. In other words, I present how Schlegel opened up this memory box at the turn of nineteenth century when German Romanticism was inaugurated. Because he was one of the most influential and famous writers of the early Romantic generation of the 1790s and continued to have an impact on the German-speaking public until the 1820s, I suggest that his opinions represent more than a generalisation of the understanding of this *topos* during the early nineteenth-century.

Golden Age and cultural transfer – Rome as displaced Greece

We find many references to the Golden Age in Friedrich Schlegel's works.[6] However, when it comes to the specific topic of cultural transfer, one cannot

4 CURTIUS, 1993 (1948), p. 79.

5 Many examples of this are analysed by LOVEJOY/BOAS, 1997 (1935) and BOAS 1997 (1948).

6 The theme of the Golden Age in Schlegel's philosophy of history shall be the topic of my forthcoming doctoral dissertation.

bypass a passage, in which Schlegel used the *topos* of Golden Age to analyse the cultural historical role of Rome as the link between the classical Greece and modern Europe. The main reason for his turning to the history of Rome was to analyse the influence of the antiquity on the European nation-building process at the beginning of the nineteenth century.[7] Schlegel's analysis of Rome is documented in his dialogue *Gespräch über die Poesie* (*Dialogue on Poetry*, 1800) that was originally published in *Athenäum*-magazine edited by the Schegel-brothers. As a part of the text, a character called Andrea reads an essay "Epochen der Dichtkunst" ("Epochs of Poetry").[8] As Ernst Behler and Roman Struc have emphasised, this small essay is probably "the first, almost excessively concise presentation of the universal as well as comparative history of literature".[9] By closely reading this text, I am able to research the displacement of the Golden Age *topos* from antiquity to the early nineteenth-century Germany.[10] My contribution shall show how this *topos* changed initially when it was taken from the Greek context to Rome and secondly from there to the early Romantic age by Schlegel.

The first significant opening of this memory box happened in Rome. It was Virgil (Publius Vergilius Maro, 70-19 BC) who gave a political connotation to the meaning of Golden Age. For Hesiod, its purpose was to justified hard agricultural labour, but after Virgil, the Golden Age was transformed to a *topos* that legitimated political rule. Rulers wanted to claim that the present age

7 Because Schlegel is considered to be among the most important members of the early Romantic circle in Jena and Berlin, his literary theory and philosophy have been intensely studied, but his work as a historian has received much less attention from scholars. Thus far, Schlegel's view of Rome has not been researched in depth, when compared to all the studies on his notion of Greece. A list of relevant literature concerning Schlegel's notion of antiquity is provided by BARNETT, 2001. See also HEINER, 1972.

8 The interpretation of this small essay implicates a source critical difficulty. It seems impossible to verify what opinions are Schlegel's own and what belong to his various fictive mouthpieces. Furthermore, sometimes it seems that his fictive characters defend positions that he has already abandoned. As Behler and Struc have written about the English translation of this text: "the dialogue form allows the author to present his previous philosophical and critical positions, even if they stand in opposition to his later points of view" BEHLER/STRUC, 1968, p. 12. In other words, it is not relevant to ask which of the characters represents Schlegel's own opinion, but to focus on the problems and questions elaborated in the dialogue.

9 BEHLER/STRUC, 1968, p. 21.

10 On the concept of *displacement* see NIVALA, 2011.

was the new Golden Age and therefore invited famous authors to their court.[11] The memory box of Golden Age was opened in Rome in order that Virgil could deposit this new content into the *topos*. Schlegel's Andrea describes this process, the change of meaning of the Golden Age *topos,* as follows:

> For the course of a few generations everybody in Rome wanted to write poetry and everybody believed he had to court the Muses and help them along. And this, the Romans called their Golden Age of poetry. It was like a barren flower in the making [*Bildung*] of that nation.[12]

The regime of the first Roman Emperor Augustus (ruling time 27 BC-14 AD; originally Gaius Julius Caesar Octavianus, 63 BC-14 AD) was considered to be the most fruitful era of Latin literature in general. Virgil made an important change in the Golden Age *topos*: as after his time, the *topos* no longer referred to an innocent stage of the first humans as presented by Hesiod, but to the artistic inauguration of national literature. *Bildung dieser Nation* is a difficult phrase to translate in this quotation. *Bildung* could mean education or the formation of a human subject, in the sense of *Ausbildung*. However, in the beginning of the nineteenth century it also referred to the biological growth (formation) of a plant or limb. Therefore we must interpret the syntagm *Bildung dieser Nation* in the context of the entire sentence. Because Schlegel is applying here an organic background metaphor (comparing the creation of the Golden Age with growing a flower), he probably meant that Romans tried to breed or raise (*aufziehen*) a new Golden Age of poetry, but failed and the end result was a barren flower of civilisation. This new blooming of poetry should serve the making of Roman "nation" (*Nation*).

The making of the Roman culture and its difficulties to gain independence from the previous Greek models was a mirror for the early nineteenth-century Germany. In 1800, Schlegel referred to the well-known *topos* of the Augustan Golden Age, for it resembled the state of modern era for Schlegel. Both Rome and modern nation states had to invent their own origin and legitimate their

11 On Virgil's role in this transformation see especially MÄHL, 1965, pp. 50-94.

12 "Während einiger Menschenalter wollte alles dichten in Rom, und jeder glaubte, er müsse die Musen begünstigen und ihnen wieder aufhelfen; und das nannten sie ihre goldne Zeit der Poesie. Gleichsam die taube Blüte in der Bildung dieser Nation." KFSA II, p. 295. (KFSA = Kritische Friedrich-Schlegel-Ausgabe.) Translation by Behler & Struc, translation is slightly modified. SCHLEGEL, 1968 (1800), pp. 65f.

status of a literary area able to produce high quality literature. This is what Virgil's *Aeneid* (29-19 BC) is about: it is an invented myth on the origin of Rome. Furthermore, during the Augustan Age, the relationship between the poets and political establishment was particularly close. In the quotation provided above, Schlegel mentions also Gaius Cilnius Maecenas (c. 74/64 BC-8 BC), who was a Roman statesman, an adviser of Emperor Augustus and a patron of letters. The etymology of the word *Mäzen* (patronage) comes from his name.

When Schlegel opened the Roman memory box of Golden Age at the turn of the nineteenth century, he was clearly conscious of how the original Greek content of this *topos* had been ideologically overwritten. Schlegel emphasises how it was the Romans themselves who wanted to call Augustus' rule a new Golden Age. Hence, this citation exemplifies how at least some past readers, such as Schlegel in this case, were not ignorant and passive to the tradition. Although Schlegel admits that the Roman version of this myth has had much influence on later generations, he also expresses critical distance to it. He claims that the fruits of the Augustan Age were infertile ("like a barren flower") and he does not take seriously the claim that this era really had been a new Golden Age of literature.

Although Schlegel was conscious of the historical load of this *topos*, he could not avoid opening himself the memory box from the early nineteenth-century perspective either. It seems that when he wrote about the making of the Roman *Nation*, he projected the early nineteenth-century German issue of cultural nationalism onto the ancient Rome. However, when it comes to the question of nationalism, one should note that Schlegel had been a republican cosmopolite during the 1790s for whom the building of nation did not yet include any of the aggressive implications of the later nineteenth-century nationalism. This kind of cosmopolitan mentality was especially typical to the early Romanticism at the turn of nineteenth century in contrast with the Late Romanticism of the 1820s.[13] Therefore Schlegel's worries about the creation of a German speaking culture were mostly connected with creating a new literary style for the modernity (i.e. early Romantic literature) and not with the formation of a great political power that would aim for the military domination of Europe. It was the older Schlegel in Vienna in 1815 who contributed to this kind of ideological project for Austrian rule. What the younger Schlegel had in mind in the year 1800 was still only "the Golden Age of poetry" and the

13 See NIVALA, 2013.

possibilities for its future recreation in his contemporary German speaking area.[14]

The necessity of a modern Golden Age

In *Gespräch über die Poesie* Schlegel presented the problem of the modern Golden Age: the building of a modern nation presupposed conscious creation and the invention of a Golden Age. In this sense, all modern nations had to imitate the Augustan Age and follow Virgil's model as the inaugurator of literature. After discussing the Roman notion of Golden Age, Schlegel's Andrea continues his speech about the so-called Golden Ages of literature during the modern period:

> The moderns have followed them; what occurred under Augustus and Maecenas prefigured Italy's cinquecentists. Louis XIV tried to force the same spiritual renaissance in France, the English, too, agreed to consider the taste during Queen Anne's reign as best. Henceforth, no nation wanted to remain without its Golden Age; each following age was even emptier and worse than the one before and what the Germans finally imagine to be their Golden Age, the dignity of this presentation prohibits from a more accurate description.[15]

According to Schlegel's interpretation, the artists and poets of the Italian Renaissance (the Cinquecentists of the sixteenth century), French classicism during the Sun King Louis XIV (1638/1643-1715) and the English literature when Anne Stuart (1665/1701-1714) was the Queen of England, all repeat this

14 The differentiation between *Kulturnation* and *Staatsnation* was first made by Friedrich Meinecke, who emphasised that cultural nationalism precedes political nationalism. See for instance OERGEL, 2006, pp. 1f. See also Juhana Saarelainen's article in this book.

15 "Die Modernen sind ihnen darin gefolgt; was unter Augustus und Mäcenas geschah, war eine Vorbedeutung auf die Cinquecenstisten Italiens. Ludwig der Vierzehnte versuchte denselben Frühling des Geistes in Frankreich zu erzwingen, auch die Engländer kamen überein, den Geschmack unter der Königin Anna für den besten zu halten, und keine Nation wollte fernerhin ohne ihr goldnes [sic] Zeitalter bleiben; jedes folgende war leerer und schlechter noch als das vorhergehende, und was sich die Deutschen als golden eingebildet haben, verbietet die Würde dieser Darstellung näher zu bezeichnen." KFSA II, p. 295. Translation by Behler & Struc.SCHLEGEL, 1968 (1800), pp. 65f.

same Roman model. It almost seems as if this *topos*, the memory box of Golden Age, had become an obsession for the modern era. Political leaders tried to declare their own age as the Golden Age of literature, hence enforcing both their own fame and the formation of a cultural nation. But the fruits were equally infertile in all those modern cases. Louis XIV opened the memory box of Golden Age in order to "force" a rebirth of the French cultural life. The English people had no other option than to follow them. As a rhetorical figure, the *topos* of Golden Age had an extremely persuasive and normative power in Schlegel's narrative.

It seems that since the Renaissance European states had to imitate antiquity in order to legitimate the making of cultural nation.[16] Schlegel claimed that the early nineteenth-century German intellectuals found themselves forced to imitate antiquity[17], but this meant actually only the imitation of Italian, French and English classicism. In other words, the Germans had to imitate something that was already an imitation.[18] Schlegel's somewhat cold attitude to the Romans is probably connected to his Protestant roots.[19] One should remember how Luther had already wanted to bypass the Latin mediation of the Bible and

16 Confer LACOUE-LABARTHE/NANCY, 1990, p. 299. This idea of Germany as a belated nation is criticised for instance by OERGEL, 2006, pp. 11, 92.

17 Schlegel argued that one should still imitate Greek antiquity in order to revise modern poetry: "Nicht *dieser und jener*, nicht ein einzelner *Lieblings-Dichter*, nicht die *lokale Form* oder das *individuelle Organ* soll nachgeahmt werden: denn *nie kann ein Individuum, ‚als solches', allgemeine Norm sein.* Die sittliche Fülle, die freie Gesetzmäßigkeit, die liberale Humanität, die schöne Ebenmaß, das zarte Gleichgewicht, die treffende Schicklichkeit, welche mehr oder weniger über die ganze Masse zerstreut sind; den vollkommnen [sic] Stil des goldnen [sic] Zeitalters, die Ächtheit [sic] und Reinheit der Griechischen Dichtarten, die Objektivität der Darstellung kurz den *Geist des Ganzen – die reine Griechheit* soll der moderne Dichter, welcher nach echter schöner Kunst streben will, sich zueignen." KFSA I, p. 346f. "One should not imitate *just anyone*, or a particular, *favorite poet*, or the *local form* or the individual organ: for *an individual 'as such' can never be a universal norm*. The modern poet who wants to strive for genuine, beautiful art should appropriate for himself the ethical abundance, the unfettered law-governedness, the liberal humanity, the beautiful proportions, the delicate equilibrium, the splendid appositeness that is more or less scattered over the entire mass. He should also approximate the perfect style of the Golden Age, the genuineness and purity of the Greek poetic forms, the objectivity of the representation – in short, *the spirit of the whole: pure Greekness*." Translation by Stuart Barnett. SCHLEGEL, 2001 (1795), p. 84.

18 Confer Plato's claim that all art is imitation of an appearance. PLATO, *Republic*, 595a-597e.

19 Confer ROECK, 2007, p. 6.

read the Greek version instead. It was typical for many nineteenth-century Germans – like for example Winckelmann, Hegel and Hölderlin in addition to Schlegel – to take Greece as a model instead of Rome that was already chosen by Italian, French and English people.[20] By imitating Greece, the German Philhellenists had the possibility to gain independence from the Latin examples. The power of rhetorical *topos* was so compelling for the nineteenth-century mind that one could not simply leave behind this pattern, but merely to search for a different model from Greece instead of the Latin model of *Romanity*.

Despite Schlegel's harsh criticism of Roman, Italian, French and English Golden Ages, his Andrea saves the most severe judgment for the German cultural life: "each following age was even emptier and worse than the one before and what the Germans finally imagine to be their Golden Age, the dignity of this presentation prohibits a more accurate description."[21] The supposed eighteenth-century Golden Age of German literature was something of such low quality that Andrea wants to save his listeners the shame to learn about the identity of the key authors of this supposed Golden Age.

As Ernst Robert Curtius discovered, later on in his career Schlegel actually had the courage to unveil what he did not want to mention in 1800, namely what the earlier eighteenth-century German critics had thought to be the Golden Age of German literature.[22] In his *Geschichte der alten und neuen Literatur* (*History of Ancient and Modern Literature*, 1812) lectures delivered in Vienna, Schlegel noticed ironically:

20 According to Suzanne L. Marchand: "This is only one of the many ironies of German philhellenism, that it owes some of its greatest debts to Latin writers and Roman copies of Greek statuary, to Italian humanists and French philosophes; access to things Greek was almost always mediated by the wider culture of Latin learning. But the Germans wished to see themselves as rediscoverers of a lost Arcadia and pioneers of a new kind of pedagogy. And the development of Germany's national self-identification with the Greeks, precisely in its explicit rejection of the culture of 'Augustan' neoclassicism, did create a new complex of ideas and ambitions." MARCHAND, 1996, p. 4.

21 " jedes folgende war leerer und schlechter noch als das vorhergehende, und was sich die Deutschen als golden eingebildet haben, verbietet die Würde dieser Darstellung näher zu bezeichnen." KFSA II, p. 295. English translation by Behler & Struc.SCHLEGEL, 1968 (1800), pp. 65f.

22 CURTIUS, 1993 (1948), pp. 273f.

> How relative the concept of a Golden Age is, at least in respect to our literature, how inclined one is to postpone [*verlegen*] it further and further [...], is confirmed by the example of an author who truly claimed this. In one of his poems, Gottsched moves [*verlegt*] this happy Golden Age into the age of Frederick, the first king of Prussia. The authors that he praised as the classics of that period, who should be for German literature approximately what Virgil was for the Romans, or Corneille and Racine for the French, were especially Besser, Neukirch and Pietsch.[23]

Now we learn that also Andrea's mock on the supposed German Golden Age in *Gespräch über die Poesie* refered to that of Johann Gottfried Gottsched (1700-1766) who was a German philosopher, author and critic.[24] In a sense, he was Schlegel's precursor, but not one that he would value very high. No wonder that Schlegel did not want to mention in his earlier essay "those poets who are nowadays not even known by their names"[25]. Where the Romans had Virgil and the French at least Corneille and Racine, the Germans should be content with Johann von Besser (1654-1729), Benjamin Neukirch (1665-1729) and Johann Pietsch (1690-1733). Those three examples, which Gottsched had tried to elevate to the status of national poets, were already forgotten *Hofpoeten* (poets laureaten) of Frederick I of Prussia (1657-1713). There was previous literature in German language, but its quality had been too low for Schlegel's standards to deserve the name of Golden Age.

From Schlegel's perspective, the start of German cultural life had been postponed. When Schlegel opened the memory box of Golden Age in 1800, its content was filled with bitterness and envy for the other European nations. Political theorist Marshall Berman has explained the rise of German Romanticism as an expression of underdeveloped identity:

---

23 "Wie relativ überhaupt der Begriff eines goldenen Zeitalters, wenigstens in Rücksicht auf unsre Literatur, wie geneigt man sei, es nur immer rückwärts zu verlegen, das kann das Beispiel eines Schriftstellers ... bestätigen, der wirklich so urteilte. Gottsched verlegt in einem seiner Gedichte diese glückliche goldne [sic] Zeit bis in die Epoche Friedrichs, des ersten Königs von Preußen. Die Schriftsteller, welche er als die klassischen in dieser Zeit preist, die also für die deutsche Literatur ungefähr das sein sollten, was Virgil für die römische, Corneille und Racine für die französische waren, sind vorzüglich Besser, Neukirch und Pietsch." KFSA VI, p. 376. English translation by Asko Nivala.

24 On Gottsched's poetics see especially Beiser 2009, pp. 72-100.

25 "Diese ‚jetzt nicht einmal dem Namen nach bekannten' Dichter" KFSA VI, p. 376. English translation by Asko Nivala.

> German intellectuals in Goethe's age were the first to see their society this way when they compared it with England, with France, with expanding America. This "underdeveloped" identity was sometimes a source of shame, at other times (as in German romantic conservatism) a source of pride, most often a volatile mixture of both.[26]

It is not a coincidence that the dialectic philosophy of German Idealism was also invented in early nineteenth-century Germany; it enabled the intellectuals to seek for a synthesis between the contradictory needs of conserving the past and creating the future. For Schlegel this underdevelopment was mostly felt in the field of literature. On the other hand, this situation was also a source of dry humour for him. The former eighteenth-century theories of German Golden Age appeared as something ridiculous at the turn of nineteenth century.

In spite of the fact that Schlegel was living during the *Goethezeit* (Goethe's time) at the turn of the nineteenth century when the German literary culture was actually on the rise, he could not have known that his own present age was the era that would have great influence on all surrounding European nations. One has to remember that even Goethe's status as the most important author of his time had not yet been established in the year 1800. Actually, Schlegel ended *Dialogue on Poetry* with an essay about Goethe's vocation as *the* German poet. There, he provided reasons why Goethe must be considered as significant a modern author as Cervantes, Shakespeare, or Dante had been for other European nations.[27] In other words, Schlegel was among the first critics and literary historians who made a conscious effort in order to elevate Goethe to the Western canon of literature.

It is remarkable how aware Schlegel seemed to be of the change of meaning in the *topos* Golden Age when it was displaced from Greece to Rome and from there to modern age. He thought that Rome was "a prefiguration" (*Vorbedeutung*) of Renaissance, for the Romans were the first people who had to embrace Greek mythology as the compulsory basis for their own poetry.[28] Schlegel even tracked this cultural transfer geographically to the Roman occupation of Greek colonies in Magna Graecia, southern Italy.[29] The Greek

26 BERMAN, 1988, p. 43.

27 See KFSA II, p. 347.

28 KFSA II, p. 295.

29 "Auch durch diese Kenntnisse, nicht durch ihre Literatur allein, als Rhetoren und Sprachlehrer, aber auch als Künstler, Mathematiker und Ärzte, empfahlen sich die Griechen den Römern, als diese nach der Eroberung von Tarent, des untern Italiens

inhabitants of Magna Graecia and their role in Roman cultural history is a perfect example of "a third area of 'mixed' zones … where the 'cohabitation' of different cultures creates something new, a 'third' thing."[30] The Roman identity was a hybrid identity from the beginning. It was based on the displacement of the Greek myth of Golden Age to Augustan era.

French philosopher Rémi Brague has condensed the position of the Romans in Western cultural history as follows: "The situation of secondarity in relation to a previous culture … constitutes what I call 'Romanity.'"[31] In this sense all we Europeans are like Romans: we feel that our obligation is to foster Greek tradition. In other words, all European nations have hybrid identities because our culture is based on cultural transfer from Greece to Rome. According to Schlegel, the Augustan Golden Age of literature (and its countless European imitations and variations since Renaissance) made the cultural transfer with the ancient Greeks to an obsession for all Western countries. Therefore Schlegel claimed: "Henceforth, no nation wanted to remain without its Golden Age."[32] The Golden Age of literature was deeply needed in order to authenticate and legitimate the German-speaking zone as a cultural area equal to Italy, Spain, England and France. Obviously Hesiod had not connected the *topos* with that kind of modern notion of national culture and national literature. For Schlegel in 1800, Golden Age was not something referring to a past stage of childlike innocence. Planning a national Golden Age implied a conscious collective project that could also result in failure.

The Augustan Golden Age as a memory box

Hence, I conclude that both Virgil and Schlegel used the *topos* of Golden Age in a significantly different way compared with its first occurrence in Hesiod. Although some characteristics of the *topos* had to stay relatively stable in order

und Siziliens, in die griechische Welt eingetreten waren, und wurden bald den Siegern unentbehrlich, so sehr diese sich anfangs der unvermeidlichen Einwirkung entgegensetzten. […] Nach der Eroberung des südlichen Italiens und Siziliens, deren Landessprache damals größtenteils noch die griechische war […] musste die Kenntnis dieser allgemeinen Sprache den Römern immer notwendiger werden[.]" KFSA VI, pp. 64f. Confere CESERANI, 2012. I owe this point to Dr. Janne Tunturi.

30 ROECK, 2007, p. 7.

31 BRAGUE, 2002 (1992), p. 43.

32 KFSA II, p. 295.

for people to be able to identify that Virgil and Schlegel were even still talking about the same *topos* as Hesiod, it also appears that every reference to this memory box in different historical situation added a new layer of meaning into it.

For Schlegel, the *topos* of Golden Age no longer referred to the original state of innocence before the inauguration of physical labour, but he was longing for the Golden Age of national poetry that was a meaning not yet present in Hesiod's version of the myth. However, what is common to both Hesiod and Schlegel is that the plot of Golden Age myth was a story of degeneration from generation to generation. For Hesiod the moral nature of mankind degenerated when the Iron Race replaced the Golden Race of man, while for Schlegel, modern literature degenerates when it is diluted to the mere mechanical classical imitation of Roman literature. Classicism appeared as an alienated style, for it did not even imitate the original Greek literature but was a modern imitation of a Roman imitation of Greece.

While the intention of Hesiod's myth was to legitimate agricultural labour as a social institution, Schlegel harnessed this *topos* to create a cultural programme for the non-existing German state. He opened up the memory box of Golden Age for his purposes; however, by doing so he also added something belonging to his own age. Virgil had already retold and overwrote Hesiod's myth, but Schlegel added a new layer as well: namely the problematic related to the formation of modern nineteenth-century nation. Therefore, not only the Golden Age *topos* was displaced from Greek antiquity to nineteenth-century Germany, but the very content of this memory box itself was a cultural transfer according to Schlegel. Of course, nineteenth-century scholars did not use our terminology to refer to this concept, but the twenty-first century scholars are not alone in having understood the basic fact of previous cultures affect those following. The memory box of Golden Age was inherited from the antiquity to nineteenth century, but every generation has filled it with new meanings.

List of References

Sources

HESIOD,Works and Days (Originally: Erga kai Hēmérai, ca. 700 BC), in: The Homeric Hymns and Homerica, trans. byHUGH G. EVELYN-WHITE, Cambridge, MA/London 1914. http://www.perseus.tufts.edu/hopper/, 23.10.2013.

KFSA = SCHLEGEL, FRIEDRICH, Kritische Friedrich-Schlegel-Ausgabe I-XXV, ed. by ERNST BEHLER/ET AL, Paderborn, München, Wien/Zürich 1958-2009.

SCHLEGEL, FRIEDRICH, On the Study of Greek Poetry (Originally: Über das Studium der griechischen Poesie), trans. by STUART BARNETT, New York 2001 (1797).

ID., Dialogue on Poetry and Literary Aphorisms (Originally: Gespräch über die Poesie), trans. by ERNST BEHLER/ROMAN STRUCK, London 1968 (1800).

Secondary Literature

BARNETT, STUART, Critical Introduction. The Age of Romanticism: Schlegel from Antiquity to Modernity, in: Schlegel, Friedrich: On the Study of Greek Poetry (Originally: Über das Studium der griechischen Poesie), trans. by STUART BARNETT, New York 2001 (1795), pp. 1-15.

BEHLER, ERNST/STRUC, ROMAN, Introduction, in: Schlegel, Friedrich: Dialogue on Poetry and Literary Aphorisms (Originally: Gespräch über die Poesie, 1800), trans. by ERNST BEHLER/ROMAN STRUCK, London 1968, pp. 1-50.

BEISER, FREDERICK C., Diotima's Children. German Aesthetic Rationalism from Leibniz to Lessing, Oxford 2009.

BERMAN, MARSHALL, All That Is Solid Melts Into Air. The Experience of Modernity, London 1988.

BLUMENBERG, HANS, Work on Myth (Originally: Arbeit am Mythos), trans. by ROBERT M. WALLACE, Cambridge, Mass./London 1985 (1975).

BOAS, GEORGE, Primitivism and Related Ideas in the Middle Ages, Baltimore/London1997 (1935).

BRAGUE, REMI, Eccentric Culture. A Theory of Western Civilization (Originally: Europe, la voie romaine), trans. by SAMUEL LESTER, South Bend 2002 (1992).

CESERANI, GIOVANNA, Italy's Lost Greece. Magna Graecia and the Making of Modern Archaeology, New York 2012.

CURTIUS, ERNST ROBERT, Europäische Literatur und lateinisches Mittelalter, Tübingen/Basel 1993 (1948).

FRANK, MANFRED, Der kommende Gott. Vorlesungen über die Neue Mythologie, Frankfurt a.M. 1982.

GADAMER, HANS-GEORG, Wahrheit und Methode. Grundzüge einer philosophischen Hermeneutik, Tübingen 1990 (1960).

HEINER, ACHIM, Der topos »goldenes Zeitalter« beim jungen Friedrich Schlegel, in: Toposforschung: eine Dokumentation, ed. by PETER JEHN, Frankfurt a. M. 1972, pp. 293-314.

LACOUE-LABARTHE, PHILIPPE/NANCY, JEAN-LUC, The Nazi Myth (Originally: Le mythe nazi), trans. by BRIAN HOLMES, in: Critical Inquiry, 16, 2 (Winter, 1990), pp. 291-312. http://www.jstor.org/stable/1343615, 01.10.2012.

LOVEJOY, ARTHUR/BOAS, GEORGE, Primitivism and Related Ideas in Antiquity, Baltimore/London 1997 (1935).

MARCHAND, SUZANNE L.: Down from Olympus: Archaeology and Philhellenism in Germany, 1750-1970. Princeton 1996.

MÄHL, HANS-JOACHIM, Die Idee des goldenen Zeitalters im Werk des Novalis. Studien zur Wesensbestimmung der frühromantischen Utopie und zu ihren ideengeschichtlichen Voraussetzungen, Heidelberg 1965.

NIVALA, ASKO, Maailmankansalaisuus 1790-luvun berliiniläisessä varhaisromantiikassa, in: Kosmopoliittisuus, monikulttuurisuus, kansainvälisyys. Kulttuurihistoriallisia näkökulmia, ed. by ANNE OLLILA/JUHANA SAARELAINEN, Turku 2013, pp. 49-83.

ID, From the Naïve to the Unnatural: Friedrich Schlegel's Early Romantic Notion of the Grotesque, in: The Grotesque and the Unnatural, ed. by MARKKU SALMELA/JARKKO TOIKKANEN, Amherst 2011, pp. 113-135.

OERGEL, MAIKE, Culture and Identity. Historicity in German Literature and Thought 1770-1815, Berlin/New York 2006.

ROECK, BERND, Introduction, in: Cultural Exchange in Early Modern Europe, ed. by HERMAN ROODENBURG, Cambridge 2007, pp. 1-30.

Providence
The Making of a Religious-political Memory Box

CATHLEEN SARTI

Using religious *topoi* in political speeches has become a common theme in today's US-politics.[1] In particular, the reference to providence, or the understanding of oneself acting in a providential manner, gives a strong legitimation to whatever the speaker claims to be providential. Through this use in relation to American politics, providence, a religious term originally, has become linked to ideas about American exceptionalism, American statehood and national culture, and manifest destiny.[2]

Today, using the topos of providence evokes certain ideas and emotions of patriotism, nationhood, America and faith as Barack Obama, among others, has shown for example in this speech from September 6, 2012: "We draw strength from our victories, and we learn from our mistakes, but we keep our eyes fixed on that distant horizon, knowing that providence is with us, and that we are surely blessed to be citizens of the greatest nation on earth."[3] The term providence has become a *topos* and can be seen as a memory box of American history.

1 GUYATT, 2007, pp. 1f.

2 The role of the topos of providence in the *Invention of the United States* is best explored in GUYATT, 2007. This topos also plays a role in the works of MERK, 1963 and BREWER, 2009, who are both concerned with special aspects of American identity and national culture.

3 MURSE, 2012. Even more known for his use of providence in political speeches is George W. Bush, e.g. when legitimising the US-attack on Iraq in 2003, see GUYATT, 2007, p.1.

In this article I am going to explore the ways in which providence can be seen as a memory box and how this may enhance our understanding of political rhetoric. I will argue that especially certain events and experiences in English and American history were seen (and talked about) as providential and thus became part of the memory box of providence. Since the *topos* of providence still plays such an important role today, these century-old meanings are still relevant for politics and for an understanding of this *topos* in political speeches.

Using the approach of the concept of memory box allows me to think of this *topos* anew. It draws attention to the ideas and connotations attached to it, therefore showing the complexity not only of the *topos* itself, but also of every time providence was used in communication. Focusing on the way of how ideas, emotions and connotations became attached to this *topos*, i.e. became the content of the memory box, and which media were used to open the box in certain situations allows for a deeper understanding of the *topos* throughout time and of its role in political rhetoric.

Providence can be understood in different ways: The original meaning refers to God's knowledge of everything in the world, or even to the act of God's hand in the world, e.g. when performing miracles.[4] Usually, it also refers to God's benevolent care for the world's welfare.[5]

The hand of God in the world was a common concept in early modern thought.[6] God was imagined as intervening in worldly affairs in two ways: first as personal providence, concerning only one person or a small group of persons, and second as national providence, concerning the fate of whole nations and determining the role of each nation and its people in the world.[7]

4 For the understanding of providence in biblical, medieval and early modern thought, see DAVIES, 1992. Davies sees providence in God's command over the physical world (pp. 14f.), in the guidance of individuals (p. 15), and in the ruling of God's will (p. 15). The New Testament also refers to different nations and their different fates after God's will (pp. 16f.). God's power is believed to form the fate of nations (p. 17).

5 See VAN BAAREN. This benevolence does not exclude punishment for sins. Quite a lot of bad things were actually seen as providential punishments; the challenge was then to figure out which sin had been committed.

6 Religion and politics were closely intertwined in the early modern period, the Bible could and was also read as a handbook on how to act, and on social interaction, see also PEČAR, 2011, p. 3.

7 The distinction into personal and national providentialism made by GUYATT, 2007, p. 5 is also used in this article in order to be able to focus more on the relationship between providentialism and political thought.

While personal providence came eventually to be regarded as superstition, national providence is a believed concept until today. In this article, I am going to concentrate on public and political uses of providence, e.g. in prints of political speeches, pamphlets or widely published documents as well as the use of the eye of providence[8] on medals. In this instances, a whole community was witness to the opening of the memory box, and these openings became thus part of the cultural memory of this community. I will first trace the appearance of providence as a memory box in certain events relevant to England's politics in the sixteenth and seventeenth century and then, in a second part, look at the uses of this *topos* in American contexts from the seventeenth until the nineteenth century. What my analysis offers is an understanding of the *topos* of providence as a memory box which helped in the case of the US to form a national identity which is still active today, and in the case of early modern England, form the national identity of a past society.[9]

The English case: The role of providence in seventeenth-century English national identity

Discussing national identity in relation to any region on the British Isles is a difficult task. Approaching this task by concentrating on English national identity at the end of the seventeenth century, i.e. before England and Scotland became one state and at a time, when belief in national providence was strong,

8 The eye of providence, also known as the all-seeing eye of God, is a symbol used to refer to God's all-encompassing knowledge and his ever watchfulness over the world. In the seventeenth century, this symbol became widely used as well as slightly changed: the eye, which was often surrounded by rays of light, now appeared in a triangle which referred to the trinity of God. Especially in England and America was this eye used in relation to rulers and national symbols emphasizing its political meaning, elsewhere in Europe it was more seen as religious symbol, used on altars, pulpits or organs.

9 Unfortunately, the very interesting question, if and when, why, the English resp. the British national identity is today no longer closely linked to an understanding of being providential or being the chosen people of God, goes far beyond the scope of this article. It touches, among others, questions of secularisation, political thought, and the English and British development since the eighteenth century.

makes this somewhat more concrete and allows me to leave out the discussions concerning British national identity.[10]

Especially one event at the end of the seventeenth century was interpreted as providential: the Glorious Revolution of 1688/89, when the English Catholic king James II was forced to leave his country, leaving behind his crown for the Protestant William III to take. In the deciding document of this Glorious Revolution, the Bill of Rights of 1689, the English parliament defined what they understood as essential to their identity: the upholding of the Protestant religion as well as of English laws and liberties according to the ancient rights. It was by God's "marvellous providence and merciful goodness to this nation"[11] that the Glorious Revolution was resolved with William and Mary taking the crown of their ancestors. The Glorious Revolution was seen as especially providential,[12] since it occurred exactly a hundred years after the defeat of the Spanish Armada, and since the important landing of William of Orange's army at Torbay on the fifth of November[13] was on the anniversary of the discovery of the Gunpowder-Plot in 1605. In 1689, providence was already linked with ideas of the English nation as well as what this nation represented: a Protestant nation with a strong parliament under monarchs given by God. Those ideas can be traced back at least to the defeat of the Spanish Armada, which was often used in comparison with the Glorious Revolution as a sign of Protestant Providence.[14] Since 1588, the defeat of the Spanish Armada, several events were represented as providential and thus filled the memory box of providence. In the following paragraphs, I am going to take a closer look at these events and what exactly made them being interpreted as providential.

10 James VI and I was the first ruler of both Scotland and England. He tried to establish a British national identity, but failed due to strong existing Scottish and English identities, which were – even worse – based on a strong mutual hostility, confer GALLOWAY, 1986, p. 10. The Welsh national identity, though it existed, was by large ignored in England, while the strong Irish identity found its expression in many revolts. For a discussion on a different aspect of Scottish identity, and how a stone becomes a memory box for Scottish, English, and British identity, confer the article by Jörg Rogge in this volume.

11 BILL OF RIGHTS, 1689.

12 See GUYATT, 2007, p. 70.

13 William could have landed a day earlier, but chose to wait, see GUYATT, 2007, p. 70. He was, after all, a master at propaganda.

14 See especially the article ISRAEL/PARKER, 1991. For the special relationship between Protestantism and providence, confer WALSHAM, 2003, p. 9 and GUYATT, 2007, pp. 14f.

In 1588, when England was under the rule of Queen Elizabeth I who also liked to present herself as "providential queen"[15], Spain under Philip II launched an attack on the island. This attack was part of the on-going undeclared Anglo-Spanish war between 1585 and 1604 and triggered by the execution of Mary Stuart in England. It was legitimated by the 1588 renewal of a papal bull from 1570, which declared Elizabeth I excommunicated and freed all her subjects from their oath of allegiance to her. The Spanish Armada, said to be the biggest naval force of its time,[16] suffered losses from storms and weather even before reaching the English coast, and more so on their way back. The biggest Armada of its time failed to win against the English navy and was mostly destroyed. Contrary to popular belief, the English navy was not helplessly outnumbered but was able to also win victories against the Spanish ships. Still, the reaction to the defeat of the Spanish Armada largely assigned the victory to the so-called Protestant winds and to providence.[17] Her destruction was even more spectacular because of her prior reputation. The perceived great danger resulted in an equally great relief and astonishment over having overcome this danger. Elizabeth I, a master at forming public opinion, used this victory to her advantage. Not only was she herself presented as a child of providence, also the nation seemed to be blessed by providence, i.e. protected against harm and chosen for a special task.[18] The memory box of providence became filled with memories of this first decisive victory over foreign Catholic forces and was linked to the English Protestant cause.

The development of puritan factions within the Anglican Church since the 1580s further encouraged these beliefs. These Puritans emphasised the ideas of John Calvin and tried to bring them deeper into English faith. Calvin's theology concerning providence and predestination is fully presented in the 1559 edition of his *Institutes of the Christian religion*. Again, providence is here understood as God's omniscience and omnipotence of worldly affairs and

15 DORAN, 1996, pp. 9f.

16 As ISRAEL/PARKER, 1991 pointed out, the Spanish Armada was indeed somewhat smaller than the Christian force at the Battle of Lepanto, but it was the biggest force to this date in the Northern Seas.

17 For further information on the comparison between the Spanish Armada and the force of William III, see ISRAEL/PARKER, 1991 as well as to the defeat of the Spanish Armada. For the interpretation of the defeat of the Spanish Armada, see also GUYATT, 2007, p. 17.

18 The idea of Elizabeth as providential queen is also explored in HALLER, 1963, especially Chapter 3, who brings attention to the role of Foxe's *Book of Martyrs* in spreading the belief of England as an elected (or: chosen) nation.

his willingness to intervene in the life of individuals and communities according to his will.[19] In addition, Calvin asserts that God uses humans as his agents in executing providence.[20]

The next commonly agreed sign of national providence appeared in 1605,[21] when on the fifth of November the so-called Gunpowder Plot to assassinate King James VI and I, and with him the entire parliament, was discovered. The design of this Catholic plot was known since the end of October, but the discovery of the culprits had to wait until the planned day, which was the opening of Parliament. The search under the House of Lords, still performed at the opening of Parliament today, revealed Guy Fawkes guarding enough gunpowder to blow up the entire Parliament. The deliverance from this danger was, and is, celebrated every year on the fifth of November as an anti-Catholic holiday since then.[22] Again, it was perceived that providence stepped in on the side of English Protestantism to prevent great danger.

Puritans, who were especially prone to search for signs of providence, were largely involved in the English civil war which eventually ended with the victory of the New Model Army over the forces of King Charles I. The New Model Army, which was the parliamentary forces in the beginning while later acting increasingly on their own, was under the command of Oliver Cromwell and composed mostly of Puritans. Their victory over Charles I, who also tried to present himself as a king watched over by providence,[23] seemed to confirm their belief in providence.[24] The deposition and execution of Charles I as well as the abolishment of the monarchy and the House of Lords was seen as providential by this radical religious group as well as by Puritans in New England.[25] They felt justified because of their victory and largely believed that Judgment Day was just around the corner and they were God's instrument in preparing for Christ's arrival on earth.[26] Most Puritans also linked providence

19 See also DAVIES, 1992, pp. 96f.
20 DAVIES, 1992, p. 101.
21 GUYATT, 2007, p. 17.
22 For further information about the celebration of the fifth of November, confer DOYLE, 2013.
23 Charles I had a medal cast depicting him under the eye of providence: BRIOT, 1633.
24 For the role of biblical beliefs in the English civil war, see especially PEČAR, 2011.
25 See GUYATT, 2007, p. 31.
26 See WORDEN, 1985, p. 55. In this article, Blair Worden shows the relevance of providential rhetoric not only for Oliver Cromwell and his followers, but also for England in general during the civil war. He emphasises that this use of providence

explicitly to England and spoke of their belief of being the chosen people of God.[27]

The delayed Judgment Day in the Commonwealth did not discourage the connection between Protestantism and the belief in being a providential nation. Even though Puritans, now called dissenters[28], were again pushed to the edge of mainstream religious belief in England, the common belief in their nation's providence as defender of Protestantism did not vanish. The interpretation of the events in the Glorious Revolution shows how deeply rooted these views still were. However, this instance also shows that the topos of providence lost some of its meaning when the political wind changed: after 1660 the regicide of Charles I was no longer considered providential. In fact, it seems as if the entire period of the rule of Charles I and of the Commonwealth was ignored on a whole. The providential character of the events of the Glorious Revolution mostly referred to the Spanish Armada and the Gunpowder-Plot and, for example, was shown by the use of the eye of providence on medals, for instance the medal by Robert Arondeaux, which depicts William and Mary under the watchful eye of providence, triumphing in the Glorious Revolution[29] or the medal by the Dutch medallist Jan Smeltzing, emphasising truth working in accordance with providence.[30]

At the end of the seventeenth century, English national identity was closely entwined with a strong belief in national providence. This meant that in opening this memory box the speakers could expect their audience to link main Protestant victories over Catholicism to the topos of providence, strong anti-

in politics and everyday-life was firstly very common and secondly not at all meant cynically but in the earnest belief in God and his power in the world.

27 See WORDEN, 1985, pp. 88-90.

28 Since the 1580s, Puritans was the term for English Protestants who wanted to go further in the English reformation than the Elizabethan religious settlement. While Puritans in England tried mostly to reform the Anglican Church from within, American Puritans often left the Anglican Church and formed their own congregations. English Puritanism became highly diverse in the English Civil War and under Oliver Cromwell. Since the Act of Uniformity, 1662, English Puritans were forced to either confirm to the Anglican Church policy or to leave the church. The approximately 2000 clerics who chose to leave the church along with Presbyterian Scots were known as dissenters from that point forward.

29 ARONDEAUX, 1689.

30 SMELTZING, 1688.

Catholic and anti-popery ideas[31], the idea of being the leading Protestant nation and the idea of having a special national relationship with God.

The American case: An English memory box relocates and becomes successful

The Puritans, who left England for the American colonies in the thousands in the 1620s and 1630s, brought with them their strong belief in providence. Their knowledge of the Bible enabled them to link their experiences in the New World to biblical experiences, e.g. comparing it to the struggles of the people of Israel. Rather than specific events of nationwide importance,[32] they labelled their experiences as providential. Leaving England for America was often due to their belief that this was what providence had them do.[33] Arriving safely in the New World after months on the Atlantic ocean was providential, surviving the first winter was providential, encountering various challenges and overcoming them was providential, and forming a "city upon a hill" (Matt 5:14) was providential, too.[34]

The small communities of English settlers in the vast world of North America stuck together. Especially the puritan communities in Massachusetts, which later spread out over the whole of New England[35], relied on their strong

31 Shown also on medals, e.g. BISHOPS STRUCK BY PROVIDENCE, 1723, telling the tale of a conspiracy of bishops to bring the Jacobites to the throne on the obverse and their judgment by God on the reverse.

32 In the seventeenth century, one cannot really speak of the American colonies as forming a nation, or even of having a separate national identity from England, or their home countries.

33 See GUYATT, 2007, pp. 28, 30.

34 An especially contested providentialism can be seen in the belief in providential signs, articulated by John Smith, Leader of Jamestown, that a French ship brought sickness to the native Americans a few years before the arrival of the Mayflower in 1620, resulting in a plague depleting the Indian settlements in Massachusetts: "God hath provided this Country for our Nation, destroying the natives by the plague", cited after GUYATT, 2007, p. 25. Guyatt points out that also the migration to America was largely seen as providential, as fulfilling God's plan in America; see GUYATT, 2007, pp. 26f.

35 Today's region of New England encompasses the states of Maine, New Hampshire, Vermont, Massachusetts, Rhode Island and Connecticut. In the seventeenth century, New Jersey and New York were sometimes also counted as belonging to New England.

shared belief explained to them by their political leaders, which were usually also their religious leaders. The social structures in Massachusetts resembled theocratic structures. One of the Massachusetts settlers, Roger Williams, whose belief differed from the political and religious leaders and who was therefore banned, founded the city of Providence in today's Rhode Island, again showing the strong belief in God's influence in worldly affairs. The firm belief of the first generation in being the chosen people of God, which showed in providential successes in their ventures, influenced the perspective these communities had about themselves. The tales of the experiences of first generation settlers were told and re-told throughout the seventeenth century. While the second generation, and even more so the third generation, did not experience such intense religious revelations as the first,[36] the stories of the first generation as well as so-called providence tales[37] exemplifying personal providence were nonetheless told and became part of the cultural memory, strengthening the community and their identity.[38] "Judgments against political or religious 'enemies' of New England could be regarded as marks of God's approval and protection of the colony, strengthening the community as well as the authority of the colony's close-knit elite of ministers, like Mather, and governors, like Winthrop."[39]

A special role was given to providence in the American Revolution[40]: not only are the United States in the Declaration of Independence from July 4, 1776 founded "with a firm reliance on the protection of divine Providence"[41], but also was the Eye of Providence chosen as part of the new seal representing

36 Membership in the church was linked to the telling of an experienced revelation and the judgement of church members as witnesses to this tale. In the second generation, church membership declined due to younger people not coming forward to apply for membership.

37 For the genre of providence tales and its relevance for the American literature, confer HARTMAN, 1999. An especially important compendium of providence tales and American history is Cotton Mather's *Magnalia Christi Americana* from 1702, see further GUYATT, 2007, pp. 49f.

38 See SEIDL, 2013, p. 193.

39 IBID.

40 Nicholas Guyatt argues that in the second half of the eighteenth century, the belief in American providence separated itself from the belief in English providence, or more concrete: while in the seventeenth and early eighteenth century American providence was seen as part of the English national providence, it ceased to be so in the later eighteenth century and became a belief in a special American national providence, see GUYATT, 2007, pp. 51f. and chapter 2.

41 The Declaration of Independence: A Transcription, 04.07.1776.

the United States of America. Even though the final design of the seal was not agreed on for six years, engaging three committees and 14 men – among them Benjamin Franklin, John Adams and Thomas Jefferson as members of the first committee – the Eye of Providence was suggested immediately and was one of four features to make it to the final version.[42] One of the men involved, Charles Thomson, explained the meaning of the Eye of Providence in the seal: "The pyramid [where the eye is placed on top] signifies Strength and Duration: The Eye over it & the Motto [Annuit Coeptis – He has favored our undertakings] allude to the many signal interpositions of providence in favour of the American cause."[43]

The use of the all-seeing eye as part of the Great Seal of the United States refers to two different memory boxes: On one hand, as Charles Thomson explained, this use can be seen as a sign of providence in American history. On the other, the use also refers to the widespread application of this symbol in the late eighteenth century, especially in Freemasonry. The picture itself was already a memory box, full of different meanings and associations. I am of the opinion that, in the case of the Great Seal of the United States, the use of the Eye of Providence on English medals is of a greater relevance than the use in Freemasonry. In England, the eye was already linked to politics and national providence, e.g. in the above mentioned medals of William III and Mary II.

In the nineteenth century, a new layer was added to providence as a memory box during the expansion of the United States of America: The idea of manifest destiny, i.e. having the divine mission[44] to expand the American nation, built on the idea of the "city upon a hill" (Matt 5:14) as well as the idea of being the elected, the providential, nation. While the idea of manifest destiny vanished after its heyday in the nineteenth century,[45] providence – being the more religious form of manifest destiny but also being much more open to different interpretations – once again took its place in political speeches and was also used in religious contexts to comment on politics. The

42 See U.S. DEPARTMENT OF STATE, BUREAU OF PUBLIC AFFAIRS, 2003, pp. 1f. To date, the reverse side of the seal, where the eye of providence is located, has never been cast since it was never necessary to use it as seal. The official design is nonetheless very much in use: on the back of the one-dollar bill as probably the most prominent place.

43 Cited after U.S. DEPARTMENT OF STATE, BUREAU OF PUBLIC AFFAIRS, 2003, p. 5.

44 For the idea of mission and the American belief in being "chosen people with a global mission", confer BREWER, 2009, p. 9.

45 MERK, 1963, pp. 265f.

idea of having a special national relationship with God was e.g. expressed in sermons such as that of Reverend Isaac N. Shannon on the occasion of the 76th anniversary of the American Independence on Fourth of July, 1852:

> What God has already wrought in this land is the pledge of still greater things to come. He has planted and prospered this nation for important purposes, and those purposes may be learned, in part, from our past history and present condition. It becomes us then not only to acknowledge His providential care in general, but to study the peculiar dispensations of His providence, with a view to determine our present duty, and our future destiny among the nations of the earth.[46]

What Reverend Shannon did not elaborate on was the controversially discussed question of his time of who was part of America's providence. Were Indians and black people part of it? Did America's national providence demand that they could – and maybe even should – become citizens? The experiences of multiple races also became attached to the memory box of providence.[47]

At the end of the nineteenth century, providence as a memory box evoked cultural memories of experiences of settlement, hardships in a hostile environment, being role models for a pious life, being independent, dealing with multiple races and establishing a new state.

Conclusion

From labelling Elizabeth I as providential queen, as John Foxe has done, to legitimising America's invasion in Iraq in 2003[48] with the extraordinary role providence has given to the United States, the *topos* of providence was used to evoke religious feelings in politics and was seen as part of national identity. Providence became a memory box which transported attached ideas, emotions and connotations from the British Isles to North America as well as from the sixteenth and seventeenth century up until the present day. Providence as a

46 SHANNON, 1852, p. 3.
47 See for further discussion on this topic GUYATT, 2007, especially chapter 5 and 6.
48 At least that was what George W. Bush in his State of the Union address claimed, see IBID., p. 1.

memory box, with the meaning of Protestant victory over Catholicism, the belief in being the chosen people of God and being chosen to lead the Protestant nations, was part of English national identity at the end of the seventeenth century. This belief drew from the cultural memory of selected events such as the defeat of the Spanish Armada or the discovery of the Gunpowder-plot and was reinforced in the interpretation of the so-called Glorious Revolution.

When the *topos* of providence was brought along with English Puritans settling in the American colonies, they attached new meanings to this memory box. Instead of events of national importance, shared experiences were added as new layers. The experiences of settlement, of struggling against a hostile environment, of independence, of piety and of being a role model for others became part of providence as a memory box and part of the American national identity. The media using this memory box predominately consisted of sermons instead of political pamphlets and medals, as was the case in England. In both instances the belief in providence included the belief in a providential role of the nation, be it England or America.

As this article has shown, the *topos* of providence can be understood as a memory box. Seeing the *topos* this way, allows identifying layers of meaning in today's use of providence. Not every recipient will immediately link these different meanings to the concept, but it will probably trigger some connotations of national identity and of belonging to the chosen people of God (or, for self-assigned non-Americans or non-English of not belonging to this chosen people). Looking at this *topos* through the lenses of the concept of memory box brought into focus the ideas, but also especially the emotions and connotations attached to the topos rather than mere intellectual meanings. Understanding a memory box as one identifiable manmade cultural artefact (in this case an abstract *topos*) and understanding this *topos* as a vessel (box) of (cultural) memories has brought forward the connection between the *topos* of providence and its role in national identity, made possible by transforming a *topos* in a portable container of different ideas, emotions and connotations.

List of References

Sources

Bill of Rights, 1689, An Act Declaring the Rights and Liberties of the Subject and Settling the Succession of the Crown, in: English Historical Documents, 1660-1714, ed. by ANDREW BROWNING, London 1966, pp. 122–128.

The Declaration of Independence: A Transcription, 04.07.1776, U.S. National Archives & Records Administration, http://www.archives.gov/exhibits/charters/declaration_transcript.html, 05.10.2013.

SHANNON, ISAAC N., Divine Providence in American History and Politics. A Discourse delivered in the Second Presbyterian Church, New-Brunswick, N.J., July 4, 1852, New-Brunswick 1852.

Medals

A medal: Bishops struck by Providence, British Isles 1723, British Museum M.8224, http://www.britishmuseum.org/research/collection_online/collection_object_details.aspx?objectId=950562&partId=1&searchText=providence&images=true&page=2, 30.10.2013.

ARONDEAUX, ROBERT, Providence in the Glorious Revolution, Netherlands 1689, British Museum G3,EM.77, http://www.britishmuseum.org/research/collection_online/collection_object_details.aspx?objectId=951601&partId=1&searchText=providence&images=true&page=2, 29.10.2013.

BRIOT, NICHOLAS, Charles I under the eye of providence, British Isles 1633, British Museum 1872,0307.1, http://www.britishmuseum.org/research/collection_online/collection_object_details.aspx?assetId=808476&objectId=952587&partId=1, 30.10.2013.

SMELTZING, JAN, Protestant Providence, Netherlands 1688, British Museum G3,EM.75, http://www.britishmuseum.org/research/collection_online/collection_object_details.aspx?objectId=951670&partId=1&searchText=providence&images=true&page=2, 30.10.2013.

Secondary Literature

BREWER, SUSAN A., Why America fights. Patriotism and war propaganda from the Philippines to Iraq, Oxford, New York 2009.

DAVIES, HORTON, The Vigilant God. Providence in the Thought of Augustine, Aquinas, Calvin, and Barth, New York 1992.

DORAN, SUSAN, Monarchy and matrimony. The courtships of Elizabeth I, London, New York 1996.

DOYLE, KEVIN Q., "Rage and Fury Which Only Hell Could Inspire": The Rhetoric and the Ritual of Gunpowder Treason in Early America, Ann Arbor 2013, http://pqdtopen.proquest.com/pqdtopen/doc/1351325640.html?FMT=ABS, 27.02.2014.

GALLOWAY, BRUCE, The union of England and Scotland, 1603-1608, Edinburgh, Atlantic Highlands, N.J 1986.

GUYATT, NICHOLAS, Providence and the invention of the United States, 1607-1876, Cambridge 2007.

HALLER, WILLIAM, The Elect Nation. The Meaning and Relevance of Foxe's *Book of Martyrs,* New York, Evanston 1963.

HARTMAN, JAMES D., Providence tales and the birth of American literature, Baltimore 1999.

ISRAEL, JONATHAN I./PARKER, GEOFFREY, Of Providence and Protestant Winds: the Spanish Armada of 1588 and the Dutch armada of 1688, in: The Anglo-Dutch Moment, Essays on the Glorious Revolution and its world impact, ed. by JONATHAN I. ISRAEL, Cambridge 1991, pp. 335–363.

MERK, FREDERICK, Manifest Destiny and Mission in American History. A Reinterpretation, New York 1963.

MURSE, TOM, 10 Highlights of Obama's Acceptance Address. Obama Speech at the 2012 Democratic National Convention, 2012, http://uspolitics.about.com/od/CampaignsElections/a/Obama-Speech-At-The-2012-Democratic-National-Convention.htm, 06.10.2013.

PEČAR, ANDREAS, Macht der Schrift. Politischer Biblizismus in Schottland und England zwischen Reformation und Bürgerkrieg (1534-1642), München 2011.

SEIDL, MARTIN, Cultural Narratology and Historical Texts: Providential Narrative in Cotton Mather's *Magnalia Christi Americana,* in: New Approaches to Narrative: Cognition – Culture – History, ed. by VERA NÜNNING, Trier 2013, pp. 187–199.

U.S. DEPARTMENT OF STATE, BUREAU OF PUBLIC AFFAIRS, The Great Seal of the United States, Washington D.C. 2003.

VAN BAAREN, THEODORUS P., Providence, in: Encyclopædia Britannica, http://www.britannica.com/EBchecked/topic/480634/providence/34003/Etymological-history-of-the-term, 06.10.2013

WALSHAM, ALEXANDRA, Providence in early modern England, Oxford 2003.

WORDEN, BLAIR, Providence and Politics in Cromwellian England, in: Past & Present 109 (1985), pp. 55–99.

Personalities as a Memory Box

HETA AALI

This section discusses persons' representations[1], personalities, and the transfer of memories about the persons as memory boxes from their own lifetime to subsequent generations. Person here refers to the actual human being and personality to his or hers later representation. The section includes two articles. In the first, the sixth-century Merovingian queen Clotilde is the personality in nineteenth-century French historiography. In the second article, twelfth-century Prince Henry the Lion becomes the personality *Enrico Leone* in a seventeenth-century libretto. The articles focus on the opening moments of the memory boxes and highlight the cultural framework of the opening moments which in both cases date hundreds of years after the actual person's death. Especially interesting is the concrete situation when the box was opened – these moments can for example be gendered, royalist, misogynistic, nationalistic or cultural. Indeed, the personalities shall not be separated from the context of the opening moment but shall be examined closely in their frameworks.

The personalities discussed here were all historical persons but the level of their later *reality* varies in both articles. Even though the focus of the articles lies in the opening moments of the memory boxes, the creation of the memory boxes are crucial as well. The process of the creation and recreation of memory boxes makes personalities more or less fictive. In other words, it makes them more or less products of imagination rather than strictly confining them to the testimonies of existing sources. The authors of this section see this process as the location of cultural transfer: especially important is the temporal aspect from a real person to a representation, to a memory box. Personalities

1 For the concept of representation, see for example ZAMMITO 2005, pp. 155-181.

thus make references to persons who are absent but who are preserved from oblivion or whose memories are revived, often in order to achieve a specific aim. The persons under discussion in this section belonged to the highest nobility, a queen and a duke with quasi-royal ambitions. Other personalities who might gain the quality of a memory box are heroes, martyrs and saints, but also artists and scientists. While a great part of personalities' memory boxes refer to more or less well-known historical figures, there are also several examples which probably have no real historical person as starting-point (or, at least, we are not able to define it), e.g. mythological heroes, as Heracles and Jason, or biblical figures, as Judith or queen Esther.

The concept of memory box is considered here as a theoretical tool which is not seen as having existed materially in history. Thanks to their non-materiality, personalities can be used by various groups simultaneously for rather different purposes. The articles focus on memories transferred uniquely in texts. The term text is understood widely and also includes sources such as opera, notes and librettos. Such a textual memory box allows us to expand the concept of memory box from its original material signification presented by Bernd Roeck in 2007 to a wider use and meaning.

Time is a crucial factor in the formation of memory boxes. Here we come close to the concept of *lieu de mémoire*. The concept of *lieu de mémoire* originally refers to a physical place containing memories and did not include transferring of memories.[2] However, it is possible to consider – as we shall see in the articles – that a person can be a *lieu de mémoire* and that personalities are memory boxes once they are removed (by death) from the original context. Very interesting is also the thought of displacement in time: personality as a memory box is no longer in his or her own time, but is displaced from it. In most of the articles the person is already dead or has been so for a long time. It follows that it is possible for the memory box to be entirely distinct from the original person and the memory box and person most likely do not have any correlation.

The first article focuses on the Merovingian queen Clotilde († 545) and on her representation. Heta Aali considers queen Clotilde as a *personality* in the context of the early nineteenth-century French historiography when the memory box was opened by historians and authors interested in early Middle Ages. The article focuses on three moments of opening the memory box, i.e. in three different works from 1820s to 1840s. Each work had a specific cultural

2 About *lieu de mémoire*, see for example NORA 1997, pp. 15f.

framework and therefore is to be separated as individual moments of opening the memory box.

The second article, written by Matthias Schnettger, examines Henry the Lion († 1195) who was the most famous ancestor of the House of Brunswick. Very soon after his death a legend arose which reshaped some elements of the life and the representation of the historical Henry in a quite creative way. Both, the real and the legendary Henry the Lion were often used by the later Guelphs as evidence of the dynasty's extraordinary nobility. Focusing on the famous opera *Henry the Lion* performed in Hanover in 1689, the article will show how Henry the Lion was enacted as veritable memory box by Ernst August of Hanover during the crucial years of the struggle for the ninth electorate in order to underline the Guelphs' claims on the electoral dignity.

The two articles are united by the same social rank of the personalities. The memory boxes are opened several hundred years after the person's death and the openings in both cases involve clear political motivations. The articles demonstrate how considering the personalities as memory boxes will provide new insight in studying representations in various contexts.

List of References

NORA, PIERRE (ed.), Les lieux de mémoire, Vol. I, Paris 1997.

ZAMMITO, JOHN, Ankersmit and Historical Representation, in: History and Theory 44, 2 (2005), pp. 155-181.

The Personality of Queen Clotilde in Early Nineteenth-Century France

HETA AALI

Rather little is known about the life of early medieval Frankish queen Clotilde who was later sanctified by the Catholic Church. She was a daughter of a Burgundian king and married Frankish king Clovis I during the last decades of the fifth century. She was Catholic and also her husband converted to Catholicism right before the turn of the century. Clotilde had at least five children of whom one died as an infant. She founded a monastery together with Clovis where she eventually died in 545.[1] She was buried in the abbey of St. Genevieve, then the Church of Holy Apostles, which was destroyed during the Revolution of 1789 but her remains were saved. Besides these cold facts, all we know about her are probabilities and interpretations, as only very few contemporary sources mention her.

A major turning point in Clotilde's history occurred in the tenth century when she began to be venerated as a saint in the Catholic Church.[2] There was a clear reason why Clotilde was granted the status of a saint. She was perceived as converting her husband Clovis to Christianity. Despite the lack of sources and information, she was probably one of the most important female figures in the history of France due to her role in Christianising France.

During the tenth century, the *Vita Chrothildis*, Clotilde's hagiographical biography, was also written. The hagiographical text and its subsequent copies

1 See for example GREGORY OF TOURS' *Ten books of Histories* (539-594), Book II. http://www.fordham.edu/halsall/basis/gregory-hist.asp#book3
Gregory's chronicles was by far the most important source about the Merovingian period before and during the nineteenth century.

2 FOLZ 1975, p. 1.

greatly affected the later images of Clotilde, particularly adding Carolingian ideals of a saint queen to the image of a Merovingian queen.[3] The texts written about her preserved the Carolingian memories of the Merovingian period and affected how she was perceived in the future. The idea of her role in the conversion survived centuries with only minor modifications and was reinforced during the nineteenth century when the French monarchy was restored after the Revolutionary Years and Napoleon's reign.

The temporal focus of this article lies on the period of French restoration and July Monarchy, from 1815 to 1848, as the interest in Clotilde increased during that time. In re-thinking the royals after the collapse of Ancien Régime, many historians referred to the earlier kings and queens and Clotilde gained great importance in the period's historiographical imagination.[4] During the years of 1815-1848, French monarchy underwent several changes and saw yet another revolution in 1830. The revolution was followed by a new form of monarchy, the July monarchy. The new king Louis Philip was no longer a king of France but the king of the French. France also received a new queen again fifteen years after the fall of Napoleon I. She was Marie Amalie who differed from previous queens in a sense that she no longer presented herself as a public figure, but identified herself more closely with bourgeois wives and mothers, thus creating a new image of queenship in France.[5]

My aim is to examine the significations Clotilde's figure held in different types of historiography[6] and how it can be referred to as a "memory box". How can we examine the moment of opening the memory box? Multiple ideas from earlier historians and contexts were transmitted to the nineteenth century through her figure and in a sense were both accumulated by earlier interpretations and as well as recharged with new significations. We are speaking of a cultural transfer from one time to another but not of a transfer in a synchronic sense from one geographic or cultural zone to another. Different epochs are thus understood as cultural zones even though they can be as problematic to define as synchronic cultural areas.[7]

A memory box refers to a physical object transferring or exchanging significations and ingredients from one context to another, both geographically

3 THIELLET 1997, p. 148.
4 See for example AMALVI 2011, p. 28.
5 MARGADANT 1999, pp. 1467-1469.
6 Historiography is understood here in a general sense thus including both academic and popular historical literature, especially biographical literature.
7 See POIRRIER 2004, pp. 355-363. Also ESPAGNE 1994.

and temporally.[8] Queen Clotilde had no physical form during the nineteenth century: she was rather just an idea. Her figure was not unchangeable during the period in question and it is possible to trace back a certain transformation starting from the revolution of 1789 and leading to the mid-nineteenth century. In my article the idea of queen Clotilde has mostly a temporal or diachronic dimension and, as so many other historical figures, hers has been modified according to the needs of every period and society. She was an *object* without a physical form or an absolute value. Her meaning and value in French history was always related to her husband and her sanctity.

I shall examine Clotilde as a memory box in three different kind of historiographical works. In other words, I shall study three unique moments of opening the memory box. Opening moment therefore refers to the moment of writing the work of historiography, not to multiple readings of the works.[9] Nor are the books themselves artificial memory boxes, but Clotilde as a personality is one memory box. The works were aimed at different audiences, thus demonstrating how the memory box of Clotilde was not similar for all readers.

The first work is written by Swiss historian and economist Simonde de Sismondi (1773-1842) and the book is entitled *Histoire des Francais*. It was first published in 1821 and only the first part interests us because there Sismondi wrote about queen Clotilde and the Merovingian period. Sismondi was best known for his work on Italian states during the late Middle Ages, *Histoire des républiques italiennes du Moyen Âge* (1807–1818). The second work was written by Jules Dubern in 1837 and it was entitled *Histoire des reines et régentes de France et des favorites des rois.* This work was a collective biography of French queens, regents and "favourites" of the kings. It belonged to a very popular genre during the first half of the nineteenth century that focused uniquely on "women worthy", women who were worth remembering.[10] The third and final work was written by Caroline Falaize and was entitled *Clotilde, ou le Triomphe du christianisme chez les Francs.* Falaize's work was published in 1848 and even though the author is quite unknown, the publisher L. Lefort in Lille was very popular in its own time and famous for publishing confessional literature for larger audiences. [11]

8 See for example ROECK 2007, pp. 11f.

9 There is no way of determining how many times and where certain books were read and therefore one must focus on the moment of writing.

10 SMITH 1998, p. 51.

11 AMALVI 2006, p. 58.

The memory box of Clotilde prior to July Revolution

Before the revolutionary years at the end of the eighteenth century Clotilde was often perceived as God's intermediary for converting Clovis and, following this logic, an intermediary for converting the entire French monarchy to Catholicism. She was seen as introducing the faith to Clovis and, by choosing her God, he won the battle of Tolbiac in 496. However, the main role in the process of conversion was held by Clovis as the father of the first Christian dynasty. For example in the *Abrégé chronologique de l'histoire de France* by famous seventeenth-century historian Mézeray, Clotilde had no other signification in the history of France than as initiating Clovis' conversion.[12] Thus, the memory she carried prior to the Revolution was that of the Christianisation of France as her sanctity was based on the conversion of the first Christian king.

It is, however, important to keep in mind that she was still a minor player in the history of France and in the process of Christianising the Franks during the first years of the nineteenth century. For example, in the text book *Epitome de L'Histoire de France* of French history written by Antoine Serieys[13] (1755-1829) in 1804 and reprinted several times during the following decades, Clotilde has practically no role at all in Clovis' conversion. The main reason for Clovis' conversion, according to Serieys, was his wish to gain more power and his desires to expand his kingdom in Gaul. There was no clear divine intervention nor had he made any promises to Clotilde to converse to Catholicism.[14] This interpretation differed considerably from the later historians' interpretations, which demonstrates well how the opening moment of Clotilde's memory box greatly affects the picture created of her – or whether she is pictured at all.

It seems that Serieys had a penchant for Republicanism during the French Revolution and in any case did not interpret Clotilde's history or Clovis' conversion from a religious perspective. He opened the memory box at a moment when the general tendency was not proactive to highlight her role in the events that lead to Clovis' conversion. One must remember that had this

12 MÉZERAY 1696, p. 31. Mézeray was also very popular among nineteenth-century historians, for example Augustin Thierry referred to him in several occasions.

13 About Serieys, see also AMALVI 2001, p. 254.

14 SERIEYS 1819, pp. 12f.

text book been written twenty years later, the interpretation would have been completely different. But it is useful to keep in mind that Clotilde was not always popular among historians and that her husband Clovis was seen as the more important figure in French history.

By the early 1820s, when Simonde de Sismondi published his *Histoire des Français,* the situation had changed both politically and socially. The restored monarchy sought justifications for its existence as not all parties were unanimous about having France once again ruled by royals. Louis XVIII was ruling and trying to restore the Ancien Régime- like monarchy. The Catholic Church was the monarchy's close ally since the two institutions had a long common history of one supporting the other in French society. *Histoire des Francais* was a long work and it took Sismondi almost twenty years to finish it. It was, however, the first work that can be labelled as French liberal historiography since he looked for impartiality in writing history and especially impartiality towards both living and dead kings and rulers. Sismondi harshly criticised those who allowed politics to dictate what they wrote about history. For him, historical writing was about what we can learn from past kings and events, and for this purpose, he argued, there was no point in embellishing the past actions.[15] Sismondi also wrote that "Our affair is to study only what truly existed and to know why it existed; to collect and present to all eyes the results of all experiences that have been tried on our ancestors and on us."[15] This was very common rhetoric in the period's historiography and should not fool us to believe that Sismondi was completely unbiased. On the contrary, many historians of the period were politically and ideologically motivated.

Sismondi mentioned Clotilde for the first time in the context of the death of her father and made clear she would have an important impact on the entire French monarchy. He wrote that "[...] he [Clotilde's uncle] only took two girls as captives, Clotilde being the other one. Later she became the wife of Clovis and had a major influence on the destiny of the French monarchy."[17] Even

15 Sismondi 1821, Introduction.

16 "Notre affaire est de rechercher seulement ce qui a réellement existé, et de savoit pourquoi cela a existé; de rassembler ainsi et de présenter à tous les yeux les résultats de toutes lesexpériences qui ont été tentées sur nos ancêtres et sur nous-mêmes." Ibid., p. XVII. All translations are by Heta Aali.

17 "[...] il ne garda prisonnières que les deux filles, dont l'une Clotilde, ensuite épouse de Clovis, eut une grande influence sur le sort de la monarchie française." Sismondi 1821, pp. 172f.

though Sismondi did not write anything else about Clotilde at this point; it is obvious he gave her a major role in French history. The sentence alone proves that her role changed considerably compared with the role given to her by Serieys some fifteen years earlier. But Sismondi also wrote about the medieval tradition of describing Clotilde and criticises very harshly those authors using false sources about Clotilde's marriage with Clovis. Sismondi pointed out that Gregory of Tours, the only near contemporary source about the marriage, did not say anything else other than Clovis wanting to marry Clotilde for her *sang royal*.[18] All the other anecdotal events related to their marriage and meeting are of a later production and according to Sismondi, should be treated like a "roman de chevalerie". Sismondi even gives an example of such an anecdote with respect to their meeting, most likely from Medieval *Chronique de Saint-Denis*.[19] Here Sismondi was thus creating a new moment for opening the memory box and *denying* the old memories attached to the figure of Clotilde. Indeed, Sismondi was intentionally creating a new memory here by refuting the old ones as not real.

The Swiss historian wrote quite extensively about the conversion of Clovis but he left open whether or not he believed that God had in fact intervened in the battle of Tolbiac where Clovis won and consequently converted to Catholicism. According to most narratives, Clovis promised to Clotilde to convert to Catholicism if he won the battle and after the victory, he indeed converted. Sismondi did not see any miracles happening in the battle but rather saw the decision as being at least partly political – Clovis wanted to ally himself with Gallic Catholic churches. But there is no doubt Sismondi saw this as a "right" thing to happen since he frequently called Catholicism the "orthodox" faith. It was "Clotilde's God" that helped Clovis to win, but that is about all there is to her role in the conversion. Her role in Sismondi's narrative ended with the victory in Tolbiac.[20]

The author of *Histoire des Français* criticised the institution of sainthood and saw the sainthood being characterised by the purity of faith during the sixth century, not so much by the virtues of the person. Sismondi expressed that during that period it was more important to make donations to the Church than to perform good deeds. Miracles marked the blessed ones, not the works of charity. Here Sismondi also defined what he saw as the "good" marks of a

18 SISMONDI 1821, p. 182.
19 IBID., p. 183.
20 IBID., pp. 186f.

saintly person and what these marks were during the Merovingian period.[21] It is not clear, however, if he intended this to also criticise Clotilde's position or to criticise the loose conditions of sainthood in the sixth century in general. Yet, this was one indication of liberal historiography in the early nineteenth century – to be critical towards the Catholic institutions even though most historians were Catholics or Protestants themselves. It was not, however, very common to criticise Clotilde's saintly position which defined her as "the mother of the French nation" and even Sismondi showed this position to be quite untouchable.

Transformations during the first decade of the July Monarchy

The 1820s were the last decade when a king of France held power in France. The year 1830 saw another revolution in France when Charles X was dethroned and Louis Philip was invited to become the king of the French. Constitutional monarchy had already been established in 1814 but the king lost his power even after the July Revolution. 1830's and 1840's were truly decades of historians since many historians became politicians and politicians became historians.[22] The most famous of these was François Guizot who worked as a Minister of Public Instruction and later as the head of the government.[23] The high hopes carried for the July Monarchy did not last very long due to economic and social problems, even though for many the new monarchy signified a new era in the history of France.

The second historian discussed in this article, Jules Dubern (1800-1880), had quite a different view on Clotilde and on women in general. Dubern's most famous and perhaps the only work *Histoire des reines et régentes de France et des favorites des rois* (1838) started with the biography of Basine who was Clovis I's mother. There are no other known works by Dubern and no knowledge of how frequently this specific work was read. The work was clearly aimed to highlight the virtues of the July Monarchy and this was done

21 SISMONDI 1821, p. 233.
22 About July Monarchy and historians becoming politicians, see for example CROSSLEY 1999, pp. 49-57.
23 THEIS, http://www.guizot.com/fr/histoire-de-sa-vie/guizot-sous-la-monarchie-de-juillet/

partly by presenting the earlier queens in a rather negative light. Dubern had a very critical attitude toward women asserting direct power and wrote in the introduction of his work that

> [s]ince the reign of unfortunate Louis XVI history does not offer any more stained pages for the glorious female sovereigns who joined all their capabilities with the happiness that has no competitors. And France can now contemplate, with pride and trust, the respected throne where shines the clearest example of marital virtues and of civil virtues [24]

In the citation Dubern refers to the situation that there had not been any female regents or powerful queens after the reign of Louis XVI. The passage clearly shows how Dubern perceived women's most ideal role as that of wives and mothers of kings, not as regents using direct power. When interpreting this citation above one must remember that no queen or empress took any part in politics after the reign of Louis XVI and both Louis XVIII and Charles X were widowers by the time they inherited the crown. Marie-Amalie, wife of Louis Philippe and queen of the French, was quite a different case compared to earlier queens. As already mentioned she was almost completely withdrawn from any politics and identified herself with bourgeois ideals, such as devotion to her family and religion. Marie-Amalie was not included in the biography; perhaps because she was still alive when the work was written. Dubern seemed to regard Napoleon's second wife Marie-Louis highly and pictured her quite positively. She did, according to Dubern, take care of politics when Napoleon was away from France but she did it only out of duty, not because she wanted to rule.[25] This is noteworthy as Dubern clearly perceived that it was unnatural for women to want to use power and those good queens only used it unwillingly. Using power was thus acceptable as long as women did not want it and did it merely out of a sense of duty.

For Jules Dubern Clotilde was not the personification of the saintly mother of a nation: in fact, he wrote that "Church has been able to name Clotilde

24 "Depuis le règne de l'infortuné Louis XVI, l'histoire n'offre plus que des pages sans tache pour les glorieuses souveraines qui joignirent à toute leur illustration le bonheur de paraître à peu près sans rivales; et la France peut contempler aujourd'hui, avec orgueil et confiance, ce trône respecté, où brille d'un si pur éclat l'exemplaire union des vertus conjugales et des vertus civiques." DUBERN 1837 (I), p. IV.

25 DUBERN 1837 (II), p. 325.

among the saints but history should remember her among the worst queens."[26] In another paragraph he described Clotilde as an "evil queen". Furthermore, he wrote that the Salic law started to exclude women from inheriting the throne of France during the sixth century and that even if this had not been the case, Clotilde would have been "unworthy of the throne".[27] In the second page of Clotilde's biography Dubern stated that she was "happy to be queen" which can be interpreted to be a negative sign as in the citation above Dubern clearly shows desire of power as being a negative feature in women. Perhaps this happiness of becoming a queen could be interpreted as a desire for power as the position did hold some power, at least morally, in the eyes of the early nineteenth-century historians. Why then was Dubern so critical towards Clotilde? One must remember that it is not this image that made Dubern critical towards Clotilde; he created such a negative image because he considered her to be a bad queen. He decided to highlight all negative aspects of Clotilde, yet without citing any sources or revealing the reasons for his interpretations. He presented his interpretation as the truth but did not justify how he had found it. The negative image was so different from other contemporary interpretations that one can suspect he had a specific reason to create it.

The new layer of Clotilde's memory box created by Dubern is very different from the other contemporary representations and, in fact, emphasises how the writer's own background affects it as well as the society and culture. Jules Dubern's political views are not known other than his support for July Monarchy and there is very little information about Dubern's background except that he came from a rather wealthy family, had a degree in law and was member of *Institut Historique*.[28] Was the reason for creating a negative image of Clotilde the will to highlight the contemporary role of the bourgeois queen? Perhaps he considered that French monarchy did not need Clovis to justify the return of the monarchy and only used the early royals as negative mirrors to reflect the superiority of his own time. It is not only due to the sources, which are most likely the same for all, but how the sources are interpreted at a specific moment. According to his source list, Dubern used *Grandes*

26 "L'Église a pu placer Clotilde parmi les Saints; mais l'histoire doit la mettre au rang des plus mauvaises reines." DUBERN 1837 (I), p. 9.

27 DUBERN 1837 (I), p. 8.

28 Revue Britannique (T. 14, 1838), p. 399. *Institut Historique* was founded in 1833. The review in Revue Britannique praised Dubern's work and expressed similar negative views about the early Middle Ages as Dubern had expressed.

Chroniques de France as one of his sources but this source does not explain his hostility as Clotilde is presented there in a highly positive context.[29]

Dubern was obviously not satisfied with Clotilde's saint position and was clearly not a fervent Catholic since criticising saints indirectly equalled criticising the Church. In fact, he presented Clotilde as taking advantage of religion when stating that "Clotilde considered her enemies as the enemies of God".[30] But was Dubern criticising Clotilde, queens in general or the early medieval saints? It seems he was not criticising all queen in general because when one examines the biography of Radegonde, a saint and Clotilde's daughter-in-law, one sees much more positive image of early medieval queen. Whereas Clotilde, according to Dubern, had a certain lust for power and vengeance, two defects that seemed to be very common in bad women in early nineteenth-century historiography, Radegonde had only hoped to retreat from her husband's court in order to become a nun.[31] Thus the criticism was not aimed uniquely at early medieval saints either. Dubern's picture of Clotilde was thoroughly negative; perhaps he just wanted criticise her actions as a queen without having a more general view about the early medieval queens or saints. Clearly though he perceived the early Middle Ages as rather barbaric when he stated in the biography of Basine, mother of Clother I, that "The cradle of France is still wrapped in the darkness of barbarism which ruled then."[32]

In order to understand the representation of Clotilde one must look at the intended audience of Dubern's work. Biographies were often read by women and especially by young women. The bourgeois ideal nevertheless often required readings to be suitable and religious, or at least in concordance with the Catholic tenets.[33] Dubern's work presented no such ideas; he even

29 I do not know exactly which version Dubern was using but the only version I have in my disposal is the one edited by Paulin Paris and Édouard Mennechet in the 1830s. It is in Gallica: http://gallica.bnf.fr/ark:/12148/bpt6k62269377/f137.image.r=Crotilde.langEN

30 "[...] Clotilde considérait ses ennemies comme ennemies de Dieu [...]" DUBERN 1837 (I), p. 6.

31 IBID., pp. 13-17.

32 "Le berceau de la France est encore enveloppé dans les ténèbres de la barbarie qui régnait alors." IBID., p. 2.

33 About good reading for French nineteenth-century school girls, see BELLAIGUE 2013, pp. 207, 209. Bellaigue shows that historiographical texts were read more and more during the nineteenth century, not only confessional literature. IBID., p. 216.

suggested that saint Radegonde was not as chaste as presented by religious authors. The same idea was also presented by liberal historian Augustin Thierry, but he is not mentioned in the list of sources in the second part of Dubern's biographies. Thierry's work, *Récits des temps mérovingiens*, was first published in the 1830s and was highly popular though also criticised by Catholic authors for its image of Radegonde. Thierry also suggested that Radegonde might have had carnal relations with a priest in her community, an idea refuted by the religious historians.[34] This might signify that Dubern's work was not approved among all religious circles and therefore perhaps not so celebrated in general, taking into consideration that confessional books were still very popular among all social classes in France.[35] Perhaps it was read by the bourgeoisie among whom biographies were well-liked, especially among women readers.

1840s and new layers in Clotilde as a memory box

The 1840s saw a lot of political and social problems in France and the situation became more aggravated towards 1848, causing another revolution that overturned the monarchy for the last time. Constitutional monarchy came to its end in the early months of 1848 and the Second Republic was created. Even though the July Monarchy had been more liberal than the Restoration Monarchy between 1815 and 1830, inequality in society was still striking and unemployment rates were high.[36] Despite the political uncertainty and the slow fall of the monarchy during the July Monarchy, early royals were as popular among authors and readers as before. In fact, history interested readers more than ever and the amount of historical literature grew constantly. In addition, after the revolution of 1830 France had witnessed a Catholic intellectual revival which induced young clergies to educate themselves further and take

34 THIERRY 1851, p. 164. Interestingly, according to Bellaigue, Augustin Thierry's *Histoire de la conquête de l'Angleterre par les Normands* (1825) was perceived as suitable reading for young women at least in some schools. BELLAIGUE 2013, p. 216.

35 Dubern's work might not have been much read even though Revue Britannique's review was very positive. See note 28.

36 For the reasons of 1848 revolution, see for example ALMOND 1999, p. 98.

part in intellectual and historiographical discussions of contemporary France. Religious historiography was revived after years of silence.[37]

My last example of a new layer in Clotilde as a memory box comes from 1848 and represents the genre of historical novel. One must, however, remember that the historiographical works and novels were still quite similar on a narrative level and presented quite similar actions from history and the Merovingian period. Caroline Falaize's *Clotilde ou le Triomphe de Christianisme* of 1848 was clearly, unlike Dubern's work, aimed for young female readers for whom Clotilde was presented as a role model. Falaize seemed to have been quite a popular author and wrote several works of historical literature. In addition, one finds for example an educational work written by her entitled *Leçons d'une mère à ses enfants sur la religion* from the catalogue of Bibliothèque National de France. The work *Clotilde* seems to have been quite well-liked as it was reprinted at least three times, which signifies that there was a demand for such a literature. In any case, it seems that *Clotilde* was read more widely than Dubern's work and most likely presented a broader picture of queen Clotilde.

When considering Falaize's work and the author's creation of new layers in Clotilde as a memory box, one should also take into consideration the context in which the work was written. The genre of religious historical novels was indeed highly popular and it is impossible to know whether Falaize wrote such novels because she wanted to or because she needed to make a living for her family and therefore, for practical reasons, chose this genre.[38] Women did not have the same opportunities to publish what they liked, but the genre options were much more limited than in the case of male authors. Biographies and educational novels, such as *Clotilde*, were an accepted genre whereas writing for example historiographical works such as the Sismondi's *Histoire des Francais*, were perceived as not suitable for women. Furthermore, women were not seen capable of writing such works.

Falaize's work follows the same chronological narrative of all contemporary works about the Merovingian period, even those written by professional historians. Since there are very few sources left about Clotilde and not one where her emotions would have been examined or described, this indicates the level of fiction in this work. Radegonde, Clotilde's daughter-in-law appeared

37 About the Catholic intellectual revival, see DEN BOER 1998, p. 25.

38 About women writing to make a living in the nineteenth century, see SMITH 1998, pp. 40, 44.

also in the novel and Falaize wrote about the meeting of these two women: "Clotilde surrounded this poor child with the most gentle interest; she pitied her destiny, supervised her from afar like a providence and ensured to give her a religious education. The court of this great queen was even more disposed toward tenderness and pity as she had made a great sacrifice [...]"[39] There are no sources telling Radegonde was ever raised by Clotilde even though she was only a child when Clother, Clotilde's son, intercepted her as a war booty from Thuringia.[40] The advantage of Clotilde as a representation is that due to the lack of sources, there is almost no negative material about her left and she can be shaped to fit all interpretations.

The new layers added to the memory box of Clotilde in this work are aimed to instruct and guide the readers. Of course, almost all historiographical works in the early nineteenth-century were written for educational purposes, at least implicitly, but the moral values were clearly emphasised in this work to create a role model in queen Clotilde. The representation of the queen presents specific values which were seen as atemporal in the mid-nineteenth century. The most important values were obedience toward the Catholic Church, husband and family, tenderness, pity, humility and modesty. And furthermore, according to the novel, Clotilde did not want to be a queen but was presented as being afraid of the role.[41] This is a similarity to Dubern's work – the lust for power, or what was perceived as such, did not fit the image of an ideal queen. Dubern, however, presented Clotilde as the opposite; yet the basic structure of the interpretation was the same.

It is rather problematic to distinguish the items of diachronic cultural transfer in *Clotilde* since the author practically mentioned no sources at all. However, one can deduce that at least the hagiographical sources were used, either directly or indirectly through other literature. Several scenes, especially from Radegonde's life and Clotilde's grandsons' death are from Gregory of Tours' *Histories* but again, it is only possible to guess where Falaize had

39 "Clotilde entoura cette pauvre enfant de l'intérêt le plus tendre; elle plaignit ses destins, veilla de loin sur elle comme une providence, et s'occupa de lui faire donner une éducation chrétienne. Le coeur de cette grande reine était d'autant plus disposé à la tendresse et à la pitié, qu'elle venait elle-même d'accomplir un immense sacrifice." FALAIZE 1848, p. 266.

40 "Saint Radegunda", *Encyclopaedia Britannica. Encyclopaedia Britannica Online Academic Edition.* http://www.britannica.com/EBchecked/topic/488379/Saint-Radegunda.

41 FALAIZE 1848, p. 192.

learned these scenes. *Clotilde* includes a lot of items that were clearly not based on any sources such as the following dialogue between Clovis and Clotilde about a construction of a basilica:

> […] - Dear husband, she said to Clovis, I dreamed last night that a magnificent basilica dedicated to apostles saint Peter and saint Paul would be elevated to this solitary place. - Géneviève had no doubt the same dream? The king answered smiling. - [Clotilde:] It could be, would it please you to fulfil the dream? - [Clovis:] *Did Clotilde think the magnitude of such attempt?* - [Clotilde:] The bigger, the worthier of my husband. - [Clovis:] Oh woman! You know the words to conquer the hearts; and you know your wishes are commands. - [Clovis:] It would be cruel of me to prove otherwise when the wishes are for saintly purposes. - [Clovis:] As I have no choice but to obey you, I will earn less good graces. [...][42] (My italics)

Géneviève mentioned in the text is saint Géneviève who was pictured in the narrative as Clotilde's dear friend and a type of a mentor. In the narrative level it is interesting that Clovis was made to refer to his wife in third person (see the italics), a style that has no foundation in any sources. Nineteenth-century transfer is visible in the way Clotilde was pictured persuading her husband by flattering him and in the way her husband obeyed her for her saintly intentions. The message seems to be that women with true faith can lead their husbands to better actions and guide them morally receiving good grace simultaneously.[43] Ever since the eighteenth-century women started to be seen as morally better than men, even though simultaneously as morally weak, and this idea of women's higher moral is visible also in this text. Of course this position greatly restricted women's ideal behaviour as they were obliged to uphold their position by their everyday actions.

42 "Cher époux, dit-elle, à Clovis, j'ai rêvé cette nuit qu'une magnifique basilique dédiée aux apôtres saint Pierre et saint Paul s'élevait en ce lieu solitaire. - Génèvieve a fait le même rêve sans doute? Répondit le roi en souriant. - Cela pourrait être, te plairait-il de le réaliser? - Clotilde a-t-elle songé à la grandeur de l'entreprise? - plus elle sera grande, plus elle sera digne de mon époux. - O femme! Tu sais les paroles gagnent les couers; mais tu sais trop aussi que tes désirs sont des lois. - Il serait cruel de me prouver le contraire, quand ces désirs ont pour objet une ouevre sainte. - Puisqu'il faut comme toujours t'obéir, j'aurai du moins le mérite de me rendre de bonne grâce." FALAIZE, 1848, pp. 221f.

43 DE GIORGIO 1993, p. 168.

Conclusion

In this article I have examined three different ways of presenting and three different moments of opening the memory box of queen Clotilde each creating a new layer there. The three early nineteenth-century works, Sismondi's, Dubern's and Falaize's, present three different genres; one being a purely historiographical work, one a biography and one a novel. One should however avoid making deductions based solely on the genres because no explicit or implicit correlation exist between genres and ways of representing a historical figure even though for example Falaize's work can be categorised in the subcategory of religious novels where all representations are quite established. Yet on a level of popularity one must recognise that Falaize's interpretation was most likely the best-selling as it was aimed to larger audiences than Sismondi's work. An early nineteenth-century phenomenon is in fact the lack of unanimity in the representations – the growing number of works led to various interpretations and to multiple openings of the memory box. The number of openings was larger than could have been in the past century which inevitably leads to more conflicting representations.

Considering the representations of Clotilde as a memory box leads to a problem related to uniqueness of the works. Are the works to be considered as unique and individual moments of opening the memory box or a part of larger models and traditions of representations? It seems that every opening is a unique moment and this is visible when looking at one later productions of Simonde de Sismondi, a work called *Histoire de la Chute de l'Empire Romain et du Déclin de la Civilisation, de l'an 250 à l'an 1000* from 1835. There he was very critical towards Clotilde being a saint and presented her quite revengeful and full of hatred.[44] Is this change in Sismondi's tone due to changed political situation or due to some personal features impossible to trace? This only proves that a memory box was very unique and even so unique that it only survived one work, or furthermore, only one instant of reading.

If we aim at making generalisations, interestingly the most important item of Clotilde's history, her sanctity, was questioned in both Sismondi's and Dubern's works. Was this a new signification related to Clotilde's figure or a transfer from the eighteenth-century Enlightenment? Questioning Clotilde's

44 SISMONDI 1835, p. 267.

sanctity could also be related to the general negative attitude towards the Merovingian period because historians often saw it as a period of decadence. In addition, one must consider that the 1830s differed quite a lot from the 1820s especially in terms of monarchy and freedom of press. Ideas that could not be published earlier found publishers some 15 years later. A separation between two poles of interpretations, between the liberal historiography and the confessional historical literature, seems to best designate the historiography during the July Monarchy as the interpretations the two genres increasingly estranged from each other.

One must acknowledge that the representation of Clotilde as a saint mother of nation did not exist as a unique interpretation in the early nineteenth-century France, even though the saint motherhood was very strong. Interestingly though her sanctity was not a new invention in the nineteenth century, her memory box got a new saintly layer which was a new product of the early nineteenth-century and included both ideas of nationalism and bourgeois idealism. But in addition, a new type of queenship born in the early nineteenth century is also visible in the representation of Clotilde and once again added one layer to her memory box.

List of References

Sources

DUBERN, JULES, Histoire des reines et régentes de France et des favorites des rois, Paris 1837.

FALAIZE, CAROLINE JACQUEMAIN, Clotilde, ou le Triomphe du christianisme chez les Francs, Lille 1848.

GREGORY OF TOURS, History of the Franks: Books I-X, transl. by ERNEST BREHAUT. http://www.fordham.edu/halsall/basis/gregory-hist.asp#book3, 30.10.2013.

MÉZERAY, FRANÇOIS EUDES DE, Abrégé chronologique de l'histoire de France. Vol 1, Amsterdam 1696.

PARIS, PAULIN/MENNECHET, ÉDOUARD, Histoire de France, par les écrivains contemporains, comprenant les annales de la monarchie française, depuis "Les grandes chroniques de Saint-Denis" jusqu'aux mémoires de la révolution, publiée, avec notes et commentaires. Vol. 1, Paris 1836–1838.

Revue britannique: Revue internationale reproduisant les articles des meilleurs écrits periodiques de l'étranger, complètés par des articles originaux. (14) Paris 1838.

SERIEYS, ANTOINE, Epitome de l'Histoire de France, Contenant L'origine Des Francs, Leurs Moeurs, Leurs Institutions, Leurs Lois, Leur Commence, Leurs Progrès Dans Les Sciences, et Beaucoup D'anecdotes Propres à Les Caractériser, Depuis L'établissement de La Monarchie Jusqu'à Nos Jours. Vol. 1, Paris 1899 (1819).

SISMONDI, JEAN CHARLES LÉONARD SIMONDE DE, Histoire de la chute de l'Empire romain et du déclin de la civilisation, de l'an 250 à l'an 1000, Vol. 1, Paris 1835.

ID., Histoire Des Français, Paris 1821.

THIERRY, AUGUSTIN, Récits des temps mérovingiens précédés de considérations sur l'histoire de France, Vol. II, Paris 1851.

Secondary Literature

ALMOND, MARK, Revolution, London 1999.

AMALVI, CHRISTIAN, Les Héros des Français. Controverses autour de la mémoire nationale, Paris 2011.

ID., Légendes scolaires du Moyen Age au XIXe siècle, in: La Fabrique du Moyen Age au XIXe siècle. Représentations du Moyen Age dans la culture et la littérature française du XIXe siècle, ed. by SIMONE BERNARD-GRIFFITHS et al., Paris 2006, pp. 473-528.

ID., Répertoire des auteurs de manuels scolaires et de livres de vulgarisation historique de langue française: de 1660 à 1960, Paris 2001.

BOER, PIM DEN, History as a Profession: The Study of History in France, 1818-1914, New Jersey 1998.

BELLAIGUE, CHRISTINA DE, 'Only what is pure and exquisite': girls' reading at school in France, 1800-70, in: French History 27, 2 (2013), pp. 202-222.

CROSSLEY, CERI, History as a Principle of legitimation in France (1820-1848), in: Writing National Histories: Western Europe since 1800, ed. by STEFAN BERGER et al., London 1999, pp. 49-57.

DE GIORGIO, MICHELA, The Catholic Model, in: History of Women in the West. Emerging Feminism from Revolution to World War, ed. by GENEVIÈVE FRAISSE, Cambridge, Mass., 1993, pp. 166-198.

ESPAGNE, MICHEL, Sur les limites du comparatisme en histoire culturelle, in: Genèses, 17, 1 (1994), pp. 112-121.

FOLZ, ROBERT, Tradition hagiographique et culte de sainte Bathilde, reine des Francs, in: Comptes-rendus des séances de l'Académie des Inscriptions et Belles-Lettres, 3 (1975), pp. 369-384.

MARGADANT, JO BURR, Gender, Vice, and the Political Imaginary in Postrevolutionary France: Reinterpreting the Failure of the July Monarchy, 1830-1848, in: The American Historical Review 104, 5 (1999), pp. 1461–1496.

POIRRIER, PHILIPPE, Les enjeux de l'histoire culturelle, Paris 2004.

ROECK, BERND, Introduction, in: Cultural Exchange in Early Modern Europe. Forging European Identities. 1400-1700, ed. by HERMAN ROODENBURG. European Science Foundation 2007.

Saint Radegunda, in: Encyclopaedia Britannica. Encyclopaedia Britannica Online Academic Edition. Encyclopædia Britannica Inc., 2013. http://www.britannica.com/EBchecked/topic/488379/Saint-Radegunda, 21.11.2013.

SMITH, BONNIE G., The Gender of History. Men, Women, and Historical Practice, Cambridge, Mass. 1998.

THEIS, LAURENT, 1830-1848: Guizot sous la monarchie de Juillet, in: http://www.guizot.com/fr/histoire-de-sa-vie/guizot-sous-la-monarchie-de-juillet/, 6.11.2013.

THIELLET, CLAIRE, La Sainteté royale de Clotilde, in: Clovis: Histoire et mémoire, ed. by MICHEL ROUCHE, Vol. I. Paris 1997.

Henry the Lion – *Enrico Leone*

A Precious Memory Box of the House of Brunswick

MATTHIAS SCHNETTGER

Henry the Lion (*Heinrich der Löwe*), the Duke of Saxony and Bavaria († 1195) was the most famous ancestor of the House of Brunswick.[1] Although he was deposed of his duchies in 1181 and sent into exile twice, he preserved this reputation for centuries. He retained considerable importance for the memory of the House of Brunswick, even more so than his son, Emperor Otto IV (who had no children and was not a direct ancestor of the later Guelphs). The exciting life of the real Henry offered some starting points for the evolution of a veritable memory box: his striking power, the conflict with Frederic Barbarossa and the German princes, the pilgrimage to Jerusalem, the marriage with Matilda Plantagenet, the exiles in England and so on. Furthermore, the portrayals of Henry inspired vivid memory, so for example in a famous illustration of his Gospel where he claimed a position similar to a king. And then there was the lion, of course, a unique symbol of the duke's strength and power.

Very soon after Henry's death, the legend of Henry the Lion arose during the thirteenth century, which reshaped some elements of the life and representation of the real Henry in quite a creative way. This legend was also adopted by the later Guelphs in order to promote their dynasty's glory. The literary version of the legend became very influential; it was composed by

1 My thanks go to Charlotte Backerra for translating the German text into English.

Heinrich Göding on behalf of Duke Henry Julius of Brunswick-Wolfenbüttel on the occasion of his wedding to Dorothea of Saxony in 1585.[2]

In the late seventeenth century both Henrys, the historical and the legendary, gained a renewed importance for the glorification of the Guelphs. During this period, the younger line of the House of Brunswick, headed by Ernest Augustus of Hanover, was on the verge of obtaining electoral dignity and thus becoming a member of the most exclusive group of princes in the Holy Roman Empire. In order to corroborate their claim to electoral dignity the Guelphs not only enacted their military strength and financial power, but also the venerable ancestry and extraordinary nobility of their dynasty. In effect, Ernest Augustus tried to demonstrate that the House of Brunswick had once ranked among the noblest dynasties of Germany and that the restoration of the Guelphs to their former position was a question of justice.

In this respect Henry the Lion played a crucial role and served as a precious memory box intended to show the old and extraordinary nobility of the House of Brunswick, filled with historical and legendary memories that could be activated, altered or enriched corresponding to the current interests and needs of the dynasty.

One of the most spectacular exhibitions of this memory box occurred in January 1689 when the new opera house of Hanover was inaugurated with the performance of *Enrico Leone* (*Henry the Lion*) in the presence of an illustrious gathering of princes and nobles. The libretto written by the Hanoverian poet laureate Ortensio Mauro was based on the legend of Henry the Lion and set to music by the famous composer Agostino Steffani.

This article shall show how the memory box Henry the Lion was utilised by Ernest Augustus of Hanover during the crucial years of the struggle for the ninth electorate. Having outlined the historical context in a first step, the article shall subsequently evaluate the importance of Henry the Lion (both in his historical and imaginary dimension) for the efforts of Ernest Augustus in a more general way. Finally, it shall analyse the image of Henry the Lion as portrayed in *Enrico Leone,* thus taking a closer look at some of the memories preserved in this memory box.

2 Werthschulte, 2007, pp. 172-175.

Ernest Augustus of Hanover and the struggle for the ninth electorate

Ernest Augustus of Hanover (1629-1698) was one of the most ambitious German princes during the second half of the seventeenth century; although the youngest of four sons of Duke George of Calenberg, he could count himself lucky to gain the Prince-Bishopric Osnabruck as Protestant prince-bishop in 1661.[3] In 1658, Ernest Augustus was married to Sophia of Palatinate, the youngest daughter of the *Winter King* Frederic V Count Palatine and his wife Princess Elizabeth Stuart. At the time of their wedding, nobody could have known that this marriage would pave the way of the Guelphs to the British throne in 1714, but the union with an elector's daughter and a king's granddaughter was certainly honourable.

In 1679, Ernest Augustus's older brother John Frederic died. He had reigned in Brunswick-Calenberg and was a convert to Catholicism. Ernest Augustus succeeded him and assumed the reins of government in Hanover while retaining his bishopric in Osnabruck. He quickly moved to secure and increase his family's position. In 1682, Ernest August married his oldest son George Louis (1714 George I of Great Britain) to Sophia Dorothea, the only daughter of another brother, George William of Brunswick-Luneburg-Celle. He thereby made provisions for his descendants to once rule over all the territories of the Guelphs' younger line. For the security of the family estate he adopted a second measure in 1682: the institution of the primogeniture in the House of Hanover. This prevented the fragmentation of the family's property by dividing the estate in the future.[4]

Despite all achievements, Ernest Augustus had indeed a noble, but by no means an outstanding status within the hierarchy of the Holy Roman Empire. The Guelphs were certainly one of the noblest German princely houses, but following the height of their reign in the twelfth and early thirteenth century they had obviously lost ground in comparison to other families (in Northern Germany especially the Hohenzollern). Unlike those, they were not part of the college of the electors. The older line of Brunswick-Wolfenbüttel even took

3 In accordance with the Peace of Westphalia, Osnabruck was ruled alternately by a Catholic and Protestant Prince-Bishop of the Guelph dynasty.

4 For Ernest Augustus of Hanover and his politics extensively SCHNATH, 1938; short and summarised SCHNATH, 1959; for individual aspects see BARMEYER, 2005; STIEGLITZ, 2001.

precedence in the house of Guelph; from 1671 they ruled once more over Henry the Lion's former seat of power, the city of Brunswick.

To overcome the older line of the Guelphs and to simultaneously gain the proper status for his family with the German princely houses, Ernest Augustus aspired to no less than the elevation to the rank of elector. In principle, the Golden Bull of 1356 by Emperor Charles IV had closed the college of electors. But since the sixteenth century there had been some changes to this illustrious circle. Emperor Charles V transferred the Saxon electorate from the Ernestine to the Albertine Wettins in 1547, after 1623 the electorate of Palatinate then passed to the Bavarian Wittelsbachs and an eighth electorate had been created with the Treaty of Westphalia 1648 in compensation for the Counts Palatine.[5]

When the House of Palatine-Neuburg inherited the Palatine electorate in 1685, the confessional disparity within the college of electors shifted further to the disadvantage of the Protestants. Of eight electors, six were subsequently Catholic, and this strong Catholic ascendancy was in contradiction to the principle of confessional parity in the Empire as was established with the Westphalian Peace. Was it therefore not advisable to mitigate the Catholic majority by creating another Protestant elector? This was one of the arguments particularly aimed at the Protestants within the Empire and was brought forward by Ernest Augustus to promote the admission of the House of Hanover to the electoral council.[6]

First of all, it was necessary to persuade Emperor Leopold I, since such an elevation of rank was not possible in the Empire without his agreement. The right to ennoble was after all one of the most prestigious imperial privileges.[7] In fact, the Habsburgs could do well with a secure Catholic majority of the emperor's electors. This is the reason why Ernest Augustus solicited intensely for the favour of the Vienna Court in the 1680s. He showed himself open-minded towards a reintegration of the Protestants into the Roman-Catholic church and granted generous military aid in the Great Turkish War (1683-1699) and in the Nine Years' War (1688-1697).[8] Temporary approaches to

5 For the transfers of electoral dignity of 1547 and 1623: RUDERSDORF, 2009; KAISER, 2004; STEINER, 1985.

6 SCHNATH, 1938, pp. 186, 474-477.

7 Admittedly, the extent at which the emperor was bound by the affirmation of the prince-electors or all of the Imperial Diet in regard to elevations of rank was contested. For elevations of rank in the early modern Holy Roman Empire: KLEIN, 1986; also SCHLIP, 1987.

8 SCHNATH, 1938, pp. 166-222, 348-354, 373-376.

France increased the pressure on the imperial court to accommodate Hanoverian ambitions.[9]

After long, tedious negotiations that intensified in 1689, Leopold I signed the so-called Electoral Treaty with the Guelph brothers Ernest Augustus of Hanover and George William of Luneburg-Celle in 1692 (dated 22nd March). In return for being bestowed with the electoral hat, Ernest Augustus promised, among other things, to deploy a corps of 6000 men against the Turks for two years, to once pay 500,000 Reichstaler, to provide military aid in the West and to grant free practice of religion for Catholics in Hanover. In December 1692 this was followed by Ernest Augustus being bestowed with the new electoral dignity. Due to the serious opposition of a number of electors and princes, Hanover was in fact admitted to the college of electors as late as 1708.[10]

Ernest Augustus, the Hanoverian opera and Henry the Lion

The Guelphs' considerable concessions were most certainly crucial for Leopold I signing the Electoral Treaty in 1692. However, this did not settle the case, as the opposition to the ninth electorate showed. An elevation of rank was only successful when met with universal approval. It was therefore important to legitimise the new dignity of the House of Guelph for the German and European public – this meant first of all a courtly public. The representation of a prince had to be according to his rank within the *Société des Princes* in the Empire and in Europe. When a prince tried to gain an elevation of rank he did well to adjust his self-imagining towards the requested status beforehand.[11]

This was exactly what Ernest Augustus did by keeping an illustrious court following the example of his older brother John Frederic's efforts in Hanover.[12] From the first moment of his rule he spent large sums on restoring

9 SCHNATH, 1938, pp. 396-437.

10 For the background and the negotiations about the electoral dignity: SCHNATH, 1938, pp. 471-505, 592-651; ARETIN, 1997, pp. 54-62. George William of Celle was at first also part of the opposition against the Hanoverian electoral dignity because he refused to see why he should step back in favour of his younger brother in this prestigious affair, too.

11 STOLLBERG-RILINGER, 1997; STOLLBERG-RILINGER, 2002.

12 MARLES, 1991, pp. 15-20, especially in regard to music and opera.

the castle's interior; with the destruction of a number of town houses, the castle gained a free forecourt towards the river Leine. He also enlarged the court and expanded the gardens at Herrenhausen.[13] Last but not least, Ernest August built a large, impressive opera house. Already during Duke John Frederic's reign there had been a golden age of Hanoverian music with first opera performances (*Orontea* and *Alceste* 1678/79).[14] Duke Ernest Augustus knew the Italian and particularly the Venetian opera very well due to his many travels to Italy.[15] Among others he may have seen Antonio Sartorio's – his brother John Frederic's chapel master – performance of Adelaide in 1672 in Venice. The title character of this opera is Empress Adelheid, the wife of Otto I the Great (936-973) of the Saxon House of Liudolfing – so Ernest Augustus had already encountered the medieval opera that referred to current rulers in Lower Saxony.[16]

And so the construction of a new court opera house followed his personal inclinations and aimed at participating in current developments of European courtly life: at the same time it was a conscious step to draw the German and European courts' attention to Hanover. In the past, the *Kleine Schlosstheater* (Little Court Theatre) by Johann Friedrich had to be used for opera performances. The new opera house, built right next to the palace within just two years in 1688/89, was "one of the greatest and most beautiful opera houses of its times, with seating for 1300 people and much admired technical features".[17] The construction costs for the building were enormous and amounted to 24,746 Taler plus an additional 5500 Taler to purchase the grounds. Even though the number of opera performances was low and the opera house itself had to be closed for financial reasons by the new Prince-

13 SCHNATH, 1962, pp. 59-87; ABBETMEYER, 1931, p. 28; RETTICH, 1992.

14 ABBETMEYER, 1931, pp. 33-67; SCHNATH, 1962, p. 69; MARLES, 1991, p. 21.

15 Ernest Augustus was during his reign in Italy in the years 1664/65, 1669/70, 1671/72, 1680/81, and for a last time in 1685/86; SCHNATH, 1938, pp. 376-381 (with dubious assessments).

16 See on *Adelaide* ABBETMEYER, 1931, pp. 53-59.

17 For the new building of the opera house: SCHNATH, 1962, pp. 69-76, citation p. 71 (translation by Charlotte Backerra); MARLES, 1991, pp. 23 f. Because of the hurried construction of the building – the result of Ernest Augustus's wish not to be later than his cousins in Wolfenbüttel which had opened an opera house in Wolfenbüttel in 1688 and had started the construction of another one in Brunswick – it needed improvements over the following years that led to further costs. The Hanoverian Estates were not least inclined to finance the building because it would prevent the Duke from further travels to Italy.

elector George Louis in 1698, the relevance of the opera is seen as very significant for the Hanoverian court under Ernest Augustus.[18]

Ernest Augustus had also a keen interest in the glorious medieval past of his house that was most fitting to legitimise the claim for an elevation of rank. For this purpose he could count on none less than Gottfried Wilhelm Leibniz, who entered into Guelph services under his predecessor and had already published a memoir *De la Grandeur de la Serenissime Maison de Bronsvic-Lunebourg* in 1685. In this, he emphasised that in former times the Guelph Dukes of Saxony and Bavaria had been electors of the emperors and were therefore in fact prince-electors. Consequently the bestowal of electoral dignity to the House of Brunswick-Luneburg merely restored the former status and rectified old injustice.[19]

Even though Leibniz never finished his great history of the Guelphs, first results of his research were immediately included in the ducal self-imagining, as can be shown with the redesign of the Hall of Knights in the Leine Palace[20] and likewise with the opera *Enrico Leone*. For Henry the Lion – and not his son Emperor Otto IV – seemed to be the fitting point of reference to historically legitimise the current claims of the House of Guelph.[21] Henry the Lion admittedly lost against his Staufer adversaries as Otto IV, but as he was a vigorous and for a long time markedly thriving territorial prince his life was a good example and starting point for the Guelphs of the late seventeenth century. In addition, Henry himself had quite successfully managed to cultivate the memory of his life. The Brunswick Palace with the bronze lion statue and the famous Book of Gospel are the most well-known examples for his efforts.[22] The legend of Henry was long since established as an element of the Guelph glorification.[23] After all Henry was ancestor to all ruling Guelphs while Otto remained childless; furthermore, Otto's reign was by no means always seen positively.[24]

18 MARLES, 1991, p. 17.

19 REESE, 1967; ID., 1995.

20 SCHNATH, 1962, pp. 64f., 67.

21 SEEBALD, 2009, pp. 65-73; REESE, 1967, esp. pp. 1-6, 31-46.

22 OEXLE, 1994; also various articles in the exhibition catalogue LUCKHARDT/NIEHOFF, 1995.

23 BEHR, 1995; METZGER, 1995; WERTHSCHULTE, 2007.

24 No one else but Leibniz was of the opinion Otto's emperorship had hurt the House of Guelph more than it benefited it; BEI DER WIEDEN/DIEHL, 2009, pp. 307-318. – The dynasty was continued by Henry the Lion's youngest son William.

Enrico Leone

Against this background, the opening of the Hanoverian opera house with *Enrico Leone* – of all operas – held a key position in Ernest Augustus's self-glorification aimed at an elevation of rank. Form and external circumstances as well as the content of the performance should demonstrate the Guelphs as one of the foremost families of the Empire and of Europe. As previously mentioned, the newly built opera house was considered one of the greatest and most beautiful in Europe. Ernest Augustus engaged Agostino Steffani, an experienced and well-known composer,[25] and Italian singers and instrumentalists from Venice, Munich and Modena came to the city on the River Leine; in addition, spectacular stage machinery was used. Consequently, the performance was visited by a number of princes, the Prince-elector of Brandenburg, the Dukes of Brunswick-Wolfenbüttel and Celle, the Landgrave of Hesse-Cassel and the Princess of Eastern Frisia as well as all their courts, and it was said to have been impressive and a sensual pleasure.[26] The propaganda was not to be limited to the public of January 1689, but to be spread all over Europe. Thus, the libretto by the Hanoverian poet laureate Ortensio Mauro was also printed. This print included so-called paratexts as the description of scenes and stage machinery to give the readers an impression of the amazing magnificence of the performance beyond the pure reading of the opera's text. By translating all texts into French – the *lingua franca* of the European courts and scholars – and German, maximum publicity was attained.[27]

Preparations for the opera event of January 1689 started early. In spring 1688, when the opera house was still being built and composer Steffani was in Munich, the Hanoverian minister Otto Grote urged Leibniz to quickly return

25 Agostino Steffani (1654-1728) was originally from Castelfranco Veneto and after first musical studies he entered the services of the Electorate of Bavaria in 1667. In 1680, he was ordained as a priest and became known as an opera composer in the service of the court in Munich since 1681. In 1688, he entered Hanoverian service and changed to the court of the Palatine Electorate in Dusseldorf in 1703. At both courts he worked as a composer and held different administrative and diplomatic functions. In 1709, he was created the Apostolic Vicar of Higher and Lower Saxony, but he repeatedly had to face challenges in the exercise of his duties; CROLL, 1961, pp. 9-75; TIMMS, 2003, pp. 3-37; KAUFOLD, 1997, pp. 13-23; for his time in Munich see also WERR, 2010, pp. 64-67.

26 TIMMS, 2003, pp. 53-56; SEEBALD, 2009, p. 71; CROLL, 1961, p. 91.

27 SEEBALD, 2009, pp. 73-75.

from his research trip concerning the Guelph history. The Duke would make plans for an opera about Henry the Lion and the scholar's expertise was urgently required. The choice of subject was thus apparently decided on the personal initiative of Ernest Augustus. At the time, Leibniz was not directly part of the writing process of the libretto. But it is quite possible that Steffani, and maybe also the theatre painter Johann Oswald Harms, supported Mauro because he apparently felt slightly insecure in this field.[28] However, the thorough preparations for the spectacular inauguration of the Hanoverian opera house clearly show that the opening of the memory box Henry the Lion by the performance of *Enrico Leone* in January 1689 was designed to play a key role in duke Ernest August's struggle for the electoral dignity.

But which were the memories to be conveyed by *Enrico Leone*? The opera's libretto begins with an *Elogio d'Henrico Leone* which powerfully visualises for audience or readers Henry the Lion's greatness with a realm covering an area from the River Elbe to the Rhine and from the Alps to the North Sea.[29] In contrast to other princes, who were overthrown by their vices, it was his virtues that doomed him: when he had declined in religious zeal to help Barbarossa, the pope's persecutor, and instead set out for the Holy Land, his envious neighbours had used the convenient opportunity of the emperor's hate, the imperial ban, and Henry's absence to rob him of his lands.[30]

The elogio, most probably also written by Mauro, thus referred to the dramatic events of the years after 1176. During that year, Henry the Lion refused to support Frederic I Barbarossa against the Lombard allies of Pope Alexander III in a meeting in Chiavenna, or rather in exchange he wanted the town of Goslar, even though the emperor beseeched him and possibly even went down on his knees before Henry. Two years later Frederic accepted the charge against Henry preferred by his Saxon adversaries. In 1179, as the Duke did not react to any summons, the emperor administered his imperial ban and –

28 CROLL, 1961, pp. 92f.

29 "[…] l'ampiezza de suoi stati, che negli antichi limiti della sassonia, e della Bauiera da esso possedute si stendeuano dall'Albi al Reno, e dall'Alpi all'Oceano". [STEFFANI]/[MAURO], [1689], p. [4].

30 "[…] furono per esso così perniciose le Virtù, come funesti per gli altri Prencipi sogliono esseri[!] i Vizi. […] Zelo di Religione lo staccò sott'Alessandria dal partito di Federico Barbarossa persecutor del Pontefice, e doppò impegnandolo nelle Guerre di Terra santa diede adito à vicini gelosi delle sue crescenti prosperità di preualersi delle inique congionture dell'odio di Cesare, e della proscrittione, e lontananza d'Henrico per usurparne le spoglie, mentr'egli spogliaua i Barbari delle Prouincie usurpate aì Fedeli." [STEFFANI]/[MAURO], [1689], pp. [4]f.

after another feudal lawsuit and a princely ruling – stripped him of all imperial feoffs. Henry was again outlawed in 1180 and was therefore without any rights. He capitulated in 1181 and lost all his territories with the exception of the allodial property around Brunswick and Luneburg. Furthermore, he was sent into exile to his father-in-law Henry II of England. Because he did not want to take part in Frederic Barbarossa's crusade, he again had to go to England in 1189, but returned arbitrarily after his wife Matilda's death in the same year. Besides all that, he achieved some successes; among other things, he conquered and destroyed the town of Bardowick whose citizens had offended him after his fall. Only in 1194 Henry finally made his peace with the new Emperor Henry VI.[31]

However, the campaigns of Henry the Lion in the Holy Land mentioned in the Elogio have never happened, because he never took part in a crusade to the Levant. He participated solely in the so-called Wendish Crusade of 1147 and made a pilgrimage to Jerusalem in 1172. The campaigns in the Holy Land are rather a key point of the Henry legend on which the actual libretto was based.

The Henry legend created in the thirteenth century was not just used exclusively by Ernest Augustus for the glorification of the Guelphs. Duke Julius of Brunswick-Wolfenbüttel had for example ordered to perform Henry's fight against gryphons and dragons at his wedding with Dorothea of Saxony (1585). For this occasion the Dresden court painter Heinrich Göding, originally from Brunswick, composed a literary interpretation of the Henry legend that was printed several times until the nineteenth century. This version of the Henry legend could also have served as the basis for Mauro's libretto.[32]

At the centre of the opera's storyline stands the legendary odyssey of Henry the Lion after his alleged fights in the Holy Land and the reunion with his faithful wife Matilda; in the opera, Henry the Lion is translated to Enrico Leone, Matilda to Metilda. To give a brief summary: After his battles in the Holy Land, Duke Enrico is on his way back to Saxony. His ship is in distress at sea; his men sew Enrico into an animal skin to save him, but a gryphon carries him away.

In the palace at Luneburg, the Burgundian Duke Almaro woos Enrico's wife Metilda – even though he is affianced to the emperor's daughter Idalba. To convince Metilda of her husband's death, Almaro allies himself to her wet

31 For the historical background: EHLERS, 2008, esp. pp. 197-211, 317-344; short JORDAN, 1969.

32 REESE, 1967, pp. 1f.; SEEBALD, 2009, pp. 79f.

nurse Errea who tries with sorcery and illusions to encourage the Duchess to marry Almaro.

At the same time, Enrico managed to free himself of the hide and escaped the gryphon. He kills a dragon to save a lion. From then on the lion follows him faithfully everywhere. Enrico and the lion are carried by a cloud on top of the Kalkberg [limestone mountain] near Luneburg. Tired, the duke falls asleep. When he is attacked by a demon, the lion's roar awakens him in warning.

Just in time, Enrico returns to Luneburg to prevent the wedding of Almaro and Metilda who was ultimately convinced of her husband's death. He announces himself as her husband by placing his wedding ring in her wine cup. Instead of the planned wedding, husband and wife celebrate their reunion. Henry forgives Almaro and with his help seizes the rebellious town of Bardowick. During the battle Idalba saves Almaro's life. Enrico announces their marriage and Idalba promises to mediate between her father and the duke.[33]

Enrico Leone was able to show – besides the artists engaged – the technical possibilities of the new opera house in the best light. Among others, the following sets were needed: a wrecking ship, a gryphon and its nest, a lion, a cloud to carry Henry to the Kalkberg, and a triumphal chariot drawn by four live horses.[34] *Enrico Leone* was in fact an enormous spectacular period opera and would accordingly have been cherished in the public's memory. To concretise the memories that should have been transported by the opera, some aspects of the plot and the elogio shall be examined in the following.

Enrico Leone has a marked heroic couple, Enrico and Metilda; their story seems to be some kind of remake of Homer's Odyssey. At the same time, both Henry the Lion and Matilda of England are the only historic figures of the libretto. Matilda however had died during Henry's exile in England and before the conquest of Bardowick on 28 June 1189.

In accordance with the Henry legend and the aim of the opera, Henry the Lion is shown as a knight in shining armour. Courage, intelligence, faithfulness and magnanimity are only some of the positive characteristics awarded to him. Mauro's characterisation of the hero is not especially original, but that is also not his point. He rather aims to show in particular the known elements

33 [STEFFANI]/[MAURO], [1689]; an extensive description of the content gives SEEBALD, 2009, pp. 81-126, with references to the noticeable influences of the Henry legend in the libretto, especially in the form of poetic arrangements by Heinrich Göding; more: CROLL, 1961, pp. 94-104.

34 KAUFOLD, 1997, p. 27.

of the Henry legend to glorify the ancestor of the ruling dynasty and at the same time the House of Brunswick-Luneburg as a whole. As Mauro writes in the elogio, instead of following Horace's rules, he complies with the ruler's dictate.[35]

After the example of the Henry legend, Mauro also did not fail to mention the difficult chapter of Henry's conflict with Frederic Barbarossa and his son Henry VI. In the elogio, he frankly speaks about the "odio di Cesare", the emperor's hate.[36] Of course, the emperor himself does not personally appear within the opera, but is represented by his fictional daughter Ibalda. And at the end, there is the chance of reconciliation with the emperor, already initiated by the marriage of Ibalda and Almaro. A real enemy is not part of the opera. The only evil human is Errea, Metilda's Mephistophelian wet nurse.

Very clearly the primary aim of *Enrico Leone* is the ruler's glorification intended to be recognised by the audience. It closely ties into an already established and known source, the Henry legend. And this legend plays a huge role in the representation of the House of Hanover during those years. In September 1688 Duchess Sophia interpreted the choice of Henry's story for the opening opera in a letter to Leibniz as a reminder for following generations to recall all the territories that were once part of the Guelph dynasty.[37] Actually, the opera related to a lesser extent to a list of Guelph territories, but rather to the greatness of the House of Guelph as seen in the person of its ancestor. Apart from this first and foremost aim to valorise the dynasty by glorifying its most famous predecessor, some more or less direct adaptations or connotations to the political events of the year 1689 are depicted.

So Mauro transferred the Guelph court – quite logically– from Brunswick, the actual town of Henry the Lion, to Luneburg. For Brunswick was reigned by the rivalling older line of the House, the Dukes of Brunswick-Wolfenbüttel, while Luneburg was admittedly not under Ernest Augustus's control, but was

35 "[…] s'è hauuto più riguardo al divertimento de' Popoli, co' quali si vive ch'alle regole de Poeti di secoli, e paesi lontani, e s'è giudicato più conveniente l'ubidir à cenni d'Augusto, che necessario l'assoggettirsi a' precetti d'Horatio". [STEFFANI]/[MAURO], [1689], p. [12].

36 IBID., p. [5].

37 "Cet Sig.r Hortance qui compose la piesse de Henri le Lion, je crois qu'on a pris ce suject afin que la posterité n'oublie point tous les estats qui ont esté autrefoys à cette maison". Duchess Sophia to Gottfried Wilhelm Leibniz. 1688 September 16. Cited from REESE, 1967, p. 2.

at least ruled by his brother George William and therefore the right line of the Guelphs.

Beginning and ending of court operas were especially good for relating to the commissioning prince. This was often done by pre- or postludes separated from the actual plot. In *Enrico Leone* the relation of ancestor and currently ruling descendant is conveniently part of the elogio. Here Mauro attests to the latter playing a "remarkable role" in Europe and following Henry the Lion's zeal in the fight against the infidels. He specifically speaks of the participation of Ernest Augustus's four oldest sons in the Turk Wars in Hungary and Greece.[38] In the year of the five hundredth anniversary of the conquest of Bardowick Mauro bridges five somewhat dark centuries in the history of the Guelphs so that the current members of the dynasty are directly following Henry's example.

The important role played by Metilda/Matilda in the plot can be seen as a reverence to Duchess Sophia's role at the court of Hanover. One comparable characteristic of the two women gained even more importance around the months of the opera's premiere: their English origins. After the expulsion of the Catholic Stuarts in the course of the Glorious Revolution of 1688, the Protestant granddaughter of James I and her descendants were a significant step closer to succeed to the English throne. However, in January 1689 nobody could have known that Sophia's son George Louis would accede to the throne of Great Britain in 1714.[39]

Lastly, the marginal reference to the conflict of Henry the Lion and Frederic Barbarossa could also be seen as a signal towards the Court of Vienna, because until the autumn of 1688 Ernest Augustus was allied with Louis XIV. This alliance ended only when he strongly supported emperor and empire in the Nine Years' War and personally led a campaign to the River

38 "Resta però degli auanzi di si gran naufragio a suoi Ser.mi Discendenti di che far nell'Europa considerabil figura, e di chè imitar felicem.te, il zelo d'Henrico à danno degl'Jnfedeli.
E che non deue la Cristianità à ualidi soccorsi mandati, e guidati dà questi Prencipi nell'Hungheria, e nella Grecia, et al valore di quattro gloriosi Fratelli, ch'in anni ancor acerbi frà le più memorabili imprese di questa Guerra si sono segnalati con attioni Heroiche, e degne dell'Augusto lor sangue?" [STEFFANI]/[MAURO], [1689], p. [5].

39 BARMEYER, 2005, p. 285. This close connection can also be seen in a medal celebrating the Act of Succession 1701, designed by Leibniz and made by Samuel Lambelet; see for images and description the British Museum online site: http://www.britishmuseum.org/research/collection_online/collection (26.09.2013).

Rhine. Only at the end of January 1689, thus at the time of the staging of *Enrico Leone*, the French envoys left Hanover.[40] When the emperor's daughter Ibalda therefore promises at the end of the opera to mediate the peace between emperor and duke, it was surely an important part of a *lieto fine*, but it could also be seen as pointing to a renewed political approach of Vienna and Hanover. Furthermore it can be stated that there is no mentioning of Henry's submission to Barbarossa, but of reconciliation – emphasising the confidence of the House of Guelph which, apart from all existing differences in rank, claims to be of equal standing even to the emperor![41] Finally it would not be wrong to assume that the character of Henry the Lion is an alter ego of the reigning duke – the image of Henry the Lion's return is already pointing in that direction, as well as the all in all preeminent importance of the Lion for Ernest Augustus's strategy to glorify his family's wealth.

Consequently, *Enrico Leone* was not the only Henry opera to be performed in Guelph territories during those years. For example, Professor Joachim Meier from Göttingen published the singspiel *Die siegende Großmuth* about the Lion's last years in 1693.[42] And in his glorifying poem *Gloria Brunswigii Leonis* Pastor Peter Richard Evers of Hameln expressly marks Henry the Lion as prince-elector and characterises Ernest Augustus as his reincarnation.[43] These examples should be proof enough to show *Enrico Leone* not as a singularity, but "only one among others".[44] It was just part of many propaganda activities aiming at legitimising the new electoral dignity in recourse to the medieval duke; it was however a prominent component of particular importance.

40 In fact, Ernest Augustus was also later prepared to put pressure on the emperor via a French alliance to coerce him to come to an accommodation in regard to the question of electoral dignity. In 1689, he led his troops another time to the Rhine for emperor and Empire. But in 1690, when negotiations faltered, he again negotiated with France and stood at the forefront of a neutral, so-called "third party" totally following French interests; SCHNATH, 1938, pp. 432-470, 502-556.

41 REESE, 1967, p. 2f., sees in Almaro's rejection of the emperor's daughter Ibalda in favour of Metilda also a valorisation of the House of Guelph.

42 MEIER, 1693.

43 EVERS, 1692.

44 So REESE, 1967, p. 5, who by the fact that he begins his description precisely with *Enrico Leone* recognises however implicitly the opera's importance.

Conclusion

Because of his political successes, his dramatic life and his care for his own memoria as well as the Henry legend that emerged a few decades after his death, Henry the Lion came to be a precious memory box for the House of Guelph. It was a requisite for showing the dynasty's prominent status with the German princely houses and played a major role in the representation of the Guelph dynasty. Henry the Lion's reputation with the aristocracy and the scholars in Christian Europe as a well-known historical character laid the foundation for using the memory box Henry the Lion successfully in competing with other dynasties.

When the House of Hanover opened this memory box with the performance of *Enrico Leone* in January 1689 it happened in a way that remained in the audience's memory and would resonate across the Empire, or even across Europe. In fact, the sensational form in presenting the memory box was perhaps as important as its contents.

With *Enrico Leone* it was less important to transport subtle content but vital to transport a vague although overwhelming message (because of the manner in which it was presented) of the dignified age and greatness of the House of Guelph. Last but not least it meant to raise the claim of a legitimate succession to Henry the Lion before the cousins of the older line of Brunswick-Wolfenbüttel who were present for the performance. The memory box Henry the Lion was, so to speak, claimed for the younger line of the Guelph dynasty; Duke Ernest Augustus was even introduced as the new Lion.

The creative combination of the historical and the legendary Henry the Lion shows that the aim was not to spread historically correct memories, but simply to claim the Guelph's rank at the top of the German princely houses even during the High Middle Ages. In some areas, as with the relocation from Brunswick to Luneburg, traditional memories were deliberately altered to match them to the current needs of the House of Hanover. Other aspects, such as the important role of Metilda/Matilda, were already based in history and legend: they had only to be embellished accordingly in reference to the very distant prospect of the succession to the English throne.

But under the circumstances of the year 1689, the claim for electoral dignity was more important. Apart from all short-term political opportunities so expertly used by Ernest Augustus in this regard, his origins in the old and noble House of Guelph should not be undervalued. In this sense the existence of the already established memory box Henry the Lion, its forceful actualisation in the years around 1690 and not least its spectacular staging in *Enrico Leone,* were important requirements for the assignment of the electoral dignity in 1692.

List of References

Sources

EVERS, PETER RICHARD, Gloria Brunswigii Leonis Cum Potentissimo quondam Electore Henrico Leone Duce Brunswicensi, Saxoniae, Angariae, Bavariae, & Vandaliae, sepulta, & hoc seculo in ... Domino Ernesto Augusto, Duce Brunsvicensi Ac Lunaeburgensi, Episcopo Osnabrugensi, Rediviva, Quum S. Caes. Maj. Auctoritate, & Potentissimi Electoralis Collegii suffragiis Ob Summa In Salutem Imperii Publicam Merita Anno M.DC.LXXXXII. die IX. Decembr. Viennae Solennissimo Ritu Elector Nonus Proclamaretur, s.l. 1692.

LEIBNIZ, GOTTFRIED WILHELM/LAMBELET, SAMUEL, Medal on the Act of Succession, s.l. 1701, British Museum, G3,BrunM.6, http://www.british museum.org/research/collection_online/collection (26.09.2013)

MEIER, JOACHIM, Die siegende Großmuth Zu Ehren dem Durchläuchtigsten und Großmächtigsten Fürsten und Herrn Herrn Ernest-August / Herzogen zu Braunsweig und Lüneburg des H. Römischen Reichs Churfürsten und Bischoffen zu Osnabrug Auff Sr. Churfürstl. Durchl. Erhöhung zur neuen und neundten Churwürde in einem Singspiel vorgestellet, Göttingen 1693.

[STEFFANI, AGOSTINO]/[MAURO, ORTENSIO], Henrico Leone. Dramma per recitarsi per l'anno MDCLXXXIX. Nel nuovo Theatro d'Hannover, s.l. [1689].

Secondary Literature

ABBETMEYER, THEODOR, Zur Geschichte der Musik am Hofe in Hannover vor Agostino Steffani 1636-1689. Ein Bild künstlerischer Kultur im 17. Jahrhundert, Göttingen 1931.

ARETIN, KARL OTMAR FREIHERR VON, Das Alte Reich 1648-1806, Vol. 2: Kaisertradition und österreichische Großmachtpolitik (1684-1745), Stuttgart 1997.

BARMEYER, HEIDE, Die Personalunion England-Hannover: Ihre Entstehung, Etablierung und Fortsetzung aus hannoverscher Sicht, in: Die Personalunionen von Sachsen-Polen 1697-1763 und Hannover-England 1714-1837. Ein Vergleich (Deutsches Historisches Institut Warschau, Quellen und Studien 18), ed. by REX REXHEUSER, Wiesbaden 2005, pp. 275-298.

BEHR, HANS-JOACHIM, Das Nachleben Heinrichs des Löwen in der Literatur des Spätmittelalters, in: Heinrich der Löwe und seine Zeit. Herrschaft und Repräsentation der Welfen 1125-1135, ed. by JOCHEN LUCKHARDT/FRANZ NIEHOFF, vol. 3: Abteilung Nachleben, München 1995, pp. 9-14.

BEI DER WIEDEN, BRAGE/DIEHL, GERHARD, "Unser Otto?" "Gnedig und sanfftmütig"? Das Bild Kaiser Ottos IV. in der Historiographie der frühen Neuzeit, in: Otto IV. Traum vom welfischen Kaisertum, ed. by BERND ULRICH HUCKER et al., Petersberg 2009, pp. 307-318.

CROLL, GERHARD, Agostino Steffani (1654-1728). Sein Leben und seine Opern, Habilitation, Münster 1961.

EHLERS, JOACHIM, Heinrich der Löwe. Eine Biographie, München 2008.

JORDAN, KARL, Art. "Heinrich der Löwe", in: Neue Deutsche Biographie, Vol. 8, Berlin 1969, pp. 388-391.

KAISER, MICHAEL, Im Kampf um die Kur und die Obere Pfalz. Maximilian von Bayern und seine Politik gegen Friedrich V. von der Pfalz, in: Der Winterkönig. Königlicher Glanz in Amberg. Vortragsreihe des Stadtarchivs Amberg zur Landesausstellung 2003 (Beiträge zur Geschichte und Kultur der Stadt Amberg 1), ed. by JOHANNES LASCHINGER, Amberg 2004, pp. 27-45.

KAUFOLD, CLAUDIA, Ein Musiker als Diplomat. Abbé Agostino Steffani in hannoverschen Diensten (1688-1703) (Veröffentlichungen des Instituts für Historische Landesforschung der Universität Göttingen 36), Bielefeld 1997.

KLEIN, THOMAS, Die Erhebungen in den weltlichen Reichsfürstenstand 1550-1806, in: Blätter für deutsche Landesgeschichte 122 (1986), pp. 137-192.

LUCKHARDT, JOCHEN/NIEHOFF, FRANZ (ed.), Heinrich der Löwe und seine Zeit. Herrschaft und Repräsentation der Welfen 1125-1135, 3 vols., München1995.

MARLES, ANN CANDACE, Music and drama in the Hanover Operas of Agostino Steffani (1654-1728), New Haven 1991.

METZGER, WOLFGANG, Greifen, Drachen, Schnabelmenschen – Heinrich der Löwe in erzählenden Darstellungen des Spätmittelalters, in: Heinrich der Löwe und seine Zeit. Herrschaft und Repräsentation der Welfen 1125-1135, ed. by JOCHEN LUCKHARDT/FRANZ NIEHOFF, vol. 3: Abteilung Nachleben, München 1995, pp. 15-28.

OEXLE, OTTO GERHARD, Die Memoria Heinrichs des Löwen, in: Memoria in der Gesellschaft des Mittelalters (Veröffentlichungen des Max-Planck-Instituts für Geschichte 111), ed. by DIETER GEUENICH, Göttingen 1994, pp. 128-177.

REESE, ARMIN, Heinrich der Löwe als Argument. Zur dynastischen Historiographie der Welfen im 17. und 18. Jahrhundert, in: Heinrich der Löwe und seine Zeit. Herrschaft und Repräsentation der Welfen 1125-1135, ed. by JOCHEN LUCKHARDT/FRANZ NIEHOFF, vol. 3: Abteilung Nachleben, München 1995, pp. 41-47.

ID., Die Rolle der Historie beim Aufstieg des Welfenhauses 1680-1714 (Quellen und Darstellungen zur Geschichte Niedersachsens 71), Hildesheim 1967.

RETTICH, HUBERT K., Der Große Garten zu Hannover-Herrenhausen. Die Sommerresidenz der Welfen im Wandel ihrer Nutzungen, in: Die Gartenkunst, N.F. 4 (1992), pp. 243-256.

RUDERSDORF, MANFRED, Kursachsen im politischen System des Alten Reiches. Staatsbildung, Religionspolitik und dynastische Rivalität im Zeichen der wettinischen Weichenstellung von 1547, in: Neues Archiv für Sächsische Geschichte 80 (2009), pp. 105-127.

SCHLIP, HARRY, Die neuen Fürsten. Zur Erhebung in den Reichsfürstenstand und zur Aufnahme in den Reichsfürstenrat im 17. und 18. Jahrhundert, in: Liechtenstein – Fürstliches Haus und staatliche Ordnung. Geschichtliche Grundlagen und moderne Perspektiven, ed. by VOLKER PRESS/DIETMAR WILLOWEIT, Vaduz/Wien 1987, pp. 249-292.

SCHNATH, GEORG, Das Leineschloss. Kloster – Fürstensitz – Landtagsgebäude. Mit Beiträgen von Rudolf Hillebrecht und Helmut Plath, Hannover 1962.

ID., Art. "Ernst August", in: Neue Deutsche Biographie, Vol. 4, Berlin 1959, pp. 608f.

ID., Geschichte Hannovers im Zeitalter der neunten Kur und der englischen Sukzession 1674-1714, Vol. 1: 1674-1692 (Veröffentlichungen der

Historischen Kommission für Hannover, Oldenburg, Braunschweig, Schaumburg-Lippe und Bremen 18), Hildesheim/Leipzig 1938.

SEEBALD, CHRISTIAN, Libretti vom 'Mittelalter'. Entdeckungen von Historie in der (nord)deutschen und europäischen Oper um 1700 (Frühe Neuzeit 134), Tübingen 2009.

STEINER, JÜRGEN, Die pfälzische Kurwürde während des Dreißigjährigen Krieges (1618-1648) (Veröffentlichungen der Pfälzischen Gesellschaft zur Förderung der Wissenschaften in Speyer 76), Speyer 1985.

STIEGLITZ, ANNETTE VON, Der teuerste Hut des Reiches. Hannovers Ringen um die Kurwürde, in: Ehrgeiz, Luxus & Fortune. Hannovers Weg zu Englands Krone. Essays zur Ausstellung (Schriften des Historischen Museums Hannover 19), ed. by SABINE MESCHKAT-PETERS, Hannover 2001, pp. 68-83.

STOLLBERG-RILINGER, BARBARA, Honores regii. Die Königswürde im zeremoniellen Zeichensystem der Frühen Neuzeit, in: Dreihundert Jahre Preußische Königskrönung. Eine Tagungsdokumentation (Forschungen zur Brandenburgischen und Preußischen Geschichte N.F., Beiheft 6), ed. by JOHANNES KUNISCH, Berlin 2002, pp. 1-26.

ID., Höfische Öffentlichkeit. Zur zeremoniellen Selbstdarstellung des brandenburgischen Hofes vor dem europäischen Publikum, in: Forschungen zur Brandenburgischen und Preußischen Geschichte, N.F. 7 (1997), pp. 145-176.

TIMMS, COLIN, Polymath of the Baroque. Agostino Steffani and his music. Oxford 2003.

WERR, SEBASTIAN, Politik mit sinnlichen Mitteln. Oper und Fest am Münchner Hof (1680-1745), Köln et al. 2010.

WERTHSCHULTE, LEILA, Heinrich der Löwe in Geschichte und Sage (Beiträge zur älteren Literaturgeschichte), Heidelberg 2007.

Artefacts as a Memory Box

ANNA-LEENA PERÄMÄKI

The following section of the book discusses material artefacts[1] as memory boxes. Compared to personalities and especially to topoi, artefacts are something quite concrete. Because of their material nature, it is at first sight perhaps easier to understand the "memory boxness" of artefacts than the other two themes analysed in the previous articles. Artefacts are something you can touch, literally remove from one place and time to another and in some cases even open up like an actual box. These material features are not, however, all that is needed in order to be able to approach an artefact as a memory box.

As Jörg Rogge and Hannu Salmi mention in the general introduction to this book, the concept of the memory box is based on the idea of isolation. Something is separated from its surroundings, isolated from its original (cultural) context. This isolation creates the boxness and is essential in the process of an artefact becoming a memory box. This can happen in a twofold manner: On the one hand, particular cultural practices in the past isolate memories and make them transferable and, on the other, the opening or recognition of a memory box is a momentum of isolation.

Of course, all artefacts can, in one way or another, be seen as access points to the past; they are *Überreste*[2] (remains) of yesterday. The materiality of the artefacts needs to be pointed out here: Many of them last longer than human life, either on purpose or accidentally. However, memory box is a specific form of *Überrest*. It is a carrier and activator of memories from the times gone, not just a passive remain.

1 The concept *artefact* is defined here as something artificial, manufactured by man.
2 See for example OPGENOORTH/SCHULZ, 2010, pp. 49-55, 86-179.

An artefact that has become a memory box thus differs from other artefacts in a sense that it is filled with specific meanings. Displacement or transfer activates it and opens up new layers, new content that was not visible or did not even exist before. Artefacts must also have the potentiality of being culturally shared before one can refer to them as memory boxes; it is possible to identify certain interests around them.

One important and differentiating factor is the question of agency. All artefacts analysed in the following articles have an easily identifiable "agent" who originally produced the memory box in question – be it an author, a film maker, a diarist, a politician or a political activist. The point of view of the producers and/or users is known. As the articles by Juhana Saarelainen and Hannu Salmi convey, in some cases also the materiality itself can be seen as an agent.

To sum up, an artefact is not a memory box if it is not possible to assign it specific meanings or content. Memory box is a combination of content and form – in an artefact itself there is only a form that structures and carries the box. In order to be approached as a memory box, an artefact must have the potential of becoming culturally shared. It has to be in a specific form and, above all, it needs to become public.

However, this publicity does not necessarily have to be very wide. In some cases, the public can be just a few people somehow associated with the memory box and/or its maker. It is even possible that this audience is the maker her/himself, opening up her/his creation after some time, living in different circumstances compared to the time when the memory box in question was produced, and attaches new meanings, adds new layers to the box. Some memory boxes get their meaning from collective memory[3] but some include more individual memories. Be it collective or individual, this memory has to become communicated somehow. To draw on Jan Assmanns's notions, memory boxes can be interpreted as vehicles between *communicative* and *cultural memory*.[4]

The authors of the articles in this section approach artefacts as memory boxes from various angles. The articles also vary in their time period and geographical context.

---

3 More about collective memory and construction of reality see BEREK, 2009. See also introduction.

4 See introduction for more discussion on these concepts.

Juhana Saarelainen centres on Finland in the nineteenth century. Saarelainen's topic is the Finnish national epic Kalevala as a memory box. In his article, he discusses the cultural historical context of transforming the Finnish oral culture into literary culture and its influence on national identity. Saarelainen focuses on Kalevala and its compiler Elias Lönnrot as an agent in this transfer.

Hannu Salmi also has a Finnish memory box as the theme of his article. Salmi's artefact of interest is the compilation film *Finland* from 1911. This compilation of 30 short Finnish travel films was produced for a travel fair in Germany. After the fair and a couple of showings in Helsinki, the film suddenly disappeared and was lost until several decades later. In Salmi's article, the isolation of the memory box from its original context is thus an especially important theme. Salmi focuses both on the spatial itinerary of this memory box between cultures (Finland and Germany in 1911) and on its travel through time from 1911 to the present day.

Anna-Leena Perämäki's article takes the reader from Finland to France during the Second World War. Perämäki discusses the idea of diary as a memory box. She especially focuses on two diaries from the 1940s kept by two young Jewish women, Hélène Berr and Elisabeth Kaufmann. The women lived and wrote their diaries in German-occupied Paris, Kaufmann also during her flight to the French countryside. Like Saarelainen, Perämäki concentrates on the moment of creating a memory box, a diary in this case. She opens up and analyses the many layers and places of cultural transfer encapsulated in this multi-faceted memory box at the time it was produced.

Books, films and diaries can have an ability to resist time, but Jörg Rogge has taken an even more durable and long-lasting artefact under his examination. Rogge's memory box is the coronation stone of the Scots. He points out how this stone has been transferred several times in different political and cultural contexts. The stone is a memory box that stores ideas about the political order on the British Isles over the time period of 700 years. Rogge analyses specific moments of opening this box in different phases of the history of English-Scot-relations, especially in the twentieth century.

The articles introduced above comprise a selection of unique artefacts and perspectives. However, in one way or another, all authors deal with the questions of agency, publicity and communicative and/or cultural memory. As mentioned earlier in this introduction, those three concepts are fundamental in the analysis of artefacts as memory boxes. Nevertheless, in addition to playing with abstract concepts, each writer of the following articles has the concrete, material world of artificial objects as her/his starting point. More than any other section in this book, the materiality of the memory boxes analysed here brings this section closer to the original meaning of the word "memory box"[5], an often wooden keepsake box used to store special mementos.

List of References

BEREK, MATHIAS, Kollektives Gedächtnis und die gesellschaftliche Konstruktion der Wirklichkeit. Eine Theorie der Erinnerungskulturen, Wiesbaden 2009.

OPGENOORTH, ERNST/SCHULZ, GÜNTHER, Einführung in das Studium der Neueren Geschichte, Paderborn 2010.

5 See introduction.

Becoming of a Memory Box: the Kalevala Sung Poetry, Printed Word and National Identity

JUHANA SAARELAINEN

In the year 1985 Matti Kuusi and Pertti Anttonen introduced a book titled *Kalevala-lipas* that translates into English as *Kalevala Box*.[1] This so called box contained almost everything one should know about the national epic of Finland. The *Kalevala* was written by Elias Lönnrot (1802–1884) and compiled different folk poems he had collected during the first half of the nineteenth century.[2] The history and cultural influence of the epic has been a topic of research and discussion without end. New ideas and perspectives have emerged constantly as it has inspired art, literature, music and popular culture. And, of course, academic studies concerning the *Kalevala* are numerous. The national epic is read in Finnish schools and one would have great difficulties to find a Finn who could not name at least a few characters or stories which appear in the *Kalevala*.

As the title *Kalevala Box* already indicates, the *Kalevala* can be approached as a memory box. Telling the story of the epic's birth, going through its social and political influence and depicting the artworks inspired by the *Kalevala*, the book by Kuusi and Anttonen traces different openings of this memory box.[3]

---

1 KUUSI/ANTTONEN, 1985. A new revised edition was published in 1999. KUUSI/ANTTONEN, 1999.

2 The first edition of the *Kalevala* was published in 1835. The second revised edition was almost double in size and was published in 1849.

3 Drawing these different historical openings of the memory box *Kalevala* together, the *Kalevala Box* itself becomes one of them.

The *Kalevala Box* is a perfect specimen of the cultural memory which the epic entails and carries within. But how it is possible for the *Kalevala* to be a memory box? Created by means of literalising oral tradition, the *Kalevala* encapsulates one culture and is able to displace it into another one. Thus the epic is a culturally hybrid artefact; it belongs partly to rural and illiterate culture of Finnish inland and partly to the canon of western civilisation.[4] The aim of this article is to investigate the actual event of transfer that occurs from oral tradition into literary culture which creates this memory box and therefore does not concentrate on the content of the *Kalevala*. The article demonstrates how already the act of crafting a memory box to be opened later in history calls for cultural transfer.

Another aim of this article is also to clarify the material conditions of an artificial memory box which is in this case a printed book known as the *Kalevala*. I argue that it was exactly the materiality of a printed book which enabled the cultural transfer from oral stories to an artificial memory box.[5] As an artefact, a printed book is of a very peculiar sort. It is manufactured as any man-made object, but any copy of one book can be replaced with another one. Even if the text is individual, one of a kind, the medium in which it is presented is replaceable.[6] Therefore, it is not a single volume of the *Kalevala* but the literary work in printed medium which is the memory box of this article. In this memory box, constantly changing oral poems appeared in a new material form that is much more lasting than an orally told story. The *Kalevala* isolated parts of the oral tradition and fixed them to a permanent form. Questions of how this fixing was done, what constitutes the materiality of the printed book and what kind of new cultural practises of identification it enables are inspected in the course of this article.

---

4 As stated in the introduction to this book, Peter Burke has emphasised that cultural transfer and exchange are transcultural in nature, interaction between cultures diffuses the borders between reciprocal participants creating new forms of cultural practices that have not existed before.

5 The subject matter of creating the *Kalevala* is thoroughly researched. See e.g. well executed and versatile anthology *Kalevala ja laulettu runo* (2004) edited by ANNA-LEENA SIIKALA et. al. Yet, I maintain that in this article the concepts of memory box, cultural transfer and materiality produce an original and informative angle to the epic.

6 Of course, different editions can differ from each other. Also when the text is exactly same from one edition to another, e.g. more expensive binding materials or illustrations can bring new meanings to the text.

I am going to begin by giving some background information concerning the historical situation in Finland at the first half of the nineteenth century. I will especially make remarks on the heritage that Lönnrot received from the Academy of Turku emphasising the importance of the Finnish language and its historicity in the formation of the national identity in Finland. Then I shall continue with Lönnrot's act of compiling the *Kalevala* and the specific problems that the transcription of oral tradition to literacy presented to him. From the notion that the *Kalevala* is oral culture displaced into literacy, I proceed to the explanation of how the epic should be interpreted as a printed text. Then I shall further develop my interpretation of a printed text as material artefact and examine what happens when poetical language is transferred from oral culture to literary culture. I conclude with a discussion about the effects of these new material conditions to national identity.

Historicity, language and Finland in the nineteenth century

As is well known, the nineteenth century was a time of the new historical consciousness and also of the recently introduced historical sciences. For example, John Edward Toews has described how the historical approach had a very deep and also intentional impact on the culture politics of Prussia in the form of architecture and music as well as the new historical academic disciplines.[7] Historical aesthetics and sciences made the nation.[8] This historical identification did not appear suddenly, but had its roots deep in the eighteenth century. The case of nineteenth-century Finland had many similarities with Germany. Both had to actively ponder upon what it meant to be a nation and how the nation should be constructed. Even though in very different political situation, Germany and Finland both had a severe identity crisis, inventing themselves as nations with their own specific cultures. Philippe Lacoue-Labarthe and Jean-Luc Nancy have interpreted that the German problem with the national identity, or the German national subject as they write, traced back

7 TOEWS, 2004, see e.g. pp. xxf.

8 It is no wonder that historicism went together with nationalism, since the first assures the latter that there is no universal human nature and therefore could ground unique local and national identities. BEISER, 2011, p. 13.

especially to the little number of great literary works in German language, when they compared themselves to other nations.[9]

But the case of Finland in the early nineteenth century was even worse than Germany's case a hundred years earlier. After hundreds of years as a part of the Swedish realm, Finland gained autonomic status in 1809 as the Grand Duchy of the Russian Empire. Emperor Alexander I then proclaimed that Finland had now become a nation among nations. Yet, not long after the birth of the autonomy, a cultural conflict within the Finnish nation was discovered: The political, economic and cultural elite spoke and wrote in Swedish.[10] The majority of the population spoke Finnish; but for a long time the only greater works in their native language were the translation of the Bible and the Evangelic Lutheran hymn book. All other literary uses of Finnish were almost non-existent. The lack of literary culture was extremely problematic since literature really defined almost all institutions considered developed and civilised.[11]

One answer to this crisis was to collect oral folklore from illiterate common people. As shall be seen, almost paradoxically, those who could not read or write themselves came to the rescue when literature was most needed. For many it was unimaginable that the Finnish language of crude farmers from the

9 LACOUE-LABARTHE/NANCY, 1990, p. 299. See also the article by Asko Nivala in this book about the yearning of a German golden age of literature. Eric A. Blackell has made this notion and, according to him, the feeling of this shortcoming did not only concern the lack of literary works, both fictional and scientific, in German language but also the capability of the language itself to express educated ideas. Especially the philosopher G. W. Leibniz (1646–1716) suffered from the present condition of German language at the turn of the seventeenth and the eighteenth century, feeling that Germany was culturally inferior especially to France. BLACKALL, 1959, pp. 2–4. Intriguing is that Leibniz himself wrote in French and Latin as he could not express himself in German, very similarly Finnish intellectuals in the eighteenth and early nineteenth century had to express themselves in Swedish or Latin when they wished for better Finnish literary language and historical knowledge about Finland. See also footnote 10.

10 SOMMER, 2012, pp. 10, 13, 18, 21. Łukasz Sommer portrays excellently this paradox. From eighteenth century onwards, many academic intellectuals in Finland considered Finnish language as the most important and defining quality of Finnishness. Yet all what was said by these individuals was written in Swedish or Latin.

11 Following the eighteenth and nineteenth century contemporaries, in this article the term *literature* indicates to all written and printed texts and not exclusively to fiction.

inland[12] could be used in poetry, science or government. On the other hand, others thought that a new literary language and literary culture could and should be invented in Finland on grounds of the native Finnish language. Both sides shared the same conviction that the Finnish language was the key factor for the culture, civilisation and the nation's self-formation; disagreement considered the question if this was possible at all.

Elias Lönnrot and the heritage of the Academy of Turku

The Finnish language was developed to slowly meet the modern standards of literary language during the nineteenth century. Elias Lönnrot was one of the most important figures in the process of creating the new Finnish literary language. He was of course only one of many but, even in his lifetime, Lönnrot was considered as one of the leading authorities on Finnish language. Lönnrot was born in 1802 in south Finland to a Finnish speaking tailor's family. Regardless of his modest beginnings, Lönnrot managed to be educated to an extent that in 1822 he could matriculate into the Academy of Turku situated at the south west shores of Finland.[13] We do not know much about Lönnrot's studentship at the Academy but after his graduation in 1827 he took up two ambitions. First, he initiated postgraduate studies to become a medical doctor. Second, he began to make journeys into the Finnish inland in order to collect folklore and poems. These travels continued during the following two decades, producing a vast collection of different materials.[14] Why was Lönnrot so fascinated with oral poetry? He most likely came to know thoughts of such individuals as J. J. Tengström (1787–1858), J. G. Linsén (1785–1848) and other intellectuals yearning for Finnish literature.

When Lönnrot enrolled to the Academy of Turku, it was occupied with many young men fascinated with Finnish mythology, language and oral

12 In a very rough division, it was considered that the coast of Finland was more Swedish speaking, more European and, by the standards of the nineteenth century, more civilized.

13 The Royal Academy of Turku was founded in 1640 by Queen Christina of Sweden. After the Great Fire of Turku in 1827 the university was relocated to Helsinki, the new capital of the Grand Duchy, where it has situated since then.

14 His collections included myths, stories, lyrical songs, riddles, proverbs, spells etc.

storytelling tradition. They were, so to speak, infected with the historical fever – historical comparative linguistics was expected to provide knowledge not only of the Finnish language but also of the old customs, poetics and culture. As Tengström wrote:

> Those folk songs, folk memories and customs which could give a hint of or illuminate older circumstances [of the Finnish nation] have been [...] cast away to the most far regions of our country, to the innermost parts of northern Ostrobothnia, Savonia and Karelia, where they should exist in their pure original form with many other characteristics of the Finnish nation.[15]

Regardless of the great interest in Finnish language and antiquity during the early nineteenth century, the contemporary condition of Finnish language made it very hard for many to imagine it being capable to operate as a language of literature, legislation, science or other literary institutions which were considered crucial for developed societies. Also Tengström made this remark. According to him, Finland is a unique nation, but it has no possibility to become a nation-state. Even if external political and material circumstances were favourable, the Finnish people would still lack more important internal qualities. The possibility of a Finnish nation was seen dependent on national history, literature and capability to form oneself according to them.[16]

Tengström made a strong argument for literary culture as the precondition for all sciences and arts. He applauded especially ancient Greeks who, according to him, had a very high or unmatched degree of culture without having the same material conditions that present day European powers possessed.[17] The great emphasis Tengström put into literary culture made his evaluation of the possibility of the Finnish literature that much grimmer: "[...] reading public in Finland is and always will be too few in order to uphold its

15 "Och de folksänger, de traditioner och plägseder, som kunde antyda eller upplysa äldre förhållanden, hafva vid culturens framsteg dels försvunnit, dels blifvit förviste till de aflägnaste trakterna af vårt land, till de innersta delarna af Norra Österbotten, Savolax och Karelien, der de dock ännu, jemte många originela drag af Finska folkets egna lynne, skola förekomma i sin urspungliga renhet." TENGSTRÖM, 1817–1818, p. 126. Unless otherwise stated, all translations are by Juhana Saarelainen.

16 TENGSTRÖM, 1817–1818, p. 72.

17 IBID., pp. 99f.

own independent literature […]"[18] According to Tengström, Finns could not achieve that kind of educated literary culture which many other nations possessed. The only and very vague possibility he saw in ancient poems and mythology.[19]

Yet Tengström was not the only one who stressed the importance of ancient Finnish mythology and poetry. For example also Linsén emphasised literature and literary language as the precondition for creating the Finnish culture. He was also evidently more positive about the possibility of cultivating ancient forms of language to be modern literature. Linsén answered directly to Tengström's article and demanded literary institutions in Finnish language. In this sense his attitude was less antiquarian. He did not want to merely discover ancient poems but also develop their language towards modernity: "What can now be expected with all good reason is that Finnish poetry will receive a romantic echo, which is the soul of all modern poetry."[20]

This looking to the future and reaching for a utopian goal of modern Finnish literature, which could as well have failed[21], was made possible only by discovering and inventing historical Finland – history of its language, culture, storytelling tradition and mythology. These were crucial for Finland's identity as a nation since historiography, written documents in Finnish, were extremely hard to come by. Linsén wrote in 1819:

> The cultivation of the language has naturally the most nearest relation with the literature: the first cannot be thought without the second. Here one must only note the sequence ordained by nature. Literature first grows in shadowy groves of songs and poems. There it leans its delicate stem to religion and oldest traditions and memories of the nation[22]

18 "[…] Finlands läsande Allmänhet alltid vara och förblifva för fåtalig, att kunna underhålla en egen sjelfbestående Litteratur […]".TENGSTRÖM, 1817–1818, p. 125.

19 IBID., p. 128.

20 "Hvad man nu med allt skäl väntar, är att den Finska poesien får den romantiska anklang, som är själern i all modern poesie." LINSÉN 1819, p. 242.

21 COLEMAN, 2010, pp. 46f.

22 "Med språkets odling står naturligtvis *Litteraturen* i den aldranärmaste förening: den förrä kan icke tänkas utan den sednare. Dervid bör endast märkas den af naturen föreskrifna ordningen, att denna Litteratur först uppväxer i sångens och diktens skuggriga lundar, och der till stöd för sin späda stängel flätar sig tillsamman med Religionen och nationens häfder och fornminnen." LINSÉN, 1819, p. 241.

Poems that supposedly were still sung in deep Finnish inland were thought still to be in touch with the ancient Finnish religion and its mythology. Therefore they were expected to provide evidence of the history of customs, culture and the language itself. When the written sources were only few, Finnish oral language and folk poetry became a living document of Finnish culture and history.

It seems that the intellectual elite of Finland, which itself made these demands in Swedish, wanted someone who could deliver them the oral culture encapsulated in the artificial form of a written text. It was not actual oral folk poetry they wanted, but a transcribed version of it. The printed medium was to them more familiar, more developed and especially more civilised than the orally sung poems. The generation previous to Lönnrot showed great interest in Finnish folk poetry, but not without contradiction. Folk poems that were believed to be treasured in the Finnish inland ensured that Finland had its own national culture and literature. But the oral culture revealed itself as a disappearing tradition of old customs and stories. It was the memory of the ancient Finland that had to be preserved for modernity. What the learned intellectuals wanted could very well be described as a memory box which would transfer the tradition of Finnish antiquity from the deep inland to the shores of the Baltic Sea. It seems that Lönnrot answered these assignments very thoroughly.

Kalevala

From 1828 onwards, Lönnrot had few anthologies of individual folk poems printed, but by 1835 he had collected and compiled enough material to publish a full length epic called the *Kalevala or Old Poems from Karelia telling the Ancient History of the Finnish People* (Kalevala taikka Vanhoja Karjalan Runoja Suomen kansan muinaisista ajoista).[23] The epic consists of 32 poems and over 12,000 verses – or half of Homer[24] as Lönnrot himself wrote in 1833, describing the goal he had set himself.[25] It is a curious combination of

23 The subtitle illustrates perfectly the connection of the *Kalevala*-project and the need of a new historical consciousness in Finland. The second edition had no subtitle and was called simply the *Kalevala*.

24 *Iliad* and *Odyssey* consist together of ca. 27,800 verses.

25 SIIKALA, 2008, p. 315.

collected folk poetry and Lönnrot's own artistic instinct. Practically every verse of the epic was obtained from different folk poetry singers, but Lönnrot arranged all the verses to form a story that he had not heard from any individual singer. The *Kalevala* is one great narrative, from a Finnish myth of World's Creation to the emergence of Christianity, which was dreamed up and written by Lönnrot.[26]

The first edition of the *Kalevala* was not a bestseller – since almost nobody could read Finnish – but even so, it was met with great enthusiasm nationally and eventually also internationally. Even the renowned German scholar Jacob Grimm (1785–1863) was very excited over the *Kalevala* and gave an extensive lecture about it in the Prussian Academy of Sciences in 1845.[27] The recognition from one of the most distinguished linguist and folklorist at the time did not go unnoticed in Finland.[28] For the first time it was thought that Finns had a literary work which could stand side by side with the canonical works of European civilisation.

Thus, when the mid-century was approaching, it seemed that, in fact, it might be possible to construct a Finnish literary culture from which the modern Finnish nation might follow. As folk poetry reassured that Finns had their own history, it also enabled imagining a shared future for the nation. This dialectic between the past and the future contributed to the creation of a national identity in the present. The need of ancient Finland was already revealed when looking into an early nineteenth-century public discussion prior Lönnrot, which was concerned with the question if a textualisation of Finnish oral culture and creating Finnish literature is possible at all. Lönnrot evidently

26 The fact that the *Kalevala* is a fictional literary work by Lönnrot has been thoroughly argued by folklorist Väinö Kaukonen with numerous publications from late 1940's onward. See e.g. KAUKONEN, 1990, p. 161, 164f. After the publication of the first edition, Lönnrot himself became even more aware of his own creative role. KAUKONEN, 1990, p. 162. As it has been suggested by Jouni Hyvönen, the fictional narrative of the ancient Finland was not the only aim of Lönnrot. He included all different kind of genres of folk poetry from myths and spells to proverbs into the *Kalevala*. Thus the epic forms an anthology gathering the whole spectrum of Finnish folklore in one volume. HYVÖNEN, 2008, p. 346.

27 See *Über das finnische Epos*. GRIMM, 1865 (1845).

28 The high praises from Grimm might well have encouraged Lönnrot to edit the thoroughly revised second edition published in 1849. WESTPHAL, 2011, p. 45. In Germany, Grimm's lecture about the *Kalevala* was received as the most important and influential notion of the epic. VOẞSCHMIDT, 1989, p. 47.

took part in this discussion, not only in the pages of journals but also in the practical action of collecting, publishing and editing Finnish folklore.

Lönnrot presented the Finns with a literary epic which met the contemporary demands of poetic beauty and authenticity.[29] But there is a deep conflict in all of the world's traditional epics from the ancient *Gilgamesh* and Homer to the modern *Kalevala* of the nineteenth century. We know these epic poems as literature but their origin is in oral culture. *Kalevala* is one of the more recent textualisations of oral tradition. What was the cultural historical context of transforming Finnish oral culture into literary culture and its influence on national identity in the nineteenth century?

I argue that Lönnrot very well understood the difference between oral and literary culture and consciously pondered upon their relationship. When he collected and scribed folk poetry, he was simply faced with the dilemma that the stories of oral culture changed constantly but when they are transformed into written form, they stay constant. Lönnrot described changing language as a living being and compared the book bindings of classical dead languages to a "shroud of dead".[30] Thus he had to solve the question of how to record oral culture and simultaneously have it live on. How did Lönnrot confront this dilemma? The *Kalevala* has been interpreted to be a literary representation of the past and would therefore be merely antiquarian in purpose. Yet this was

29 The question of authenticity was crucial to any folklore anthology after the scandal that the *Songs of Ossian* published by James Macpherson (1736–1796) caused. Lönnrot himself noted in 1851 to Léouzon Le Duc, the French translator of the *Kalevala*, that the one who has doubts about the authenticity of the *Kalevala* can travel to the Finnish inland or search the archives and find all the collected verses there in, LÖNNROT, 1993, p. 472. (Apparently the total revision of the order of the verses was not considered as a problem by him) It was no wonder that Finns had no suspicions about the authenticity of the *Kalevala* since Lönnrot's journeys were well known to the reading public. Also the international audience was convinced. The depiction of Jacob Grimm is very revealing: "[…] Elias Lönnrot durch längeren aufenthalt in Karelien und Olonetz unmittelbar aus dem munde des volks und der kundigsten sänger eine reiche samlung solcher lieder treu und gewissenhaft zu stand brachte." [sic!] GRIMM, 1865 (1845), p. 78. It was Grimm's judgment that the *Kalevala* is an actual folk epic that had survived from the Finnish antiquity. See VOẞSCHMIDT, 1989, p.73f. Of course, today definitions of folk poetry are very different from the notions of the early nineteenth century and one should be aware of the possible anachronisms when judging the past interpretations. See also footnote 26.

30 LÖNNROT, 1991, p. 116.

not Lönnrot's only intention. Bearing in mind the task of creating modern Finnish literature, he also aimed for a new literary language.

Already as young man, at the age of 28, when beginning his journeys Lönnrot wrote to C. A. Gottlund (1796–1875), an older college and one of the pioneers of the nineteenth century in the study of Finnish folklore, and explained his choices of writing down the oral poetry:

> I have selected over the other practices of writing the one that allows me to express myself so that I can mediate between Savonian and other Finnish dialects, and this I have done for that reason that Finns even from other provinces than Savonia and Karelia would be able to read and understand the Poems of their ancestors full of wisdom in their simple and powerful language.[31]

The letter depicts how the evident differences between spoken and written word were at the very core of folklore collecting. We can see how the findings in oral and aesthetical language from deep Finnish inland raised the question of how Finnish should be written. The scriber, may it have been Lönnrot, Gottlund or any other folklore enthusiast in the early nineteenth century, had to make many choices when oral poetry was transformed into written form. The task could not be done without the question: How should this transformation be done? The rules of writing had to be invented, since there was no Finnish standard language, grammar or orthography upon which a writer could rely. Very early on, Lönnrot was convinced that the written word should be made to be something else than oral culture. Literary culture should be shared by all Finns, in other words it should be more general than provincial oral culture.[32]

31 "Jag har dock framför andra skrifsätt valt den såsom, att jag så må uttrycka mig, en medlare emellan den Savolaxiska och de andra Finska dialekterna, och detta af det skäl, att Finnarne äfven på andra orter än i Savolax och Karelen måtte kunna läsa och förstå sina förfäders visdomsfulla Runor i deras enkla, kraftfulla språk." LÖNNROT, 1990, p. 18.

32 In his letter, Lönnrot defended his choice, since Gottlund was not in the favour of a standard language but thought that every dialect and even every writer should have their own grammar and orthography. Mark Sebba has argued that there is no writing system or orthography which could be neutral technology. They always have social and cultural connotations. SEBBA, 2012, p. 9. Nonstandard orthographies seem to be more expressive than standard orthography but it also seems that this quality is apparent only in comparison to the standard one. JAFFE, 2012, p. 221.

But simultaneously he also wanted to preserve the simple and powerful language of the oral folk poetry. In the *Kalevala,* oral culture is displaced from its origins in the rural and uneducated inland provinces of the Savonia and Karelia into literary culture of Finland's southern and western coastline. Clearly it can be argued that according to Lönnrot, the textualisation of folk poetry should be and was a preparatory work for a literary language which would be understood by all Finns and thus transcend provincial dialects. Based on this notion it is possible to study Lönnrot's *Kalevala* as a medium – or a material artefact – which tries to transmit, or mediate as Lönnrot writes, between inland's oral culture and the literary culture of modern Europe.

Materiality of oral tradition and materiality of literary tradition

The notion of the materiality of printed texts in this article is based on a simple remark that the folk poetry collected from illiterate singers and transformed into literature is displacing oral culture into literary culture. This transfer between different spheres of cultural practises is simultaneously transference between different material mediums. This transformation has irreversible effects on the content of folk poetry because the form and the content cannot be separated from each other. This has been stated in many different ways. For this article, I find interesting how Marshall McLuhan described a medium as the message. With this he means that how any medium, the form in which any content is represented, changes the content. According to McLuhan, new media – that is new technologies – contain aspects of older media. Writing contains the older medium which is speech. But speech in new written form is no longer the same.[33]

What is especially interesting in McLuhan for this case is his definition of new media as new extensions of human senses and other capabilities both individual and collective.[34] For example, writing enables communication over vast geographical areas in comparison to speech.[35] But we can also interpret writing as a material extension of the human memory. This approach is not new. Already Plato in his dialogue *Phaedrus* refers to writing as an

33 McLuhan, 1964, p. 82.
34 Ibid., p. 35.
35 Ibid., p. 85f.

externalised continuation of memory but also its corrupter, since it transfers the memory from human individual to letters outside of the individual.[36]

Like nineteenth-century Finns, also Plato considered himself being in a breaking point between oral culture and literary culture. Even though the canonical literary works of Homer were already 300 years old at the time of Plato and the technique of writing much older – so old that its origin had to be told with myth[37] – the process of literalisation of the culture was slow in Greek. In fact, it was the time of Plato which was the decisive moment for the emergence of literary culture, but even then written works lingered in the sphere of the spoken word since they were most often read aloud or performed to an audience[38], as happens also in Plato's dialogue. Yet Plato was in different situation than Lönnrot. In ancient Greek, all written documents were manuscripts which could not spread as widely and quickly as printed text. As Finnish became to be a written language at a very late point in history, Finns passed the time of manuscripts and began to write in the modern technological era of the printing.[39] The oral culture was not only transferred to written form, but this was done with the advanced reproducing capabilities of book printing. Therefore, we must consider the materiality of the printed book.

The *Kalevala* is a book written by Elias Lönnrot.[40] There are two sides to this notion. As it has been suggested by Lauri Honko, the *Kalevala* can be called a traditional epic in the sense that practically all of its content was collected from illiterate poem singers.[41] On the other hand, no singer had or could have had a recollection of that kind of extensive literary epic which Lönnrot constructed. When the amount of the collected folk poems and lore began to multiply, Lönnrot stated that he could have compiled seven such Kalevalas, all different from each other.[42] From all these possible seven unique

36 PLATO, *Pheadrus*, 275a.

37 IBID., 274c.

38 WERNER, 2012, pp. 183f.

39 Of course, there had been manuscripts in Finland before the invention of printing technology but Finnish language had not been used. Finnish as a literary language had to be created for the first time in the sixteenth century when the church in Sweden was reformed and the translation of the Bible was initiated by Bishop Mikael Agricola (1510–1557).

40 See footnote 26.

41 HONKO, 2002, p. 9.

42 KAUKONEN, 1987, p. 29. The publication of the first edition of the *Kalevala* infected many Finnish intellectuals with a folklore fever and they rushed to Karelia in order to provide supplements to Lönnrot's collections.

Kalevalas it is only the printed specimen which we know today – not the other possible six ones.

As folklorist Satu Apo has realised, the goal to reproduce the original oral poems cannot ever be reached since the oral singing of the poem and its literal representation are too different from each other.[43] Furthermore, Apo has systematically shown how the *Kalevala* is in many respects modern literature.[44] In fact, all literary representations of the Finnish folk poetry, from Lönnrot's *Kalevala* to the more current attempts, have the same tendency to always use the standards of literature. But the original oral presentations of Finnish folk poetry were performances that used sound, tones of voice and gestures. The singer would react to the audience according to their reception and would make up new verses as well as modify the recalled ones.[45] These all are material conditions of the singing performance. Unlike the ancient Greek reciters of Homer, Finnish poem singers had no written document to which the story would compare, so the stories would always change with every performance. For the illiterate poem singers every performance was new and unique. What was written and printed by Lönnrot does not change any more. Written word and printed book as media are in that way more inflexible as oral storytelling but also more permanent. What happens when a unique oral performance is transformed into literature?

According to McLuhan's posthumous work *Laws of Media* (1988) there are some questions that we can always ask from any medium. Two of these are: (1) What does the medium *enhance* or make possible? (2) What does the medium make *obsolete*?[46] Applying these questions to the current case, we can enquire what happens when oral medium of folk poetry is displaced into literature.[47] Interesting is that we do not need to make up the answers to these questions. We can ask Elias Lönnrot and let him tell us, since he has pondered upon the same problems in the documents he has left behind. He wrote in the Foreword to the *Kalevala*'s second edition:

43 APO, 2010, p. 19.

44 APO, 2002, see e.g. p. 108.

45 APO, 2010, pp. 19f. See also HIRVENLAHTI, 2004.

46 SANDSTROM, 2012, p. 4. The remaining two questions are: What does the medium retrieve? What the medium can reverse into? According to McLuhan, these four questions are the laws of media or the four effects that all media and also artefacts have.

47 And they should be applied, as Asa Briggs and Peter Burke have reminded that the consequences of new media and technologies are not necessarily the same in every different social and cultural context. BRIGGS/BURKE, 2009, p. 10.

> From now on [after the publication of the *Kalevala*] they [the amount of folk poems] will begin to reduce rather than multiply, since anyone who wants can have them in a form of the ready-made book, and in broader form than any individual memory can anything uphold. Therefore will the value of singing disappear from the memory and after the value has disappeared will also the singing itself be forgotten.[48]

Here Lönnrot takes the same position as Plato when he reveals the two-sided nature of writing as extension and corrupter of memory. According to Lönnrot, written word exceeds the capabilities of human memory – it is *enhanced*. Yet Lönnrot also sees the inventible consequences: As there is available a printed book, a new medium, in which the oral poetry is presented, the memory of individual poem singers fades as the words are externalised from the human memory to an artificial object – the older medium is made *obsolete*. Therefore it could be said that in this certain sense the *Kalevala* as a material product of printing technology has non-human agency or capability.[49]

McLuhan says that media are extensions of man. Plato describes how writing enhances memory with objective letters but degenerates subjective human memory. Both lack an extensive analysis of objects superseding the individual human life span. If not explicitly then implicitly, Lönnrot takes this into consideration when he describes how folk stories are in constant change when they pass from one singer to another and especially from generation to generation. Lönnrot acknowledges very precisely that his book will end this variation – which has led to ever growing multiplicity of folk poetry. This multiplicity, Lönnrot writes, will now begin to decline. But as McLuhan writes, content of any medium is another medium. And the content of written text is speech but also human thought and memory.[50] Writing generates almost Hegelian *Aufhebung*[51]: that which is left behind is not cast away but found in a

48 "Tästälähin alkavat ne taas pikemmin supistua, kun uusilla lisäyksillä enetä, sillä kun, ken ikänänsä tahtoo, saapi ne valmiina kirjana käteensä, ja täydellisempänä, kun minkä kenen erinäinen muisto kannattaisi, niin katoaa muistolta laulamisen arvo, ja arvon kadottua itse muistolta laulaminenki." LÖNNROT 1993, p. 411.

49 This is not to say that it is an intentional or conscious agent but insofar as it has capability to produce effects in social and material reality, it has certain kind of and amount of agency.

50 MCLUHAN, 1964, pp. 23f.

51 G. W. F. Hegel (1770–1831) is known among other things for his philosophical method of dialectics. He claimed that in the historical process of all phenomena there is rational logic in which previous contradictory categories of reality are

new form in the next step of historical process. Therefore, the memory of oral culture is encapsulated into this literary work and preserved there as it would be in a box.

Philosopher Hannah Arendt has written that an artificial object manufactured by men lasts beyond the makers' lifetime.[52] Thus artificial objects create stability and continuity for the human world and preserve it over generations.[53] Also, or perhaps especially, written and printed texts have this quality. As already Plato noted, written word and human memory have a relationship whether one wanted that or not – once a technology such as writing is invented, there is no returning to the time beforehand. It is not far from revolutionary how writing supersedes spoken communication. Thoughts and ideas can be communicated over vast distance, both in place and time. Thinkers, poets and scholars long dead still share their words with us today. Technology of printing multiplies the possibilities of distributing and receiving these ideas. Lönnrot seems to be aware of this when he describes how printed medium exceeds the individual memory. But he also takes into consideration that printed text prevails over generations. In a Swedish literary review *Litteraturblad*, Lönnrot wrote with the title "Remarks to the new *Kalevala* edition" (1849) that he cannot believe that the folk poems of the nineteenth century would be the same as in ancient times. He explains that in his experience, one poem goes through significant changes if it passed over ten different singers, and continues:

> If I now change the mentioned ten singers to ten centuries through which the poems of the Kalevala could have come to us, I should not have to add anything else to declare my opinion about the character of present day poems in comparison to the original ones.[54]

---

united "in such a way that they are not only preserved but also abolished (to use Hegel's term of art for this paradoxical-sounding process, they are *aufgehoben*)." FORSTER, 1993, p. 132. The German noun *Aufhebung* and verb *aufheben* have many different meanings indicating simultaneously preserving and abolishing something.

52 ARENDT, 1958, pp. 167f.

53 IBID. For Arendt it is the work of art that culminates the property of lasting in artefacts.

54 "Förvandlar jag nu de nysomtalte tie sångare till de tie sekler, genom hvilkas mun Kalevala sångerna kunna havfa kommit till oss, så torde jag ej behöfva tillägga något ytterligare, för att tillkännagifva min tanke om deras närvarande beskaffenhet i förhållande till den ursprungliga." LÖNNROT, 1993, p. 407.

Lönnrot acknowledges that oral folk poetry presented by individuals cannot create as vast an amount of works of poetry as literary culture, but he also has notion that for the same reason – inefficiency of individual memory – the oral culture experiences constant change. Poetical works in literary culture on the contrary stays constantly the same. Once the *Kalevala* was written, printed, published and distributed there was no more need to sing the poems. According to Lönnrot, the change of oral culture will disappear and the printed version of the poems will become canonical.[55] It is the materiality of the printed book which enables this. Even if the technology by which it is created and the meanings that are assigned to it are man-made, the printed medium has, so to speak, a life of its own which cannot be entirely controlled by human intentions.[56] On the contrary, a printed book has the capability to affect the socio-cultural world of men by, for example, enabling a creation and distribution of a national epic and on the other hand obsoleting oral performances of folk poetry singers.

Conclusion

Written and especially printed words are artificial objects produced by human technology. Yet, due to their material characteristics, they have non-human qualities. They are more precise and in large numbers more extensive in memory than humans. Even further, they can spread language, poetry, news, ideas, science etc. over a vastly greater geographical area than individual person. With the notion by Hannah Arendt that artefacts prevail beyond human life, one can realise that they thus do not spread widely merely in space, but also in time. As the text is an extension of a memory that lasts over human generations, it becomes a vehicle for historical consciousness and may

55 According to Jan Assmann, both oral and literary societies have had their experts to carry and uphold the cultural memory of the society's mythical origin. In oral societies this was the task of poets. ASSMANN, 2008, p. 114. It was Lönnrot's conviction that the literalisation of the oral tradition belonged its normal life cycle. HYVÖNEN, 2004, p. 329. Thus it was only natural that in one point of history the oral culture would transform into literary one.

56 This, of course, can also apply to other material artefacts (as well). Also it should be remembered that it is not only the materiality of the medium which has effects but also the thoughts and ideas by men that fill the pages of printed books. BRIGGS/BURKE, 2009, p. 19.

contribute i.e. to the national thought as it did in the nineteenth century. When a memory is engraved in artefacts that last longer than organic life, it is very easy to imagine that this kind of memory must then belong to a subject which transcends individuals. Thus the new historical consciousness made possible by printing technology was able to renew the metaphor of body politic. Nation could now be perceived as a body *with* spirit, capable to remember the past and imagine the future and therefore having subjectivity of its own. It was not by chance that the so called memory institutions, such as library, archive and museum, were developed to their modern form in the nineteenth century.

In Finland, the *Kalevala* had functions similar to all these institutions. For the contemporaries, it was a library of oral poetry, an archive for events in ancient history and museum of old customs and culture. This entire ancient culture was encapsulated in a little book which could be multiplied and distributed endlessly. It could be said that the *Kalevala* was made to perform as a memory box. It displaced ancient oral culture and transformed it into modern literary culture. As a memory box it transferred between different cultures and thus transcended them. It merged two cultural spheres by being a culturally hybrid artefact. Lönnrot had the dilemma that he wanted both, the ancient, powerful and living language of the oral Finnish tradition and also the modern European literary language. The concept of memory box can explain how he managed, or at least presumed that he could, to simultaneously preserve the past and create something new for the future.

It was possible for the *Kalevala* to become a memory box because the creation of this artefact was an event of cultural transfer itself. The epic as a memory box was filled by Lönnrot with memories from the (imagined) ancient Finland. As the oral poems were expected to inform the modern people about the ancient culture of the Finnish nation, it became a carrier of those memories. The *Kalevala* was perceived to encapsulate in written form the Finnish antiquity documented and engraved to the "simple and powerful language" of the poem singers of the Finnish inland. Thus the cultural transfer that created the memory box of the *Kalevala* was twofold. First, it transferred the sung poems from the Finnish inland to the shores of Baltic Sea and into literary culture. Second, the cultural transfer happened also from ancient past to the present day, the modern age of book printing, literature and science. Therefore, culture is transferred in the *Kalevala* both geographically as well as in time from the ancient past to the present modern day – and of course for the future of the Finnish nation.

List of References

Sources

GRIMM, JACOB, Über das finnische Epos, in: Kleinere Schriften. Zweiter Band. Abhandlungen zur Mythologie und Sittenkunde, Berlin 1865 (1845), pp. 75–113.

LINSÉN, JOHAN GABRIEL, Om Finsk Nationalitet (Forts.och slut fr. N:o 60), in: Mnemosyne 61 (1819), pp. 241–244.

LÖNNROT, ELIAS: Valitut teokset 1. Kirjeet, ed. RAIJA MAJAMAA, Helsinki 1990.

ID., Valitut teokset 3. Kirjoitelmia ja lausumia, ed. RAIJA MAJAMAA, Helsinki 1991.

ID., Valitut teokset 5. Muinaisrunoutta, ed. RAIJA MAJAMAA, Helsinki 1993.

PLATO, Pheadrus, trans. Robin Waterfield, Oxford et. al., 2002.

TENGSTRÖM, JOHAN JAKOB, Om några hinder för Finlands litteratur och cultur, in: Aura. Första häftet, 1817, pp. 67–90. Andra häftet, 1818, pp. 93–129.

Secondary Literature

APO, SATU, Milloin kansanrunoutemme kehitys saavutti huippunsa?, in: Tieteessä tapahtuu, 4–5 (2010), pp. 15–20.

ID., Kertojan ääni Kalevalassa, in: Lönnrotin hengessä, ed. by PEKKA LAAKSONEN/ULLA PIELA, Kalevalaseuran vuosikirja 81, Helsinki 2002, pp. 108–122.

ARENDT, HANNAH, The Human Condition, Chicago 1958.

ASSMANN, JAN, Communicative and Cultural Memory, in: Cultural Memory Studies. An International and Interdisciplinary Handbook, ed. by ASTRID ERLL/ANSGAR NÜNNING, Berlin 2008.

BEISER, C. FREDERICK,The German Historicist Tradition, Oxford et. al. 2011.

BLACKELL, A. ERIC, The Emergence of German as a Literary Language 1700–1775, London/New York 1959.

BRIGGS, ASA/BURKE, PETER, A Social History of the Media. From Gutenberg to the Internet, Cambridge 2009.

COLEMAN, C. MICHAEL, "You All Might Be Speaking Swedish Today": Language change in 19th-century Finland and Ireland, in: Scandinavian Journal of History, 35, 1 (2010), pp. 44–64.

FORSTER, MICHAEL, Hegel's dialectical method, in: The Cambridge Companion to Hegel, ed. FREDERICK C. BEISER, Cambridge et. al. 1993, pp. 130–170.

HIRVENLAHTI, LAURI, Vakiojaksot ja muuntelu kalevalaisessa epiikassa, in: Kalevala ja laulettu runo, ed. ANNA-LEENA SIIKALA et. al., Helsinki 2004, pp. 194–214.

HONKO, LAURI, Foreword. The Kalevala on the world epic map, in: The Kalevala and the World's Traditional Epics, ed. by LAURI HONKO, Studia, Fennica Folkloristica 12, Helsinki 2002, pp. 9f.

HYVÖNEN, JOUNI, Kalevala Elias Lönnrotin tieteellisenä projektina, in: *Kalevalan kulttuurihistoria*, ed. by ULLA PIELA et. al., Helsinki 2008, pp. 330–359.

ID., Lönnrotin eläytyminen kansanrunojen maailmaan, in: Kalevala ja laulettu runo, ed. by ANNA-LEENA SIIKALA et. al., Helsinki 2004, pp. 299–339.

JAFFE, ALEXANDRA, Transcription in practice: Nonstandard orthography, in: Orthography as Social Action, ed. by ALEXANDRA JAFFE et. al., Boston/Berlin 2012, pp. 203–224.

Kalevala ja laulettu runo, ed. by ANNA-LEENA SIIKALA et. al., Helsinki 2004.

KAUKONEN, VÄINÖ, The Kalevala as Epic, in: Religion, Myth, and Folklore in the World's Epics, ed. by LAURI HONKO, Berlin, New York 1990, pp. 157–179.

ID., Kalevala Lönnrotin runoelmana I. Tutkielma ja kirjoituksia viiden vuosikymmenen ajalta. Snellman-instituutinjulkaisuja 6, Oulu 1987.

KUUSI, MATTI/ANTTONEN, PERTTI, Kalevala-lipas. Uusi laitos, Helsinki 1999.

ID., Kalevala-lipas, Helsinki 1985.

LACOUE-LABARTHE, PHILIPPE/NANCY, JEAN-LUC, The Nazi Myth, trans. Brian Homes, in: Critical Inquiry, 16, 2 (1990), pp. 291–312.

MCLUHAN, MARSHALL, Understanding Media: The Extension of Man, New York 1964.

SANDSTROM, GREGORY, Laws of media – The four effects: A McLuhan contribution to social epistemology, in: Social Epistemology Review and Reply Collective, 1, 12 (2012), pp. 1–6, http://wp.me/p1Bfg0-uc, 11.2. 2014.

SEBBA, MARK, Orthography as social action: Scripts, spelling, identity and power, in: Orthography as Social Action, ed. by ALEXANDRA JAFFE et. al. Boston/Berlin 2012, pp. 1–19.

SIIKALA, ANNA-LEENA, Kalevala myyttisenä historiana, in: Kalevalan kulttuurihistoria, ed. by ULLA PIELA et. al., Helsinki 2008, pp. 296–329.

SOMMER, ŁUKASZ, A Step Away from Herder: Turku Romantics and the Question of National Language, in: Slavonic and East European Review, 90, 1 (2012), pp. 1–32.

TOEWS, JOHN EDWARD, Becoming Historical. Cultural Reformation and Public Memory in Early Nineteenth-Century Berlin, Cambridge et al. 2004.

VOßSCHMIDT, LIISA, Das Kalevala und seine Rezeption im 19. Jahrhundert. Eine Analyse von Rezeptionsdokumenten aus dem deutschen Sprachraum, Frankfurt am Main et. al. 1989.

WERNER, S. DANIEL, Myth and Philosophy in Plato's Phaedrus, Cambridge et. al. 2012.

WESTPHAL, WERNER, Sprache, Bildung und Identität im Diskurs von Martin Luther, Gottfried Herder und Jakob Grimm, in: Kommunikation für Europa II: Sprache und Identität, Hrsg. JÜRGEN SCHIEWE et. al., Frankfurt am Main 2011, pp. 37–50.

Encapsulating Visions of Nationhood

Finland (1911) as a Memory Box

HANNU SALMI

At the turn of the nineteenth and twentieth centuries there was a growing interest in Finland to increase tourism by making the home country known among its own citizens and by arousing international interest in travelling to the shores of the Baltic Sea. In 1911, an international fair for tourism, *Die Internationale Reise- und Fremden-Verkehr Austellung*, was planned to be organised in Berlin, and the initiative was taken in Finland to produce a promotional film for the exhibition. This was exceptional in the sense that no previous film advertising an entire country is known to have been produced in the history of cinema.[1]

The urge to apply modern technology in building an international reputation, or at least in giving a sign of existence for the international community, was deeply rooted in the upheaval of national sentiments in Finland that was still a part of the Russian empire at the time. The policy of Russification was particularly oppressive during the years 1899–1905 and 1908–1917. Finns have traditionally called these periods *sortokaudet* (years of oppression) and interpreted them in terms of national threat; yet, they were in

1 On Finnish travel films, see SALMI, 2002, pp. 26-29, SEDERGREN/KIPPOLA, 2009, pp. 200-236. The credit of the first film to market an entire country has often been attributed to the long documentary *Finlandia* (1922), produced in the newly independent country. This credit may well be given to *Finland* which was made eleven years earlier despite the fact that Finland was still part of the Russian empire.

fact part of a larger interest to abolish the autonomy of non-Russian minorities within the Russian empire.[2]

During these years of turmoil, a compilation film entitled *Finland* was produced. Finland had already been invited to the Berlin fair in 1909, but only a year later the idea about the film was conceived.[3] At this point, the schedule looked tight. The Finnish Tourism Association (Suomen Matkailuyhdistys) contacted the engineer Karl Emil Ståhlberg who owned the pioneering Finnish film company Atelier Apollo.[4] Within just a few years it had produced the first fiction film in Finland, *The Moonshiners* (Salaviinanpolttajat, 1907), and dozens of short documentaries. It seems obvious that no shootings were made for *Finland* because of the rushed schedule and the film was edited on the basis of previous Apollo documentaries that portrayed Finnish cities, historic monuments and landscapes. At that time, films were usually very short, only a few minutes in length. In this respect, it is noteworthy that *Finland* turned out to be a long piece, 508 metres of film lasting almost 25 minutes.[5] It was still in one reel and thus easy to perform.

Finland was compiled of 30 short travel films, produced by Atelier Apollo between 1906–1910, and many of the early Finnish films had actually been preserved through this particular copy. The final premiere copy also included German intertitles, of which 27 have been preserved.[6] The film was shown in Berlin and Helsinki in 1911, but after this, the only copy suddenly disappeared for decades. When *Finland* was finally found again in the Finnish Military Archive it was like a memory box that did not only reveal rare, unseen moving

2 MOSS, 2005, pp. 481f., LAVERY, 2006, pp. 74-80.

3 The film was made for German audiences, or the audience in the German fair, but the name of the film remained in Swedish, which means that there is only one 'n', *Finland*. In German it would have been *Finnland*. The evolution of the name is depicted in detail by SEDERGREN/KIPPOLA, 2009.

4 SALMI, 1999, p. 83.

5 This is based on the assumption that the film was screened with the speed of 16 fps (frames per second). The question of frame rate is essential in estimating how long early film screenings lasted. Today, most of the films are projected with the speed of 24 fps and 25 fps in the case of video recordings. If shown with 24 fps, *Finland* would last over 18 minutes. Reducing the frame rate significantly influences the reception of the film. It is most probable that *Finland* was filmed and projected with 16 fps, which means that the shots left a much more peaceful impression on the audience than with 24 fps. I have previously discussed the frame rates of early Finnish cinema in SALMI, 2002, pp. 16-18. See also the filmographic details of *Finland* at http://www.elonet.fi/fi/elokuva/162301, 16.03.2014.

6 SALMI, 1999, pp. 84f. 1.

images and glimpses of early film history, it also offered an access to early twentieth-century Finnish landscapes and sceneries as the contemporaries wanted them to be seen through foreign eyes and perhaps even how they consciously aimed at transmitting this heritage to future audiences.

This resembles the way Aleida Assmann has characterised the complex nature of memories. She notes that places of memory should not be analysed only from the perspective of temporal dimension, since memories always include also horizontal qualities. Therefore it is illuminating to study what kind of spatial implications memories can have.[7] In the case of *Finland*, the memory box seems to have an itinerary of its own, in the bygone world of the year 1911, but at the same time carries meanings about the past. Bernd Roeck also writes about these materialisations when he refers to "packets or boxes of memories" containing legacies from the past.[8] From our present day perspective, *Finland* carries memories about the past but, to draw on Roeck's point, brings forward historical signification as early as at the time of its production by referring, for example, to different previous traditions of depicting Finnish *lieux de mémoire*.[9]

In her book *Framing the Nation: Documentary Film in Interwar France* Alison J. Murray Levine interpreted, although in passing, documentaries as memory boxes. She writes:

> When all of the human interactions surrounding documentary production are pulled into focus alongside the frame and the framer of a film, documentary films serve as a different kind of memory box. Neither faithful records of bygone practices, nor outdated documents that are patently untrue; they become dynamic sites of negotiations and exchange.[10]

Levine analyses mainly films from the 1930s, and her thoughts are not completely applicable to early cinema, but she makes the point of interpreting a film as a material object, comparable to a memory box that can be a site of negotiation about the past or a site of cultural exchange, both in temporal and spatial terms.

7 ASSMANN, 2011, p. 101.
8 ROECK, 2006, p. 11.
9 On the notion of *lieux de mémoire*, see NORA, 1989, pp. 7-24.
10 LEVINE, 2010, p. 161.

The aim of this article is to elaborate these thoughts further and to analyse *Finland* as a memory box by focusing on two different aspects of its memory-box-ness, on its spatial itinerary between cultures, between Finland and Germany in 1911 and on its temporal trajectory, its travel through time from 1911 to the present day. The latter is closely connected with the materiality of *Finland*, with the fact that this rare nitrate cellulose film has been preserved in the first place. Therefore, my essay starts with the history of the film reel which became a memory box also due to the fact that it remained on the dusty shelves of the archive unopened for such a long time. After that I change focus by considering the contents of the film and how it encapsulated visions of Finland, its culture and nature. As a conclusion, I shall return to *Finland*'s dual nature as a memory box.

Rebirth of *Finland*

In 1911, *Finland* was screened 75 times during the tourism exhibition in Berlin and only four times in Helsinki.[11] This clearly shows that it was originally planned to attract foreign audiences and was made for performances abroad rather than domestic screenings. The itineraries of the actual film copy remain unclear. It is just as difficult to estimate how many copies there actually were. The only existing copy has survived at the Military Archives of Finland. It is likely that the reel was returned to Finland after the intensive use at the exhibition and was archived into the collections of the army, which was known as the last station for touristic materials. And it was this archive where the copy was finally "found" in the 1990s. The copy was subsequently restored under the guidance of the Finnish Film Archive to celebrate the centenary of cinema in 1995.[12] At that point also a soundtrack was inserted, emphasising Finnish brass music typical of the popular concerts of the late nineteenth and early twentieth centuries, but no evidence is available on the type of music and sound effects used in the screenings in Berlin. This is important from the

11 KIPPOLA/SEDERGREN, 2003. Jari Sedergren and Ilkka Kippola argue, however, that the film might have been screened more often than the written sources suggest. This is based on the fact that the only existing reel was in a rather bad condition before its restoration. A film reel should stand around 80 performances without being so worn out as the copy was. See SEDERGREN/KIPPOLA, 2009, pp. 205f.

12 SALMI, 1999, pp. 80-84. KIPPOLA/SEDERGREN, 2003.

perspective of interpretation: only the visual appearance of the film is reliably similar to the copy that was screened in 1911, but the particular meanings attached to the images was, of course, produced by the interplay of sound and image in the original presentations. Today, we only have access to the image, not the sound.

As *Finland* as a cultural artefact had been hidden for almost 85 years, it was concretely an invisible and silent object. It was not lost in the sense that it *had* been archived together with other kinds of exhibition material and footage, but it became a memory box, without any possibilities of becoming part of cultural communication as it was forgotten. Thus, also its contents remained in secrecy.

When the box was finally opened, the finding proved to be sensational. Nitrate cellulose material is in itself extremely fragile; it is flammable, even explosive, and can dissolve into such a bad condition that nothing can be saved through restoration efforts.[13] If the copy had been preserved somewhere else or if the reel had been archived in a wrong position, the memory box may have closed for ever. But since *Finland* had been stored under proper conditions, it could be restored for viewing. All this means that there are grounds to argue that, at least in this case, materiality has agency. The memory box is not only born out of human intentions and meaning-making: the chemical processes that constitute a film are an essential basis for *Finland* from the perspective of its memory-box-ness.

Before the end of the 1990s, the history of early Finnish cinema looked quite different.[14] No fiction film prior to 1917 had ever been completely preserved. Some documentary films existed, however, but only around 20 titles were available. Before Finnish independence in 1917, a total of 326 Finnish documentaries are known to have been made. All footage that had been preserved could be presented within one hour.[15] The first Finnish film known to have been made was shot in 1904 and featured children in their schoolyard in Helsinki.[16] After 1906, film production became more regular, and the leader of the market was the company Atelier Apollo, headed by Karl Emil Ståhlberg.

13 On the nitrate film material, see SALMI, 1993, pp. 57-62.

14 Confer previous accounts of early Finnish cinema in UUSITALO, 1965; UUSITALO, 1972; HIRN, 1981.

15 I have explained this in detail in SALMI, 1999, pp. 80-83.

16 SALMI, 1999, p. 81.

The first fiction film *The Moonshiners* (Salaviinanpolttajat) was produced by Atelier Apollo in spring 1907.[17]

The audio-visual memory of Finland was distorted not merely by the fact that only a few films were available; it was also filtered by later opinions on what kinds of films were valuable for future generations. At the turn of the 1940s and 1950s, the leading Finnish newspaper *Helsingin Sanomat* commissioned a documentary on its own history to celebrate the 60th anniversary of the paper. The filmmaker Veikko Itkonen was hired to complete the film and, finally, the long documentary entitled *Thus Was the Present Day Born* (Näin syntyi nykypäivä) was premiered in January 1951.

During the production process, Veikko Itkonen contacted many of the early film companies and gathered footage for his film. He was especially interested in political events in Helsinki during the first decades of the twentieth century and took only those films that fitted his conception of the anniversary documentary. The rest of the material, portraying scenes from other parts of Finland, was abandoned, and since there was no film archive in Finland, it was soon destroyed.[18] Thus, the making of the documentary *Thus Was the Present Day Born* became the distorting filter for the audio-visual heritage in Finland.[19]

The early films included in Veikko Itkonen's documentary depicted such events as the opening of the senate, the visit of the General Governor and the Czar in Helsinki, the funeral of Senator Leo Mechelin and the confirmation ceremony of the University of Helsinki.[20] Contrary to this, film programmes and announcements reveal that many of the early films showed sceneries from the countryside and portrayed historic monuments and smaller cities of Finland, but none of these films had been preserved.

The finding of *Finland* – the opening of the audio-visual memory box – completely changed the view on early Finnish cinema. *Finland* was compiled of earlier travel films, presumably shots between the years 1906–10 and, thus, it mediated 25 minutes of unseen material, views on cities such as Turku and Tampere, natural sceneries from northern and eastern parts of Finland and sites of memory such as the castle of Kajaani and the Valamo monastery.

17 UUSITALO, 1965, pp. 12f; HIRN, 1981, pp. 187-201; SALMI, 1993, pp. 74f.

18 The Finnish Film Archive was founded in 1957.

19 I have discussed this earlier in SALMI, 1996, pp. 145-163.

20 See Lauri Tykkyläinen's documentary *Suomalaisen lyhytelokuvan vuosikymmenet* (1985).

Itineraries of Finland: cartographic view and spatial imagination

Finland was composed in the form of a tourist route across the country. It starts with sceneries from Turku (in Swedish, Åbo) showing, for example, the Turku castle and the cathedral. In the existing copy, the route ends by the river Tornio in Lapland. The surviving list of intertitles tells, however, that there was one more location at the end of the film, Rovaniemi, but this scene has disappeared. In German, the last intertitle read: "Berg Ounasvaara bei Rovaniemi. Endpunkt der Eisenbahn am Polarkreis."[21] As this text reveals, the filmmakers wanted the audience to note that it was possible to travel by train up to the polar circle.

Clearly, the film is made to resemble an itinerary through Finland, almost as if it were meant to portray how Finland opens up for a foreigner that comes by ship from the Baltic Sea. The first harbour is Turku, and from there the traveller is expected to move forward following the coastal line. The film includes scenes from Naantali (Nådendal), Parainen (Pargas), Tammisaari (Ekenäs) and Hanko (Hangö) and continues further to Helsinki. The intertitles of the film can be listed here as an illustration of the cinematic itinerary:

0 [Turku Castle and the river Aura]
1 Turku Cathedral
2 River Aura
3 Naantali
4 Manor Joensuu
5 Manor Mustio
6 Parainen on the southern coast
7 City and sea bath Hanko
8 City Tammisaari
9 Ruins of the old fortress Raasepori
10 Aspects from Helsinki
11 The old city of Porvoo
12 Industrial city Tampere
13 Tourist route going down Mankala rapids

21 The intertitle list has been published by SALMI, 2001 according to the film copy, and later by KIPPOLA/SEDERGREN, 2003 and SEDERGREN/KIPPOLA, 2009, pp. 206f according to the archival sources.

14 The old castle of Viipuri
15 Imatra rapids
16 Saimaa Canal
17 Castle Olavinlinna at Savonlinna
18 Isle of Punkaharju
19 Castle Käkisalmi
20 Island cloister Valamo at Lake Ladoga
21 Island in Lake Ladoga
22 Mount Koli
23 Kuurna Canal at Pielis river
24 Tar boat in Kajaani
25 Departure of tourist boat from Vaala at Oulu river
26 City of Oulu and Merikoski rapids
27 Midnight sun over the Tornio river[22]

22 This list is written down from the film. See also SALMI, 2001. Jari Sedergren and Ilkka Kippola have found the original intertitle list from the archives, and there are three missing elements: the first intertitle was "Åbo. Alte Burg". Today this sequence exists but not the intertitle. The second missing part has been after the city of Oulu (Uleåborg). There was the intertitle "Stadt Torneå", followed by moving images from the city of Tornio. The third missing sequence is the end, with the intertitle "Berg Ounasvaara bei Rovaniemi". See SEDERGREN; KIPPOLA, 2009, pp. 206f. From the perspective of interpretation these differences are not a problem, since the film has been preserved almost in a complete form.

Figure 1: Map of Finland with cinematic stations

If these cinematic stations are positioned on a map (figure 1), the itinerary becomes more obvious. The route makes a quick sidestep to Tampere, one of the oldest industrial cities of Finland, giving evidence that Finland is also an industrial country, but right after that the camera returns to rural sceneries, and the cavalcade continues in the lake district, in Carelia and then moves towards the north. *Finland* offers a pathway through the country and is thus strongly cartographic by nature.

In his *Cartographic Cinema*, Tom Conley argued that a film often serves as a locational machinery; it establishes its own geography.[23] This also happened in *Finland*: the film implies a map, or merely a route through the country,

23 CONLEY, 2007, pp. 1f.

although this map is never openly shown. When the locations are put on a concrete two-dimensional map, it seems evident that the film reveals only a partial look over Finland, first concentrating heavily on the southern-western corner of the country, the most historical region of Finland, then moving eastwards, noting both Tampere and the capital Helsinki, subsequently focusing on Eastern Finland and following the railroad track towards Lapland. It is noteworthy that Ostrobothnia and Middle Finland are not depicted in the film. The reason might be, of course, that train and ferry connections were not ideal from the traveller's point of view in those parts of the country; however, the most obvious reason is the fact that Finnish national self-understanding had predominately been built on Eastern Finnish, especially Carelian cultural heritage.[24]

The existing film consists of a total of 81 shots. Since the film was compiled of earlier short travel films, it is likely that images after particular intertitles are derived from separate films. The original short films might have been longer that the selected shots, but it seems that every film or item consisted of two or three shots. Many of the shots are like moving photographs, reminding of the very early films of the late nineteenth and early twentieth centuries.[25] The density of shots, and thus the use of montage, is at its highest in the sequences portraying tourist activities in Finland. The passage shot in Punkaharju consists of four images where travellers are seen wandering and admiring natural sceneries. The passage depicting Koli is based on three shots, and the tourist boat in Oulu river has as many as six shots. This sounds irrelevant as such, but the amount of shots indicates the effort to try to capture the dynamism of tourist activities and portray Finland not only as a series of beautiful landscapes but also as a site of action.

In its emphasis on Finland, the film particularly stresses waterways: if added up, the film owes almost one third of its duration to rapids, rivers, lakes and channels. The water-focused character of the film is already emphasised in the first images showing Naantali, Parainen and Tammisaari: the camera is on board, approaching these towns from the sea. This decision is carefully considered since the first images of the film give an impression of approaching Finland from abroad, by ship. This effect has been created by editing separate

24 Confer Juhana Saarelainen's essay on Kalevala and the Carelian cultural heritage in this book.

25 See, for example, SCHWARTZ, 1999, p. 187; MARSH, 2003, p. 71; BEUMERS, 2009, p. 5.

shots together but, obviously, this draws on the fact that moving camera shots were frequently seen in early cinema.[26]

The centrality of moving, immersive shots is striking. To be sure, this feature can be linked with the touristic aims of the production, but can be also interpreted as a cartographic feature which, instead of topographic bird's-eye views, stresses locational navigation through the landscapes.[27] The camera has been positioned in the view of a potential tourist visiting Finland: s/he arrives by boat, continues by railway, takes a boat trip down the rapids and walks over the hills of Punkaharju. All this makes sense, considering the fact that the film was intended for the *Internationale Reise- und Fremden-Verkehr Austellung.* On the other hand, it is even more striking that there was suitable footage to be used in the editing of the film in the first place. If the material included in *Finland* is compared to the films that were previously known to have been preserved, the difference becomes obvious.[28] There is one immersive shot in the material that was incorporated into *Thus Was the Present Day Born* and all the other shots were rather stable, showing people passing by or focussing on street scenes. *Finland* was a memory box already for these aesthetic reasons: it included stylistically unique shots that have not been preserved in any other remaining reels. After the opening of the memory box, the view on the history of early Finnish cinema was radically changed. It is known that the setting of a camera on a boat, on a car or on a train was a regular practice in creating moving shots in other countries[29], and it was likely that this was also the case in Finland. But the finding of *Finland* proved that this technique was known and employed also in Finnish production. In this sense, the opening of the memory box had an impact on how the audio-visual heritage was, and will be, remembered.

26 See, for example, MUSSER, 1994, pp. 150, 248.
27 CONLEY, 2007, pp. 1f.
28 Confer the documentary *Suomalaisen lyhytelokuvan vuosikymmenet* (1985) by Lauri Tykkyläinen.
29 For further details, see HOLMBERG, 2003, pp. 129-147; MUSSER, 1994, p. 150.

Figures 10 and 11: Immersive shots in Finland

Finland draws on immersive shots and aims at mobilising the gaze. The supposed viewers, the passers-by of the Berlin exhibition, are like urban *flâneurs* who, instead of window shopping, can consume a virtual tourist trip to a distant country.[30] *Finland* is a commodity, aimed at arousing interest in travelling. According to Tom Conley, a film "encourages its public to think of the world in concert with its own articulation of space".[31] This happens in the case of *Finland*, too, as it persuades its spectators to join the travel and experience Finland only through its ready-made itinerary. Cinema can be interpreted as a technology of mobilising the gaze but, almost paradoxically, is simultaneously a technology of limiting the ways of seeing. It offers a particular selection of Finnish scenes, sceneries and routes and serves a mnemonic filter, remembering some locations and forgetting others.

Whose memory box?

As already argued, *Finland* can be conceived as a memory box, without which the remembrance of Finnish cinema would be completely different. It has had an impact on how the past of Finnish filmmaking is remembered – and, in fact, can be remembered. It enabled the activation of latent memories. It is important to ask, however, who the holder of memories finally is, whose memories they are and whose memory box the old dusted reel actually was.

The reel and its projection have become a memory box to those people, mostly film historians, who discovered the reel and opened the box in the 1990s.[32] For them, it was a memory box *in relation* to the former understanding of Finnish film history. This is, however, only a limited view on *Finland*'s memory-box-ness; the meaning of the word 'memory' can be interpreted in a more complex way.

It is possible to interpret that *Finland*, irrespective of its character as a tourist commodity, or perhaps because of it, was already a memory box in 1911, at the time of its original screening in Berlin. As a memory box, *Finland* has travelled in time, from 1911 to the 1990s and to the present day, but it also travelled in space, from the Finnish filmmakers to the Berlin audience in 1911.

30 On the idea of window shopping and cinema, see FRIEDBERG, 1993, pp. 1-10.

31 CONLEY, 2007, p. 1.

32 I belonged myself to the first film historians to analyse *Finland* and its cultural ramifications in the late 1990s. See closer SALMI, 1999, pp. 80-88; SALMI, 2001.

In addition to this, it may be argued that even its constituent parts, the separate travel films made prior to 1911, tried to capture 'memories' of Finland.

Pierre Nora has pointed out that there are "sites where a sense of historical continuity persists" and that there are "*lieux de mémoire*, sites of memory, because there are no longer *milieux de mémoire*, real environments of memory".[33] *Finland* and its raw material, the short films depicting different locations in Finland, were portraying *lieux de mémoire*, sites that had already changed, that were under continuous transformation and that were layered by historical memories. Already the first images of *Finland*, with the castle and the cathedral of Turku, symbols of the medieval past of the country and perhaps unarticulated references to Finnish past under Swedish realm, refer to this point of departure. The Swedish connection might even have a political undertone, considering that *Finland* was compiled in 1911.

There are further aspects in the layered memories of the film. An eminent Finnish author of the nineteenth century, Zacharias Topelius (1818–1898) had written popular books such as *Finland framställdt i teckningar* (Finland in Drawings, 1845) and *Boken om Vårt Land* (Book on Our Land, 1875) which became influential transformers of the notions of Finnish nature and culture.[34] They stressed provincial landscapes in a way that is echoed in the cinematic interpretation of *Finland* in 1911. Even the short travel films made prior to 1911 were in fact Topelian depictions of Finnish landscape, and early filmmakers wanted to create a certain filmic assemblage of Topelius' views.[35] Therefore, even the constituent parts of *Finland* were stratified by memories, and the images from Koli and Punkaharju, for example, had already been etched into the national symbolic capital.

Finland seems to capture both diachronic and synchronic strategies in defining nationality. The original short travel films were mostly made for domestic audiences,[36] and national landscapes were employed in the construction of Finland as an emotional community at the time of the national upheaval. Still, these very same images were used to attract foreign audiences to come to Finland. Of course, it is impossible to know what kinds of images

33 NORA, 1989, p. 7.

34 KLINGE, 1998, pp. 271-274.

35 For further details, see SALMI, 1993, pp. 77f; SALMI, 1999, pp. 81f.

36 It seems, though, that the early film pioneer K. E. Ståhlberg had a plan of exporting Finnish travel films in the late 1890s. See Ståhlberg's interview in the newspaper *Nya Pressen* 22 January 1897. See also SALMI, 1999, p. 82. There is, however, no evidence of any successful export activities.

were consciously set aside and not regarded as worthy of showing. It may be argued, however, that there is no fundamental difference between intended audiences, and domestic footage could be easily used for tourist purposes, too. Finnish filmmakers had portrayed *lieux de mémoire* to their fellow countrymen, and these same images could be used to widen the basis of remembering outside the community.

If a nation is an imagined community[37], this imagination has both internal and external ramifications that are bound together: the questions of how a community sees itself and how others see it, are inseparable – as well as the questions of how a community wants others to see it, how it imagines others to imagine it and how this imagination, in the end, influences the way others see it and a community sees itself.

Conclusion

In the beginning of the 2000s, it often looked as if the previous century was completely dominated by audio-visual culture. The new technologies such as CDs and DVDs have also left an impression that everything from the past would be available. It has, however, been estimated that only one third of the titles produced during the history of cinema has been preserved, meaning that most of the films are lost.[38] The transient nature of history is especially obvious in the first decades of cinema, and it is as clear that contemporaries did not usually see any lasting value in the films that were shot. When *Finland* was compiled during the years 1910–1911 it was not considered that someone could be interested in screening it after a century. *Finland* was made for contemporary purposes. Yet, as the film was made for the audience in Berlin, it also encapsulated visions of nationhood, and when it was shelved after the screenings in Berlin and Helsinki the reel became a silent object without possibilities to communicate with new generations.

Finland was already a memory box for the audience in 1911, both in Finland and abroad, but the memories it held were mixed in nature. The circulation of imagery on Finnish culture and nature in the early twentieth century resulted in persistence of memory which emphasised the "boxness" of

37 This refers to Benedict Anderson's idea of a nation as an imagined community. See ANDERSON, 1983, p. 6.

38 ALLEN/GOMERY, 1985, p. 29.

Finland already in 1911. At the time of its making, there was an urgent need to create an image of the country, and there probably was no notion of the permanence of film as a historical medium, as something that could transmit messages to the future.

The curious history of the actual film reel led to it becoming a memory box in another sense in the 1990s. Its plain materiality played a role in this process but also the fact that *Finland* had been completely forgotten. This oblivion created necessary inertia that made it a memory box of audio-visual heritage. As this box was opened and the film had once again the possibility to communicate with the audience, it became – to draw on Alison J. Murray Levine's words – "a dynamic site of negotiation and exchange".

List of References

Sources

Films

Finland. Produced by K. E. Ståhlberg. Atelier Apollo, Finland 1911. The film can be viewed at the database of Finnish cinema at http://www.elonet.fi/fi/elokuva/162301

Suomalaisen lyhytelokuvan vuosikymmenet. Documentary in six parts. Directed by Lauri Tykkyläinen. Finnish Broadcasting Company, Finland 1985.

Newspapers

Nya Pressen 22 January 1897

Secondary Literature

ALLEN, ROBERT C./GOMERY, DOUGLAS, Film History: Theory and Practice, New York 1985.

ANDERSON, BENEDICT, Imagined Communities: Reflections on the Origin and Spread of Nationalism, London 1983.

ASSMANN, ALEIDA, Cultural Memory and Western Civilization: Functions, Media, Archives, Cambridge 2011.

BEUMERS, BIRGIT, A History of Russian Cinema, New York 2009.

CONLEY, TOM, Cartographic Cinema. Minneapolis 2007.

FRIEDBERG, ANNE, Window Shopping: Cinema and the Postmodern, Los Angeles 1993.

HIRN, SVEN, Kuvat kulkevat. Kuvallisten esitysten perinne ja elävien kuvien 12 ensimmäistä vuotta, Helsinki 1981.

HOLMBERG, JAN, Ideals of Immersion in Early Cinema, in: Cinémas: revue d'études cinématographiques, 14, 1 (2003).

KIPPOLA, ILKKA/SEDERGREN, JARI, Finland (1911) - ensimmäinen matkailuelokuva Suomesta, in: Ennen & Nyt 4 (2003) (Internet publication: http://www.ennenjanyt.net/4-03/finland.htm, viewed 1 December 2013).

KLINGE, MATTI, Idylli ja uhka. Topeliuksen aatteita ja politiikkaa, Porvoo 1998.

LAVERY, JASON, The History of Finland, Westport, CT 2006

LEVINE, ALISON J. MURRAY, Framing the Nation: Documentary Film in Interwar France, London 2010.

MARSH, ANNE, The Darkroom: Photography and the Theatre of Desire, Adelaide 2003.

MOSS, WALTER G., A History of Russia. Vol. I: To 1917. Second edition, London 2005.

MUSSER, CHARLES, The Emergence of Cinema: The American Screen to 1907, Los Angeles 1994.

NORA, PIERRE, Between Memory and History: Les Lieux de Mémoire, in: Representation 26, Spring 1989.

ROECK, BERND, Introduction, in: Cultural Exchange in Early Modern Europe. Vol. IV: Forging European Identities, 1400–1700, ed. by HERMAN ROODENBURG, Cambridge 2006.

SALMI, HANNU, Kadonnut perintö: Näytelmäelokuvan synty Suomessa 1907–1916, Helsinki 2002.

ID., "Ansichten aus Helsingfors": kotimaisen elokuvan historiaa verkossa, in: Agricolan Tietosanomat 3-4 (2001) (Internet publication: http://agricola.utu.fi/julkaisut/tietosanomat/numero3-4-00/helsinkielokuva.html, viewed 1 December 2013).

ID., Tanssi yli historian: Tutkielmia suomalaisesta elokuvasta, Turku 1999.

ID., Kaupunkikuvan ongelma mykkäkauden suomalaisess näytelmäelokuvassa, in: Kuva ja historia, ed. TIMO SOIKKANEN/VESA VARES, Turku 1996.

ID., Elokuva ja historia, Helsinki 1993.

SCHWARTZ, VANESSA R., Spectacular Realities: Early Mass Culture in Fin-de-siècle Paris, Berkeley and Los Angeles 1999.

SEDERGREN, JARI/KIPPOLA, ILKKA, Dokumentin ytimessä: Suomalaisen dokumentti- ja lyhytelokuvan historia 1904–1944, Helsinki 2009.

UUSITALO, KARI, Eläviksi syntyneet kuvat: Suomalaisen elokuvan mykät vuodet 1896-1930, Helsinki 1972.

ID. Suomalaisen elokuvan vuosikymmenet. Johdatus kotimaisen elokuvan ja elokuva-alan historiaan 1896–1963, Helsinki 1965.

Diaries, Material Memory Holders

Creating a Memory Box

ANNA-LEENA PERÄMÄKI

Memory boxes have a capability to move in time and space. My first contacts with the memory boxes I am going to discuss in this article, i.e. two diaries from the 1940s, took place almost 70 years after they had been created. One of them was sent to me by e-mail in form of scanned documents from Washington D.C. in October 2009. I first came across the other as a published and translated book in 2009. My encounter with the original diary – or its photocopy on the computer screen, to be accurate, since no one is allowed to touch the original – did not happen until October 2010 at an archive in Paris. These moments of opening the memory box differed much from the moments when these memory boxes were created and written. The diaries had a long journey through decades, changing circumstances and, in the case of the diary now archived in Washington, across the ocean before they ended up in my hands. Let's take a closer look at the one I had a chance to read in Paris:

> There are two parts in this diary. I can see it now when reading the beginning: I wrote the first part from a sense of duty to preserve the memory of what must be told […]. It makes me happy when I think that if I will be arrested, Andrée has stored these pages, something of me and of the most precious, since I do not care about anything else material nowadays; what must be saved is your soul and memory.[1]

1 "Il y a deux parties dans ce journal, je m'en aperçois en relisant le début: il y a la partie que j'écris par devoir, pour conserver des souvenirs de ce qui devra être raconté [...]. Cela m'est un bonheur de penser que si je suis prise, Andrée aura

This is how 22-year-old Hélène Berr, a Jewish student from Paris, writes in her diary in the autumn of 1943. She is living in the midst of terror and persecution. The hard times have made her realise something very important about the nature and purpose of the diary. Diaries are in essence material memory holders, memory boxes of their time. That thought I am going to tackle and develop further in the article on hand.

In the diary quote above one can see how this particular memory box, Hélène Berr's diary, was born. Its conscious creator was the writer herself and she was also its first audience. Berr going back in time and once again reading her first diary entries can be considered as one of the first moments of opening the memory box. By analysing the motives behind her diary-keeping and noticing that her diary consists of two parts, she immediately started adding new layers to the box. This shows how the memory box's creator and audience, which is what an artefact needs in the process of becoming a memory box, can actually be the same person. However, Berr's diary has subsequently achieved much wider publicity by its publication in 2008 and translation into several languages. When Berr wrote the entry quoted here she had no idea how many people would re-open the memory box she created and give new meanings, add new layers, to it in the future. I, as a researcher and analyser of her diary, am one of them.

Diary as a memory box and its maker

This article discusses the idea of a diary as a memory box. My aim is to show how the concept of a memory box can bring new viewpoints to the analysis of diaries as sources for historical research. The main questions are: How is a diary made a memory box? What kind of levels does this special memory box hold? I am thus concentrating especially on the moment of creating a memory box, and I am not going to specifically touch the further meanings attached to the box by its later openings.

gardé ces pages, quelque chose de moi, ce qui m'est le plus précieux, car maintenant je ne tiens plus à rien d'autre qui soit materiel; ce qu'il faut sauvegarder, c'est son âme et sa mémoire." The diary of Hélène Berr (in the following footnotes BERR, 1942-44), 27.10.1943, Centre de Documentation Juive Contemporaine, Mémorial de la Shoah, Paris (CDJC). All translations by Anna-Leena Perämäki.

My focus is on the diaries written by young Jewish women who lived in the German-occupied Western Europe in the 1940s, during the Jewish persecution and World War II. I am especially going to take a closer look into the diaries of two girls from Paris: Hélène Berr and Elisabeth Kaufmann. Hélène Berr (1921-1945) kept her diary between the years 1942-1944. She was a French-born university student who lived in Paris with her parents until she was arrested and transferred into a concentration camp in March 1944. Berr died in Bergen-Belsen in April 1945, only a few days before the camp was liberated. Elisabeth Kaufmann's (1924-2003) diary was written in 1940. Kaufmann was born in Austria, but her family had to leave to France after the German annexation in 1938. She kept her diary – written in her mother tongue German – before and during the German occupation of Paris and during her and her mother's flight from Paris into hiding in the southern French countryside. Kaufmann (later Koenig) managed to survive the war and later moved to the United States where she died in 2003.[2]

Berr's and Kaufmann's diaries were written in two different styles by two writers of different age and interests. Berr was clearly a very talented writer and had literal ambitions which she expressed and practiced by writing her diary; whereas Kaufmann just wanted to write down what was happening in her life and around her for the purpose of remembering it later and thus might not have paid as much attention to the form of her writings as did Berr. However, these two diaries written in difficult times offer an interesting insight into the concept of memory box.

Like Bernd Roeck,[3] I see memory box as an encapsulation and a vehicle of cultural transfer. In this article, cultural transfer means the transfer that already happens when a memory box is created. In the case of diaries, this transfer is related, on the one hand, to the different traditions and conventions of diary keeping and, on the other, to the often varied and complex cultural and historical context(s) influencing the way a diarist sees and represents him/herself. When a diarist writes his/her diary notes, s/he makes these transfers visible. In this article, the diary is thus approached as a memory box that captures both memories and cultural transfer and puts them in a movable form.

A diary is first and foremost an artefactual memory box, but when someone opens this imaginative box, they can see that it has also immaterial dimensions

2 JOB, 2008, pp. 299-305; ZAPRUDER, 2002, pp. 37-41.
3 ROECK, 2007, pp. 11-14.

or layers. This article's structure is based on these different layers[4]. First, I am going to discuss the layers that are material and give the box its form. After that, it is time to look beyond the strictly material questions and take into consideration the other layers telling about the time of diary's/memory box's birth. At the bottom of the box, one can finally find the level of thoughts and ideas of its creator, the diarist.

Material memory box – the artefactual layers in a diary

A diary[5] usually has a cover, a back and pages that one can feel and touch (if an archivist allows this[6]). If the diary in question is not written by typewriter or computer, one can also try to analyse the diarist's handwriting. In some cases, the research stops there because it is impossible to actually read and understand the workings of his or her pen. But this material level – book covers (if any), the quality of the paper and pen used, handwriting – can already tell us a lot about the time and place when a certain diary was written. Therefore, even if our focus is on strictly material questions, a diary can be seen as a memory box that holds the traces of its time in its cover and pages.

The diary of Elisabeth Kaufmann, who was the younger of the Jewish diarists discussed here, consists of three small notebooks. The first notebook has a French word "Cahier" – meaning a notebook in English – printed on its cover. Under this rubric there are four lines with printed "de" – probably leaving space for a notebook owner to write her/his name on the first line – and "à M" – apparently directing the owner to specify to whom (*Madame/Monsieur*) the notebook is dedicated. This might refer to a teacher, which indicates that this notebook was probably originally meant to be a school exercise book. Kaufmann has left these lines empty. Instead of the diarist's name, for instance, there are some very unclear drawings on the cover. It is hard to say what they depict. The cover looks ragged and shabby and is

4 I am interested here in the layers that were put in the memory box when it was made.

5 My focus here lies on handwritten diaries. I am thus not going to discuss the modern electric or online diaries.

6 In the case of Hélène Berr's diary that is held at the Shoah Memorial Museum in Paris, researchers are only allowed to see the photocopy of the original diary.

edges are not sharp, as they most likely used to be, but rounded and curled by time.[7] In addition to the influence of time, careless preservation prior to being handed over to the archive and/or a sloppy diarist, one possible explanation to this worn-out cover is that the owner of the notebook has lived through some rough times. One can also speculate solely by looking at the cover – although it can indeed be nothing but *speculation* at this point – that this notebook might have been very important to its possessor and it is likely that she carried it everywhere.

The pages inside Kaufmann's first notebook are of very simple lined paper with thin red margins printed on the right side of the paper. Her large text, written with black ink, goes across the margins and fills every line, but she has not written on the white space before and after the lined area. It seems that this diarist did not worry that she could run out of paper – maybe Kaufmann's notebook had not cost much and she thought she could easily buy a new one after coming to the last page or she had got it for free from school. On the last page, she does not refer in any way to the fact that this notebook is full now and she needs more paper but simply continues her notes in the next notebook that is very similar to the first in terms of paper and lining.

The last notebook of Elisabeth Kaufmann is different from its two predecessors. It does not have anything printed on its hard cover but has been originally empty. However, Kaufmann has filled the empty space with a stylised "Isabeau" written on it. Above the name she has drawn a neat picture of a maiden, a decorated cone-shaped hat with a veil on her head, flowers and a castle silhouette in the background.[8] There are also a much smaller and lighter pencil drawing of a female face and even lighter sketches of flowers on the cover, not to mention some unrecognisable drawings similar to those on the first notebook.[9] Kaufmann's passion for art and drawing is apparent here – she studied at an art school in Paris, after all.[10] When one flips through her notebooks one can also find many other sketches that usually illustrate her written diary notes. During her flight to the countryside she has pictured the

7 The diary of Elisabeth Kaufmann (in the following footnotes KAUFMANN, 1940), United States Holocaust Memorial Museum, Washington (USHMM).

8 *Isabeau* might refer to Isabeau of Bavaria, the Queen of France (the wife of King Charles VI) of German origin, who was called Elisabeth before she became queen at the end of the fourteenth century. See for example ADAMS, 2010.

9 KAUFMANN, 1940, USHMM.

10 ZAPRUDER, 2002, p. 39.

big crowd of people and cars leaving Paris when the German troops were about to occupy the city, for example.[11]

Like in the case of the first notebook, the cover of Kaufmann's third notebook is worn-out but somehow still slightly better preserved-looking than the older notebooks. This is interesting because she started her flight from Paris at the time of this last notebook. It might tell something of the importance of diary keeping to Kaufmann. It is possible that the true value of her notes became clearer to her through the worsened circumstances and she started to take greater care of the notebooks during the flight.

However, the traces of Kaufmann's dangerous flight are apparent, if not on the cover, on the graph paper pages of the last notebook. The flight has left its mark on her texts. Kaufmann's handwriting is not the tidiest, but the notes written during the flight are even messier and harder to read than the writings at the beginning of the diary.[12] Both Kaufmann's physical and mental condition, not to mention the lack of proper places to write, had an effect on her handwriting. She had more important things to worry about than the readability of her diary entries at the time.

Unlike Elisabeth Kaufmann's, Hélène Berr's diary[13] was not written in notebooks but on the loose sheets of simple, unlined paper that resembles stationery. Berr used a bigger paper folded around the sheets as a cover. On this – then possibly white, now yellow – "cover" she has written, probably shortly before she was arrested and deported: "Ceci est mon journal. Le reste se trouve à Aubergenville."[14] When Berr started keeping a diary in 1942, two years after Elisabeth Kaufmann, the war and the German occupation of Paris had already been going on for a long time and there was shortage of almost everything. Paper was not an exception.[15] That might be a reason Berr used loose paper sheets instead of purchasing a notebook. On the other hand, these sheets appear to be in better condition than Kaufmann's notebooks.

It is maybe too far-fetched to make any comparisons considering these two diarists' living conditions merely based on the condition of their diaries – and

11 KAUFMANN, 1940, 13.6., USHMM.

12 See for example KAUFMANN, 1940, 13.6., USHMM.

13 I have seen the original only as a photocopy. I cannot thus describe the material side of Berr's diary in much detail.

14 "This is my diary. The rest is at Aubergenville." BERR, 1942-44, CDJC. Aubergenville refers to family Berr's summer house near Paris.

15 See more about the conditions in Paris and France during the war, POZNANSKI, 2001, pp. 471-475; WEINBERG, 2001a, pp. 213-222.

the wear and stains on Kaufmann's notebooks might also be the result of later years – but their situations were indeed different. Berr lived at her childhood home in Paris the entire time she kept a diary. Kaufmann on the other hand, whose family felt more threatened already in the beginning of the war because they were foreigners and not native Frenchmen like Berr, fled from Paris even before the German occupation of the city had officially begun.[16] Author Virginia Woolf – as mentioned by cultural historians Maarit Leskelä and Ritva Hapuli – as well as researchers Suzanne L. Bunkers and Cynthia A. Huff, have emphasised the importance of the material conditions for writing.[17] Berr's writing conditions were better than Kaufmann's even in the midst of the persecution and are reflected on the well preserved pages of her diary.

Also, Hélène Berr's handwriting is much clearer than that of Kaufmann. Her tidy notes written with blue ink are always arranged in almost straight lines, although the sheets have no lining. However, also Berr's handwriting style varied with her moods and the overall state of affairs. For example, her handwriting is different than usual when she writes about a card from her father, who spent three months under arrest at the Drancy transit camp[18] in 1942. In that card, Berr's father is expecting to be deported soon and says his goodbyes to his wife and children. Berr's note on the card shows how worried she is about her father's situation, although she only mentions her mother's distress. Her handwriting suddenly becomes very small in size, and she has not written the whole page full like usually.[19] Changes in handwriting can reveal the writer's feelings even when s/he does not actually write about them.

The material aspects of a diary can tell a lot about its writer and when and where the diary in question was written. Already the first layers brought to daylight thus show what kind of interesting encapsulation of a specific time and place a diary is as a memory box. However, there is much more to uncover beneath the artefactual side in the box. Next, I am going to analyse the motives

16 Foreign Jews living in France had been treated worse than native-born citizens already before the war. However, the German occupiers turned out to be more lenient towards them in the beginning than they had expected. The harsher anti-Jewish measures were introduced not earlier than in summer 1941. WEINBERG, 2001a, pp. 215, 217f.

17 See for example HAPULI/LESKELÄ-KÄRKI, 2005, pp. 69, 71f.; BUNKERS/HUFF, 1996, pp. 6, 20.

18 Drancy was situated in a Paris suburb. Approx. 70,000 French Jews were sent to this camp during the course of the war prior to their deportation to the extermination camps in Poland. WEINBERG, 2001b, p. 159.

19 BERR, 1942-44, 22.7.1942, CDJC.

and traditions of keeping a diary that can be found behind the handwriting of my diarists – the layer of conventions.

The encapsulation of western and Jewish – the motives and conventions of diary-keeping

The researcher who uses diaries as their source material and is able to read and understand what is written in these memory boxes from the past, will find other layers hidden in the diary pages and between the lines that reveal further details about the situation in which the diary was born. Here we come to the cultural transfer in diary writing. In the case of the young Jewish diarists analysed in this article, their diary notes were the children of two traditions of keeping a diary. On one hand, they followed the Western tradition of confessional diary, *journal intime*[20]. On the other, the effect of these diarists' Jewish background is also apparent in their notes.

Like Maarit Leskelä-Kärki has argued in her dissertation on the writing of the Krohn sisters, a diary is not only something private but always at least on some level dependent on the conventions of its time, a culturally constructed phenomenon.[21] That is noticeable also in Hélène Berr's and Elisabeth Kaufmann's diaries. The conventions of a traditional, western type of diary-keeping have had a strong influence on the diarists' way of constructing their notes. They knew how diaries are usually structured and followed that convention. Both of the young women almost always started their notes with a date, in some cases also with the time of the day, and Kaufmann sometimes with a place, too, especially during her flight. On the other hand, they did not stick to another common feature in a traditional diary, especially in the case of younger diarists: to start every diary note with a greeting like "Dear diary".[22] The best known young Jewish diarist and also an example for many teenage diarists after her, Anne Frank, even gave her diary a name and greeted it with "Dear Kitty".[23] Frank also read girl books that were written in diary form and were very popular among young people in the first half of the twentieth century, which probably influenced her considerably when writing her own

20 See for example MAKKONEN, 1993, p. 363.
21 LESKELÄ-KÄRKI, 2006, pp. 36, 73f.
22 MAKKONEN, 1993, pp. 364-369; see also LESKELÄ, 2000, p. 215.
23 PERÄMÄKI, 2009, pp. 28f.

diary.[24] It is not known if Berr or Kaufmann had ever read those kinds of books. However, many features of their diaries fit well into the picture of a traditional, conventional diary.

As mentioned earlier, Berr's and Kaufmann's diaries are characteristic western type diaries not only in their structure, but also in their content. In many ways they can indeed be seen as classical examples of confessional diaries (*journal intime*). That type of personal diary including much self-examination has its roots in religious diaries kept by English Puritans in the 1600s and became popular during the nineteenth century. This can be interpreted as diachronic cultural transfer: the puritan way of keeping a diary in early modern England – although somewhat different in its motives and purpose – was transferred through centuries and applied to the needs of subsequent diarists. At the same time, a diary became an especially feminine way of writing and a tool to examine oneself and observe one's own moral, considered suitable for young girls in particular.[25] Berr and Kaufmann used their diaries as a private channel to pour their feelings onto paper and write about things that they could not discuss with anyone else.

Especially Hélène Berr acknowledged that writing often made her feel better. Having opened up about a certain relationship that she is trying to end and feels very upset about, she concludes: "*It sufficeth that I have told thee,* my piece of paper; everything is already better."[26] Berr did not want to bother her mother with her troubles – although she sometimes yearned for it – but she could tell all to a "piece of paper". That was her solace. Berr herself states in the diary that she writes because she does not know with whom to talk.[27]

However, Berr had a long break from her diary, lasting from autumn 1942 until autumn 1943. During the break, the persecution of Jews in France had intensified and come closer – many of Berr's friends had been arrested and she herself had narrowly escaped a roundup at her workplace UGIF.[28] When Berr

---

24 See more about the literature Frank read LEE, 2011, pp. 237, 418f.

25 LESKELÄ, 2000, p. 214. See also VATKA, 2005, pp. 39-57; MAKKONEN, 1993, pp. 362f.

26 "*It sufficeth that I have told thee*, mon bout de papier; tout va déjà mieux." BERR, 1942-44, 11.4.1942, CDJC. Italics in the original.

27 BERR, 1942-44, 15.4.1942, CDJC.

28 UGIF (l'Union générale des israélites en France) was established in November 1941. It worked as a legal mediator between the occupiers, the Vichy government and the Jews. UGIF's most important task was to help the French Jews and their families. Hélène Berr volunteered as a social worker in the organisation from

began to write again, it appears that she understood even better than before the true value of keeping a diary. Clearing her thoughts and feelings by writing soothed her so much that she decided not to hold back any longer and to tell everything troubling her to the diary from that moment on.[29]

Unlike Hélène Berr, Elisabeth Kaufmann does not explicate in her diary what keeping it meant to her. However, also Kaufmann appears to have used it as a channel to confess and share her deepest feelings and thoughts – just like so many western diarists before and after her. By keeping a diary, Kaufmann had a chance to open up about things she did not want the others to know. She wrote what she really thought about her schoolmates and was also very open about her opinions on politics. The following quote from March 1940 is a good example:

> Nothing else at all is done at school than talked about politics. Even more there, where the most different political opinions are gathered. […] If the girls were serious and thought at first through what they say would it surely be very interesting. But they are all unlearned in politics and simply pass on the things that they catch at the dinner table without forming their own opinion. I love political debates. However, it would be meaningless to participate in these and so I take an eminent mediating position between the fighters in the class, even though it wouldn't otherwise conform to my character.[30]

Kaufmann thought that her schoolmates were foolish and did not actually know anything about politics, but she did not want to take part in their debates. What she hid at school she shared with her diary.

Sometimes the diary was also Kaufmann's only comfort and company, so at her sixteenth birthday, for instance, when she was alone at home and it

summer 1942 until the raid. MODIANO, 2008, pp. 12f., 99, 215, 241; KADOSH, 2001, p. 368; MICHMAN, 2001, p. 373.

29 BERR, 1942-44, 10.10.1944, CDJC.

30 "In der Schule wird überhaupt nichts anders gemacht, als politisiert. Umso mehr, da die verschiedensten politischen Meinungen versammelt sind. […] Wenn die Mädels seriös wären, und zuerst durchdächten, was sie redeten, wäre es ja recht interessant. So sind sie aber all politisch uninstruiert und reden einfach nach, was sie beim Mittagessen aufschnappen ohne sich selbst eine Meinung zu bilden. Ich liebe politische Debatten. Sich aber an diesen zu beteiligen, wäre Unsinn und so nehme ich in der Klasse einen ausgesprochen Vermittelnden Posten zwischen den Streitenden ein, wiewohl das sonst nicht meinen Charakter entspräche." KAUFMANN, 1940, 17.3., USHMM.

seemed that no one would come to celebrate with her: "I sit in the kitchen now, write in the diary and am sad."[31] The diary also kept her company during the flight from Paris. Even then, Kaufmann kept writing whenever she had a chance to do so. That must have alleviated her excitement and fear. The western tradition of the confessional diary thus proved to be a very helpful survival tool for these young Jewish women when everything else around them was about to collapse. They passed on this tradition in the memory boxes they created.

The diarists discussed here were not, however, only influenced by the western conventions of keeping a diary. Their Jewish background must not be forgotten. It is common to many diaries kept by Jews during the Holocaust that the diarists had a strong need to testify about the persecution of their people, a desire to remember. According to James E. Young, this need to testify is in essence based on the texts and background of the Jewish holy writings. There is a profound idea of literary testifying or the will/testament behind them.[32] It can be criticised how well Young's thoughts fit to younger and often quite secularised diarists who were not necessarily as aware of this long Jewish tradition of testifying as the older generations. Perhaps it was only the hard times and fear of death in the near future which naturally induced even young Jews to see the potential of their diaries as important testaments of the terrifying events during the war and persecution. However, the diaries analysed in this article fit very well into that category, especially in the case of Hélène Berr, who was the older of the two diarists.

Just as Young states about the writing Jews, one of Hélène Berr's motives for keeping a diary was the idea of a wider public to which she wanted to testify about her suffering and the suffering of Jewish people in general. Berr wanted to remember the persecution of Jews and show also to the later generations what happened during that time. She often writes about that in her diary. She even thought it was her downright duty to tell about these things, as this entry from October 1943 makes clear: "[W]riting is a duty that I have to fulfill since the others must know. [...] [T]he others don't know, [...] they don't even imagine others' suffering and the evil certain people inflict on others. And I always try to make this hard effort to tell. [...] I should thus write

31 "[J]etzt sitze ich in der Küche, schreibe im Tagebuch und bin traurig." KAUFMANN, 1940, 7.3., USHMM.

32 YOUNG, 1988, pp. 17-19.

in order to be able to later show the people what kind of era this was."[33] Berr thought that her gentile contemporaries did not know enough of what was happening to the Jews and felt it was thus her task to write the truth about her time. However, she also thought that she did not have time to write a book in the midst of it all and found it important that she would at least note her every experience in the diary for the later.[34] Berr had thus a strong desire to testify. That connects her diary to the long Jewish tradition of testimonial writing, although it does not become clear in the diary how well she knew this tradition herself.

Elisabeth Kaufmann's diary is not so clearly meant to be a testimonial about the Jewish persecution for later generations as is Berr's diary. However, it seems that also Kaufmann thought it important to write down what was going on around her. She appears to have felt that she must note everything exciting and unusual, even unpleasant that she experienced because of the persecution. Especially the diary entries written during the flight sometimes resemble an adventure novel, the self-evident heroine being Kaufmann herself. It is typical for diarists to colour their life events.[35]

Already at the beginning of her flight Kaufmann seems to have wanted to write down her experiences throughout in great detail. She even mentions the time and weather, in a dramatic tone: "So they were not in Paris anymore. It was about ½ 11 before noon, Wednesday the 12th of June 1940. The weather was unchangeably murky. They both wandered, a windy journey in the great chain of plight, rousing a silent lament in the midst of the great suffering."[36] Kaufmann's diary entry about a night under arrest at a police station is an especially apparent example of this diary's significance in documenting important events. In that entry, Kaufmann writes that she has just explained to

33 "[J]'ai un devoir à accomplir en écrivant, car il faut que les autres sachent. [...] [L]es autres ne savent pas, [...] ils n'imagent même pas les souffrances d'autres hommes, et le mal que certains infligent à d'autres. Et toujours j'essaie de faire ce pénible effort de raconteur. [...] Il faudrait donc que j'écrive pour pouvoir plus tard montrer aux hommes ce qu'a été cette époque." BERR, 1942-44, 10.10.1943, CDJC.

34 BERR, 1942-44, 10.10.1943, CDJC. See also BERR, 1942-44, 18.7. and 12.9.1942, 10. and 25.10.1943 and 14.-15.2.1944, CDJC.

35 KAGLE/GRAMEGNA, 1996, pp. 38, 41.

36 "So waren sie nicht mehr in Paris. Es war zirka ½ 11 vormittags, Mittwoch den 12 Juni 1940. Das Wetter war unverändert trübe. Sie zogen beide, ein windiges Glied in der großen Elendskette, bildend, ein unbeklagter Jammer im großen Leid." KAUFMANN, 1940, 12.6., USHMM.

a curious man also arrested at the station that an experience like this must be written down.[37] Kaufmann thus understood the importance of a diary – if not as a direct testimony about the persecution of Jews – as a preserver of memories and her own past, at least. The diary was a memory box to her, the memory box that she had made herself.

Literature researcher Rachel Feldhay Brenner, who has written about the diaries of young Jewish women, argues that diaries offer their writers an opportunity to read "backwards" and write "forwards". A diarist can compare the present moment with the events s/he has described before and thus form an insight into the historical course of their life.[38] It was especially important to the young diarists described here to understand themselves as historical agents who leave their traces in the past because, being Jews, their right to their own history was under threat.

The extreme living conditions under which these diarists wrote their notes make their diaries not only part of the more common western tradition of confessional diary-writing, but also part of the tradition of Jewish testimonials. These diaries can be seen as memory boxes that encapsulate the cultural transfer and exchange from and between different cultures of diary-keeping. In the following chapter, I am going to look into the deepest layer in these boxes analysed here that is also closely connected with the concept of cultural transfer. It is the layer of identity.

Beyond the material and conventions – identity building written in a diary

As it has become clear in this article, diary as a memory box consists of various different layers that are, however, closely intertwined. The last layer examined here does not make an exception. Keeping a diary is not just about notebooks, handwriting, conventions and writing traditions – it is also a channel to construct and represent one's identity. The level of identity is therefore an important layer attached to this memory box already at the time when it was made. It can be analysed by looking at the box's creator's

37 KAUFMANN, 1940, 13.6., USHMM.

38 BRENNER, 1997, p. 139. Quotation marks in the original.

individual thoughts and ideas expressed behind the common and recognisable conventions of diary writing.

The concept of identity is, first and foremost, understood here as cultural identity. It is the aspect of a person's identity that is connected with belonging to some distinct ethnic, linguistic, religious or national culture. Cultural researcher Stuart Hall argues that no one receives that kind of identity at birth, but they are formed and change their shape as part of and vis-à-vis the meaning systems, representations, attached to them. That is related to the question of symbolic communities. National culture, for instance, is merely a discourse – a way to build meanings that direct and organise our actions and perceptions of ourselves.[39] Being a Jew can be seen as this kind of cultural and constantly shape-changing part of one's identity.

> I suffered, there, at that sunny court of Sorbonne, in the middle of all my study mates. I suddenly felt that I wasn't myself anymore, that all had changed, that I had become a stranger, like I would be in the middle of a nightmare. I saw familiar faces around me but I sensed everyone's sorrow and astonishment. It was as if I had a mark of a red branding iron on my forehead. On the stairs, there were Mondolini and Mrs Bouillat's husband. They looked aghast when they saw me. [...] I was natural, superficially. But I was living a nightmare.[40]

This is how Hélène Berr describes one of her first visits to the university with a yellow Star of David on her chest in June 1942.[41] Berr had apparently not talked much about her Jewish background before – it seems that many of her study mates and teachers had not even known that she was a Jew. When the law about the yellow star came into effect, she had to face her Jewish identity and others' reactions to it in a dramatic way. The feelings of being labelled and an outsider are strongly presented in the quote above.

39 HALL, 2002, pp. 19, 46f., 227-229.

40 "J'ai souffert, là, dans cette cour ensoleillée de la Sorbonne, au milieu de tous mes camarades. Il me semblait brusquement que je n'étais plus moi-même, que tout était changé, que j'étais devenue étrangère, comme si j'étais en plein dans un cauchemar. Je voyais autour de moi des figures connues, mais je sentais leur peine et leur stupeur à tous. C'était comme si j'avais eu une marque au fer rouge sur le front. Sur les marches, il y avait Mondolini et le mari de Mme Bouillat. Ils ont eu l'air stupéfaits quand ils m'ont vue.[...]J'étais naturelle, superficiellement. Mais je vivais un cauchemar." BERR, 1942-44, 9.6.1942, CDJC.

41 An order that forced the Jews to wear the yellow star came into effect in France on 29.5.1942. See for example BERR, 2009, 42 (note 8).

Deborah Dwork, who has researched the fates of persecuted Jewish children, states that many children and young people became fully aware of their own Jewishness only when their separation and labeling started. Especially the forced use of the Star of David, which also Hélène Berr had to experience, had that kind of effect.[42] The system that oppressed the Jews had the power to make especially the younger of them see and feel themselves as somebody Other. As a reaction to that, some young people even wanted to deny that they were Jews.[43] The force from above to face one's own Jewishness was thus sometimes very traumatic to the youngest Jews. It was traumatic even to already 21-year-old Hélène Berr.

The Jews of Western Europe were tightly integrated into the secular society in the beginning of the twentieth century. They were often from wealthy and well-educated families. They supported western liberalism and aimed at an individual identity beyond religion and nationality. The young people did not necessarily know much about their Jewish roots.[44] This applies also to the two diarists analysed here. Based on their diaries, at least, one can assume that their families were relatively secularised. Elisabeth Kaufmann's diary includes no reference to Jewish traditions or religious festivities. Even if her parents practiced their religion, their daughter did not think that Jewish traditions were worth mentioning in her diary.

Hélène Berr, on the other hand, did not remain completely silent about her Jewish background in the diary, although she did not necessarily talk about it to her gentile acquaintances. Berr even writes about her visit to a synagogue once, although she had not enjoyed the visit much because there were no young people and she knew only few persons attending the service.[45] She also mentions the Jewish fest Jom Kippur in autumn 1942 but does not describe how her family celebrated it. It seems, however, that the Berrs did not fast before and during the fest that year according to the tradition. At least Hélène herself opted out of fasting because, according to her own words, she rather

42 DWORK, 1991, pp. 20-27. See also BRENNER, 1997, p. 8.

43 HALL, 2002, p. 228; ZAPRUDER, 2002, p. 68. Hall's example is about the effect of colonisation on the identity of the black indigenous people.

44 BRENNER, 1997, pp. 8, 17; TURTIAINEN, 1995, p. 26. Philosopher Hannah Arendt argues, however, that the Jews were never fully accepted as members of the European society. In spite of their efforts to assimilate, they always remained outsiders and could not wholly escape their roots, whether they wanted to do so or not. See ARENDT, 1978 (1944), pp. 67f.; FELDMAN, 1978, p. 18.

45 BERR, 1942-44, 11.9.1942, CDJC.

wanted to help others. She names her fasting work mates at UGIF in her diary, though.[46] Although she did not always follow all its rules, Jom Kippur must thus have been a somehow meaningful fest to Berr. Maybe her family had celebrated it more properly before the war and persecutions.

Nevertheless, Berr also mentions Christmas – but not Hanukkah – in the diary in December 1943. She writes about Christmas trees she has decorated to delight the – at least partially – Jewish children whom she helps.[47] One can also read between the lines that Berr and her family possibly ate pork that is forbidden in the Jewish religion.[48] The Jewish traditions and festivities appear to have been a bigger part of Berr's identity than they were to Kaufmann but even the Berrs were not very strict with their religious practices. One can see the effect of the eating habits of western gentiles and even Christianity in Berr's writings – synchronic cultural transfer from western culture to a girl with a Jewish background.

Berr's stance on the Jewish part of her identity was very complex. This complexity is already apparent in the diarist's thoughts about wearing the Star of David. At first, she plans not to obey the new law at all because wearing the star would be a shameful sign of submitting to the German orders. However, Berr finally decides to obey the law since doing the contrary would be cowardly towards the other Jews. "But if I wear it, I always want to be very elegant and dignified so that people see what it means."[49] Berr was thus able to feel at least a little proud about her Jewish background. On the other hand, it appears that she had hidden her religion even from her new, catholic boyfriend before the yellow star revealed the truth.[50] Berr's diary does not tell why she did that, but it seems that she was afraid that he would start treating her differently if he knew about her Jewishness. On the whole, she wanted people to see her as herself, not as the representative of all the suffering Jews who must be commiserated. Berr notes in her diary that wearing the star has turned walking on the streets into a constant, forced representation. She must have

46 BERR, 1942-44, 20. and 22.9.1942, CDJC.

47 IBID., 22.12.1943.

48 IBID., 16.6.1942. The family Berr had an own farm in Aubergenville. According to the diary, they got their fruit and vegetables from there but brought also pig meat to the city. Berr does not clarify, however, whether the meat was sold or the family ate it themselves.

49 "Seulement, si je le porte, je veux toujours être très élégante et très digne, pour que les gens voient ce que c'est." BERR, 1942-44, 4.6.1942, CDJC. See also BERR, 1942-44, 9.6.1942, CDJC.

50 BERR, 1942-44, 8.6.1942, CDJC.

found that particularly problematic. Elsewhere in the diary, she often points out that Judaism is just a religion, nothing else. Berr strongly resisted an idea of Jews as a unified nation, not to mention as a race.[51] Nevertheless, the law about the Star of David forced Hélène Berr to re-construct her identity. As everyone could now see her background, being a Jew also became a bigger part of her own perception of herself.

However, being a Jew was only one side of Berr's and Kaufmann's cultural identity. It appears in their diaries that a sense of belonging to some nation and having a home country was at least as important to them, if not more, as their Jewish background. They transferred the idea of national identification to their texts. It is important to an individual to be able to identify him/herself as a part of something bigger – as a member of a certain group, state or nation, for instance. As noted by Hall, social anthropologist Ernest Geller has stated that the absence of the feeling of national identification would cause a deep sense of subjective loss.[52]

Especially Elisabeth Kaufmann, whose family had fled to France after the annexation of Austria, seems to have based her identity strongly on her Austrian roots. She saw herself first and foremost as an Austrian, not as a Jew. In fact, she never even directly mentions that she is a Jew in her diary. One of the rare cases when Kaufmann uses the word Jew is when she compares her friend Vilma to the Jews fleeing from Egypt. Even there, she does not give any hint about her own Jewish background but writes as if she were an observer from outside.[53] She writes about "us Austrians" instead, with whom she identifies herself and distinguishes from the others, especially from the Frenchmen. She describes her family's flight from Vienna to Paris with the word "emigration" – she seemed to think, or wanted to think, that they were emigrants, not Jewish refugees.[54] Kaufmann also often expresses her longing for Vienna and the good old times, when her family, although not so well-off as the previous generations, could still hold on to the bourgeois lifestyle:

> How can […] these girls understand that I can indeed ice-skate and own also skates that I still have from Vienna but don't have the money to pay the entrance fee? […] When I lived in Vienna I wasn't aware of it, but it becomes

51 BERR, 1942-44, 29.6. and 27.7.1942, 9.11. and 31.12.1943, CDJC.

52 HALL, 2002, pp. 45f.

53 KAUFMANN, 1940, 11.6., USHMM.

54 IBID., 26.2., 10., 17. and 24.3., 13. and 22.5., 6. and 13.-14.6.

> clear to me now that we were living much beyond our incomes even then and still permitted us the pleasures that didn't meet our material situation. […] [H]ere in the emigration the attempt to maintain the culture and tradition doesn't die out, yet the means have shrunk from minimum to nothing. […] [W]e still try, with all the possible and unlikely means, to cut out the so called "Luxus" […] as little as possible. So […] I couldn't refuse to go skating.... to some extent as a social duty.[55]

The group Kaufmann identified herself with and felt pride for was the Viennese well-off bourgeoisie. Even in the "emigration", her family, who had almost completely lost their incomes, still tried to live like they used to in Vienna. Kaufmann tried to keep up especially with her school mates at the art school and did not want them to notice the poor state of her family.

Kaufmann emphasises her Austrian identity in the diary but the years in Paris had an effect on her, too. Although Kaufmann's diary is written in German and she uses Austrian expressions like "Servus" in it, there is also some French in the diary.[56] Before the German occupation of Paris, she often expresses her support to and trust in the French army and the allied forces. She even once refers to France with the pronoun *wir* (we) in that context.[57] In addition to the language and the country at war, also the city influenced and inspired Kaufmann. She learned to love Paris and describes its beauty with great enthusiasm: "The broad alley […] gives me certain euphoria through its beautiful green area […]. It's difficult to decide what I love the most in Paris.

---

55 "Wie können […] diese Mädchen verstehen, dass ich zwar eislaufen kann und auch Schlittschuhe besitze, die ich noch aus Wien habe, aber nicht das Geld mir den Eintrittspreis zu zahlen? […] Als ich mich in Wien lebte wusste ich es nicht, aber jetzt wird es mir klar, dass wir schon damals recht weit über unsere Verhältnisse hinaus lebten und uns immer noch Vergnügungen leisteten, die unserer materiellen Lage nicht entsprechen. […] [H]ier in der Emigration das Bestreben Kultur und Tradition aufrecht zu erhalten nicht erloschen, die Mitteln jedoch von einem Minimum zum Nichts vertrocknet sind. […] [W]ir versuchen noch immer mit allen möglichen und unwahrscheinlichen Mitteln möglichst wenig von dem alten, sogenannten 'Luxus' […] aufzugeben. So […] ich es mir nicht versagen konnte Eislaufen zu gehen.... gewisser Massen als gesellschaftliche Pflicht." KAUFMANN, 1940, 5.5., USHMM. See also KAUFMANN, 1940, 4.4., USHMM.

56 KAUFMANN, 1940, 13. and 28.5., 10. and 14.6., USHMM.

57 IBID., 18. and 24.5., 5.6.

It's just clear that I love it. […] [T]he charm of Paris doesn't end […]. It gives me joy…"[58]

Based on her diary, Elisabeth Kaufmann built her identity especially on her former home country Austria and still wanted to live like the members of the Viennese well-off middle class. However, two years in Paris had already started to shape her identity into new direction. Belonging to a certain nation appears to have been more important to her than being a Jew, though. Nevertheless, it must be pointed out here that Kaufmann's diary is from the year 1940, when no Jew in France had to carry the labeling Star of David yet. Being in exile, or an emigrant, as Kaufmann wanted to be called, the feeling of otherness was, then again, already familiar to her.

Whereas Elisabeth Kaufmann identified herself with the Austrians, Hélène Berr's beloved country was France. It appears in Berr's diary that being French was at least as important a part of her identity as being a Jew, if not more. She started to hate and despise the Germans she had to face on the streets of Paris every day and who thought that she, a native French, did not belong in her own home country. One of those encounters made Hélène open up in her diary: "[T]hose men there, those *foreigners* who would never understand Paris or France, claimed that I wasn't French and considered that Paris belonged to them, that rue de Rivoli was their property."[59] The presence of the occupiers strengthened Berr's national feelings. How some foreigner dared to march proudly through her home town like its owner and, at the same time, denied her nationality only because she happened to be a Jew? Berr also uses an expression "by us in France" and wonders why the Germans do not seem to realise how much the deported Jewish families miss the country where many of their ancestors have already settled themselves centuries ago. Based on the diary, also Berr's parents had a strong French identity.[60] Belonging to the French people thus formed a firm basis in Hélène Berr's identity. Even though

58 "Die breite Allée […] gibt mir durch ihre schöne Anlage ein gewisses Hochgefühl […]. Es ist schwer zu bestimmen, was ich an Paris zum meisten liebe. Fest steht, dass ich es liebe. […] [D]er Charme von Paris hört nicht auf […].Ich habe meine Freude daran…" KAUFMANN, 1940, 28.5., USHMM. See also KAUFMANN, 1940, 8.4., USHMM.

59 "[C]es hommes-là, ces *étrangers* qui ne comprendraient jamais Paris ni la France, prétendaient que je n'étais pas française, et considéraient que Paris leur était dû, que cette rue de Rivoli leur appartenait." BERR, 1942-44, 30.10.1943, CDJC. Italics in the original.

60 BERR, 1942-44, 9. and 14.11.1943, 13.12.1943, CDJC.

the persecution made her also think more about her Jewish background, national identity was still very important to her.

The analysis of these two Jewish diarists' identity, as they express and present it in their diaries, has brought to light yet another layer of cultural transfer written in the memory box discussed in this article. The cultural identity of a persecuted young Jew was very complex and flickering – a combination of a fortified, partly forced identification with the fellow Jews and, on the other hand, often strong sense of national identity. Being in exile from one's home country, as in case of Elisabeth Kaufmann, made identity building even more complicated. When one approaches a diary as a memory box, the encapsulation of this complex process of identity construction becomes apparent in its pages.

Conclusion

I have used the concept of memory box as a tool to analyse diaries in this article. I argue that the diary fits well to this concept. It has an easily identifiable agent or creator (a diarist), it is in a form that has great potential to become public and it has its own audience (the readers) – even if only the diarist him/herself is the public. This audience attaches different, specific meanings to the diary by reading and interpreting it from their own perspectives and starting points. If one approaches memory boxes in a less abstract way, the diary as a concrete artefact that you can open and touch, carry and move, is very easy to picture as a box. It is a box that encapsulates and makes movable the memory of the time and place in which it was created, in all its complexity and variety.

Approaching the diary as a memory box opens up new possibilities and viewpoints to a researcher. It is a tool that can be very helpful for the historical and cultural analysis of diaries. Imagining a diary as a box that has many different layers inside is an eye-opening experience. It is a very concrete and at the same time, in-depth way to approach one's source material. In case of the diaries analysed in this article, I have taken three specific layers into consideration: I started from the material side of the diary and looked at the cover, paper and handwriting, continued with the layer of conventions and motives behind diary writing and, finally, picked the layer of cultural identity of the diarists from the box. Already this short glimpse has showed how many-sided diaries can be. All their dimensions deserve to be taken into consideration.

As mentioned earlier, memory boxes are vehicles of cultural transfer. The makers of the memory box discussed in this article, Hélène Berr and Elisabeth Kaufmann, made their memories into a movable form by keeping a diary. The other thing made movable, more or less unconsciously, was the cultural transfer in diary writing and in diarists' evolving identities. Thinking of a diary as a memory box helps to see the cultural transfer present in all its dimensions. The young diarists living in the middle of war and persecution were influenced from both western and Jewish cultures and ways of life. That is apparent already in their ways and motives of keeping a diary and, above all, in their identity construction process analysed through their diary notes.

In this article, I have mostly concentrated on the time when the diaries analysed here were written – the memory box was created – and given voice to the diarists. However, it is not only the agent or creator of the memory box that gives meanings to it. Also the subsequent openers – the public of the box – have an important role in filling it. It should not be forgotten that the publicity that constantly shapes and modifies a certain memory box can include also academic research. Berr's and Kaufmann's diaries moved in time and were displaced into my subjects of analysis. I, as a twenty-first century European reader, approach a Jewish diary from the 1940s with retrospective eyes. That affects the reading. The diarist did not know what their fate would be – the reader knows. Today's reader also has more general knowledge about the persecution of Jews and the Second World War than the diarist living those events could have. I am aware that I look at this memory box from a different perspective than its creator. Even the process of writing the article on hand has thus added yet another layer to the box.

List of References

Sources

Unpublished Sources

The diary of Elisabeth Kaufmann (26.2.-14.6.1940), United States Holocaust Memorial Museum (USHMM), Washington.

The diary of Hélène Berr (7.4.1942-15.2.1944), Centre de Documentation Juive Contemporaine (CDJC), Paris.

Published Sources

BERR, HÉLÈNE, Päiväkirja 1942–1944, Helsinki 2009.

ID., Journal 1942–1944, Paris 2008.

Secondary Literature

ADAMS, TRACY, The Life and Afterlife of Isabeau of Bavaria, Baltimore 2010.

ARENDT, HANNAH, The Jew as Pariah. Jewish Identity and Politics in the Modern Age, New York 1978.

BRENNER, RACHEL FELDHAY, Writing as Resistance. Four Women Confronting the Holocaust: Edith Stein, Simone Weil, Anne Frank, Etty Hillesum, Pennsylvania 1997.

BUNKERS, SUZANNE L./HUFF, CYNTHIA A., Issues in Studying Women's Diaries. A Theoretical and Critical Introduction, in: Inscribing the Daily. Critical Essays on Women's Diaries, ed. by SUZANNE L. BUNKERS/ CYNTHIA A. HUFF, Amherst 1996, pp. 1-20.

DWORK, DEBÓRAH, Children With a Star. Jewish Youth in Nazi Europe, New Haven et al. 1991.

FELDMAN, RON H., Introduction. The Jew as Pariah: The Case of Hannah Arendt, in: HANNAH ARENDT, The Jew as Pariah. Jewish Identity and Politics in the Modern Age, New York 1978, pp. 15-52.

HALL, STUART, Identiteetti, Tampere 2002.

HAPULI, RITVA/LESKELÄ-KÄRKI, MAARIT, Kirjallisia edelläkävijöitä. Virginia Woolf, oma huone ja naisten traditiot, in: Avaintekstejä kulttuurihistoriaan (Cultural History - Kulttuurihistoria 6), ed. by HANNA JÄRVINEN/KIMI KÄRKI, Turku 2005, pp. 69-83.

JOB, MARIETTE, Une vie confisquée, in: HÉLÈNE BERR, Journal 1942–1944, Paris 2008, pp. 299-307.

KADOSH, SARA, Joint Distribution Committee, in: The Holocaust Encyclopedia, ed. by WALTER LAQUEUR, New Haven et al. 2001, pp. 367-370.

KAGLE, STEVEN E./GRAMEGNA, LORENZA, Rewriting Her Life. Fictionalization and the Use of Fictional Models in Early American Women's Diaries, in: Inscribing the Daily. Critical Essays on Women's Diaries, ed. by SUZANNE L. BUNKERS/CYNTHIA A. HUFF, Amherst 1996, pp. 38-55.

LEE, CAROL ANN, Anne Frank 1929–1945, Helsinki 2011.

LESKELÄ, MAARIT, Kaipaava, haluava, seksuaalinen nainen Aino Kallaksen päiväkirjoissa, in: Modernin lumo ja pelko. Kymmenen kirjoitusta 1800–

1900-lukujen vaihteen sukupuolisuudesta, ed. by Kari Immonen et al., Helsinki 2000, pp. 211-244.

LESKELÄ-KÄRKI, MAARIT, Kirjoittaen maailmassa. Krohnin sisaret ja kirjallinen elämä, Helsinki 2006.

MAKKONEN, ANNA, Valkoisen kirjan kutsu eli löytöretkellä päiväkirjojen maailmoissa, in: Hiljaista vimmaa. Suomalaisten naisten päiväkirjatekstejä 1790-luvulta 1990-luvulle, ed. by SUVI AHOLA, Helsinki 1993, pp. 360-374.

MICHMAN, DAN, Judenrat, in: The Holocaust Encyclopedia, ed. by WALTER LAQUEUR, New Haven et al. 2001, pp. 370-377.

MODIANO, PATRICK, Préface, in: HÉLÈNE BERR: Journal 1942–1944, Paris 2008, pp. 7-14.

PERÄMÄKI, ANNA-LEENA, Nuoret naiset juutalaisvainojen varjossa. Anne Frankin ja Etty Hillesumin selviytymiskeinoja toisen maailmansodan aikaisessa Amsterdamissa päiväkirjojen valossa (master's thesis), University of Turku 2009.

POZNANSKI, RENÉE, Paris, in: The Holocaust Encyclopedia, ed. by WALTER LAQUEUR, New Haven et al. 2001, pp. 471-475.

ROECK, BERND, Introduction, in: Forging European Identities, 1400–1700. Cultural Exchange in Early Modern Europe (Vol. IV), ed. by HERMAN ROODENBURG, Cambridge 2007, pp. 1-30.

TURTIAINEN, JOUNI, Sionismi, in: Ikkuna juutalaisuuteen - historia, usko, kulttuuri, ed. by JOUNI TURTIAINEN, Helsinki 1995, pp. 26-28.

VATKA, MIIA, Suomalaisten salatut elämät. Päiväkirjojen ominaispiirteiden tarkastelua, Helsinki 2005.

WEINBERG, DAVID, France, in: The Holocaust Encyclopedia (2001a), ed. by WALTER LAQUEUR, New Haven et al. 2001, pp. 213-222.

ID., Drancy, in: The Holocaust Encyclopedia (2001b), ed. by WALTER LAQUEUR, New Haven et al. 2001, p. 159.

YOUNG, JAMES E., Writing and Rewriting the Holocaust. Narrative and the Consequences of Interpretation, Bloomington et al. 1988.

ZAPRUDER, ALEXANDRA, Salvaged Pages. Young Writers' Diaries of the Holocaust, New Haven et al. 2002.

“We wanted a parliament but they gave us a stone”
The Coronation Stone of the Scots as a Memory Box in the Twentieth Century

JÖRG ROGGE

In this article a memory box is presented, in which and to which different meanings were contained and attached in the course of seven centuries.[1] This memory box is the coronation stone of Scottish kings, nowadays on display in Edinburgh Castle, the external form of which has remained for the most part unchanged. The roughly 150 kg heavy, 67 cm long, 42 cm wide and 28 cm high sandstone block was used in the Middle Ages at the inauguration of Scottish kings.[2] In the course of history, however, it was removed from its original functional context and transferred to other cultural and political contexts. In this connection, both diachronic and also synchronic transfers of the coronation stone and the concepts of political order in the island of Britain stored in it were carried out. At present it is still an important memory box filled with political concepts, and it was and is a starting point for research into the relationship between the Scots and the English over the past 700 years. It is remarkable that this stone was used by nationally emotional Scots and also by the Government in London as symbol in important debates in the twentieth century. Historical recollections are transported by the Scots and the English with the stone that one may certainly call a container of memory. Here I

1 My thanks go to John Deasy for translating the German text into English as well as to the editors for finishing the final formatting.

2 The description of the stone is in AITCHISON, 2000, p. 39 and HILL, 2003, p. 11.

concentrate on the question which memories the Scottish Nationalists and Unionists have projected at the stone or *read into* it; memories which they have at times made into the guideline for their political action.[3] My focus thus lays on the certain opening moments of this memory box in different contexts. I am especially interested in the meanings attached to it in the twentieth century. However, before analysing those meanings in more detail, I shall briefly discuss the earlier phases of the box.

From Scone to Westminster Abbey in 1296

It is undisputed that Edward I, after having defeated the Scottish troops and deposing King John Balliol in 1296, had a stone, upon which new Scottish kings were initiated into their office, transported from Scone near Perth to London.[4] Together with the Scottish regalia (sceptre and crown), the king donated the throne stone to St. Edward the Confessor, whose tomb is still in Westminster Abbey today. In 1300 or 1301, the stone was incorporated into the English kings' so-called coronation chair in Westminster Abbey. With this transfer, King Edward I placed the stone in a new political-cultural context. The stone was now no longer seen as the memory box for the political independence and self-governance of the kingdom of Scotland, but it showed that Scotland had now lost its independence.[5] The memory box Stone of Scone now had different meanings, or better two strands of meaning, attached to it. Every English king seated on the coronation chair was at the same time also made king over Scotland.[6]

For centuries, the stone remained in Westminster Abbey in London, even though King Edward's successors did not succeed in establishing permanent English sovereignty over Scotland. Rather, in 1328, in the Peace of Northampton, King Edward III recognised the Scottish independence gained

3 One can argue with NORA, 1990, p. 13, that the recollection or memory adheres to something concrete, whether it is a space, a gesture, a picture or – as in our case – an object.

4 For the political and military disputes see BARROW, 2005, here particularly pp. 95-97.

5 AITCHISON, 2000, p. 117: "The chair celebrated Edward's triumph over the Scots".

6 AITCHISON, 2000, pp. 119-120 with written and pictorial documentary evidence for coronations since 1308 (Edward II).

by Robert Bruce.[7] In the course of these negotiations, the return of the stone to Scotland was also discussed. The English government was prepared to give the stone back. However, this will was not included in the treaty, but Edward III instructed the chapter of Westminster to hand over the stone. However, the Abbot of Westminster refused to return the trophy donated to St. Edward the Confessor. He was supported by parts of the London populace who did not want to hand over the stone on any account.[8] Therefore, the stone remained in Westminster Abbey and in the coronation chair on which James VI and I was crowned King of England and Scotland (Union of Crowns) in 1603 as the successor to Queen Elizabeth I. In March 1707, the Scottish parliament accepted the Act of Union with England. From then on there was a joint parliament in London; 45 Scottish members sat in the House of Commons. It was to take until 1999 before a Scottish parliament convened once again.

From Westminster Abbey to Arbroath and back in 1950/51

In the twentieth century and, in particular after the Second World War, the coronation stone became an important memory box in the Scottish Covenant Movement's struggle for Scottish self-administration or the restoration of a separate parliament and separate government in Scotland (*Home Rule*).[9] The activists were of the opinion that they had to remind their compatriots of their Scottish identity as well as of the political independence as a kingdom in order to thus motivate them to fight for their own parliament in the present. Between 1947 and 1950, some two million people signed a petition drafted by the movement for political self-government.[10] At this time, the fighters for a separate Scottish national assembly as a place for political self-determination *discovered* the stone as a memory box of their old freedom and independence. The representatives of Scottish freedom and the national idea adopted a special interpretation of Anglo-Scottish history linked to the stone in London and propagated this. A link was created between the refusal of the government in London to allow Home Rule and keeping the Scottish coronation stone in

7 BROWN, 2004, p. 229; ROGGE, 2012, pp. 101-116.
8 BARROW, 2003a, p. 204; AITCHISON, 2000, pp. 132-33.
9 HARVIE, 1998, pp. 169-173; LEVITT, 1998, pp. 33-58.
10 On this also the article Bis die Engländer froh sind, 1950.

Westminster Abbey. The stone became the symbol of the continuous suppression of Scottish endeavours for more independence by established politics. If one could free the stone from its English captivity, then that would be a beacon signal for all Scots to participate in the struggle for political independence. So thought at least Ian Hamilton who, together with two further students, Gavin Vernon and Alan Stewart and the teacher Kay Matheson, wanted to bring the stone back to Scotland.

> The stone had been taken away from Scotland to show that we had lost our liberty. Recovering it could be a pointer to our regaining it. A promise had been made by the Treaty of Northampton of 1328 that it would be returned, and that promise had never been kept. Why should fulfilment of that promise not be wrung from them by spiriting the stone away at dead of night? […] An empty chair speaks out louder than a full house. Much louder than a full house if that house is a House of Westminster Parliament. It might just speak loud enough to awaken the people of Scotland.[11]

With the abduction of the stone the group wanted to arouse their Scottish compatriots, the majority of whom seemed to have come to terms with their subordinate position in the realm at the end of the 1940s. With their action they wanted to demonstrate that Scots can achieve great things and were precisely not second-class Englishmen. Hamilton, at least, was motivated by the high-handed manner of British governments as well as the general public, whose representatives he even accused and accuses of racism.[12] He was of the opinion that Scotland would be better off without administration by a government in London. But to achieve this goal, the Scots' fighting spirit had to be aroused. According to Hamilton, shame dominated the emotional state of nationally-moved Scots in the years around 1950.

> The shame was that we were not English. We had lost our sense of community. English customs, English pronunciations, English table manners were the mark of success. You were nothing if you did not speak proper […]. People even tried to think as the English did, and if there is one thing a people cannot do, it

11 HAMILTON, 2008, p. 13.

12 "There is more racial abuse towards us in the English papers than we would ever think of using toward England", so Ian Hamilton in his blog, HAMILTON, 2012.

> is to use the thought processes of another people. Most Scots thought of themselves as a sort of second-class English.[13]

In addition he deplored that the Scots had lost their singularity; they ignored their undoubtedly extant capabilities. The cultivation of a nation's soul was a matter for the people, but the Scots had no longer taken care of their nation's soul – with grave consequences for the Scots' conception of themselves and their identity, because: "When we give away our soul, we have nothing left to give".[14]

Hamilton and his comrades-in-arms wanted to set an example against this. With an action, such as fetching back the stone, which was difficult but also spectacular and symbolic, they could shoot the English right in the heart; an old injustice would be rectified and the Scots aroused for the struggle for independence and political self-determination. In 1950, he and his comrades-in-arms considered themselves as "a representative group of our own generation. We belong to a generation that saw the need for change and who set about making it."[15]

With the liberation – as Hamilton put it –of the stone from Westminster Abbey, he wanted above all to remind his compatriots of their forefathers' struggle for independence and their own government.[16] Therefore he prefaced the first edition of his report on the abduction of the stone published in 1952 with a section "For the English" in which he declared that he did not harbour any hatred against the English. Rather, he deplored the attitude of those Scots who would compare themselves with the English and then assess their being Scottish as better as or worse than being English. What was important was rather that the English and Scots should recognise that they are different nations. In addition he warned that if the problem of Scottish home rule was not resolved, Scotland could become a second Ireland.[17]

In summer 1950, Hamilton reconnoitred the location of the stone in Westminster Abbey and thought about how it could be removed from the chair and taken out of the church unnoticed. He planned the transport to Scotland

13 HAMILTON, 2008, p. 8.

14 HAMILTON, 2008, p. 10.

15 IBID., p. 211.

16 In an interview in The Daily Telegraph (14.12.2008), Hamilton stressed that he and his comrades-in-arms had not committed any theft in 1950: "It was a liberation. A returning of a venerable relic to its rightful ownership", CRAIG, 2008.

17 HAMILTON, 1952.

and thought out a diversionary tactic in order to make pursuit more difficult for the English police. For this purpose, he and his comrades-in-arms used two cars. On 24 December 1950, the group succeeded in forcing their way into the church and extracting the stone from the chair with the help of a chisel. However, in the process it fell to the ground and broke into two parts. That made it easier to transport the stone, which Hamilton first hid in a wood near Rochester for some days, because strict checks were conducted at the Anglo-Scottish border after the theft had been discovered. Only on 31 December did Hamilton and his helpers succeed in bringing the larger part of the stone to Scotland. Hamilton reported full of pride that they had brought back the symbol of Scottish freedom and, for the first time after over 600 years, were able to expose it to Scottish air again.[18]

The reactions to the act in England were foreseeable. The deed was immediately blamed on Scottish Nationalists.[19] The Home Secretary called the burglars thieves and impudent vandals. For the Dean of Westminster the purloining of the stone was not, of course, liberation. He considered the deed to be not just a theft, but a sacrilege, because the stone had been in the possession of the abbey for almost 700 years. On the other hand, many people in Scotland were pleased about the act, because they thought the stone should come home and because the English police were not in a position to find the stone's hiding place. However, the majority of Scottish politicians proved to be less enthusiastic, criticised the action and appealed to the culprits to return the stone.[20] All in all, most Scots were probably satisfied with the blessings of the British Welfare State which were making themselves noticeable in Scotland, too, in the 1950s. The Labour Party did not have a separate government or administration for Scotland on its political agenda, the Conservatives were achieving great approval on the other side of the border and the Scottish National Party (founded in 1928) achieved just one to two percent of the votes in elections.[21]

The abduction of the stone did not trigger a political change, but the activists did achieve one of their objectives. Scotland's constitutional position was discussed by a broad section of the public. The spectacular action surrounding the disappearance of the stone from London was also taken up by

18 HAMILTON, 2008, p. 194.
19 No trace of missing Stone of Destiny – already over the border?, 1950.
20 AITCHISON, 2000, p. 141.
21 DEVINE, 2012, pp. 565-568.

satirical review performers who made their own suppositions about the whereabouts of the stone. Because there had been complaints about the poor quality of coal, the rumour was also going round that the stone had been taken over by the Coal Board. Finally the BBC received the order to show consideration for the mood in Buckingham Palace and refrain from all jokes about the stone.[22]

The question arose for the students and their supporters what should happen next with the stone. At some time the authorities would find its hiding place and the members of the group around Hamilton would presumably be arrested and convicted. If the stone were to be shown publicly, it would quickly be seized by the police and brought back to Westminster. One idea was therefore to link the return of the stone with the demand that it might remain in Scotland. Finally it was decided to lay the stone, the two parts of which had been put together again, in front of the altar of Arbroath Abbey at Easter 1951. This abbey was closely associated with the struggle for Scottish independence because of the renowned *Declaration of Arbroath* of 1320.[23] The stone was handed over to the police by James Wishart, the custodian of the abbey. Wishart stated that he had not recognised the persons who had brought the stone into the abbey. He emphasised, however, that he was pleased that the stone had come to this historic site. [24] The stone was then taken back to London under guard and once again installed in the coronation chair in February 1952.[25] In June 1953, Elizabeth II sat on this chair during her coronation.

From Westminster Abbey to Edinburgh in 1996

In the years following Hamilton's deed, many Scots were aware of the significance of the stone as a memory box for Scotland's political independence; however, support for the Scottish Nationalists remained low, interest in self-government was slight. From the 1980s on, Scottish nationalism once again gradually developed political force. Owing to the oil finds off the Scottish coast, some Scottish politicians saw a possibility of making Scotland

22 Diebesgut in Ihrer Kirche, 1951.
23 Confer for more on the declaration BARROW, 2003b.
24 Return of the Stone, 1951.
25 MUNRO, 2003, p. 232.

financially more independent from England and thus have an economic basis for the demand of more political independence. In the awareness of this economic potential, the question of Scottish self-government was again discussed intensively.[26] The demand for devolution, coupled with a constitutional reform, was the core of the political programme of the Scottish National Party whose chairman, Alex Salmond, demanded the return of the stone to Scotland in 1995. Salmond knew that the removal of the stone by Edward I 700 years before would be recalled in 1996 and did not want to miss the opportunity to bring the stone and its significance for Scotland back into national awareness again. The Government in London did not react to this demand and it was not likely that the stone would ever return to Scotland.

Therefore, the surprise was great when on 3 July 1996 the Prime Minister, John Major, announced in the House of Commons that the coronation stone, also called the Stone of Destiny, the oldest symbol of the Scottish kingdom, was to return to Scotland. Admittedly, only the transfer of locality was linked with this, because the stone was to remain in the possession of the Crown and be used at future coronations of rulers of the United Kingdom. But because the stone had a special place in the hearts of the Scots, Major continued, 700 years after its transfer to London by Edward I, it was to return to its historic homeland again and be kept in safe custody in an appropriate manner.[27] In the course of the ensuing debate, the prime minister emphasised that the stone was a sign of the unity of the United Kingdom. An attitude that was also shared by Conservative MPs. Tim Renton observed that the return of the stone should be regarded as a sign of unity and not one of discord in the United Kingdom. The Scottish Conservative MP, Bill Walker, supported this opinion a few days later. The stone was, on the one hand, a symbol of the independent Scottish nation, he said, but on the other hand it was also a sign of the Union between England and Scotland. And finally he explained: "It is part of the cement that holds the Union together. Returning the stone strengthens the Union".[28] The Minister of State for Scotland, James Douglas-Hamilton, emphasised that since the Union of the Crowns in 1603 the stone had been part of the common history of Scotland and England.[29]

26 DEVINE, 2012, pp. 591-617.

27 The announcement by Major is also printed in MUNRO, 2003, the announcement verbatim, pp. 232f. For the ensuing debate in the House of Commons on 3 July 1996 see: House of Commons Debate Stone of Destiny 03.07.1996.

28 House of Commons Debate Stone of Destiny 16.07.1996, Column 1053.

29 House of Commons Debate Stone of Destiny 16.07.1996, Column 1056.

Scottish Labour Party MPs, in particular, saw this differently. Tony Blair, the Chairman of the Labour Party, saw in the return of the coronation stone a sign of the acknowledgement of Scotland's special position within the United Kingdom, because Scotland was a nation different from England, with its own traditions, own history and culture. For the Government in London, the stone was a memory box of the unity in difference existing since 1603, whereas Scottish MPs have interpreted the stone rather as a memory box of the self-rule and independence existing in former times. In 1996, more separate responsibility as well as self-government in their home country was a political objective for Scottish politicians in the House of Commons. The MP for Tweeddale, David Steel, declared that the majority of Scots did not just want to have a symbol, but also the content linked with the stone, namely independent control over Scotland's internal affairs.[30] The Labour MP, Andrew Faulds, also emphasised that they did not just expect a symbol of Scotland's independence, but concrete measures for this from the Government in London. John Maxton (Glasgow) stated even more sharply that the return of the stone was irrelevant for those who wanted a Scottish parliament, because the stone was a symbol of medieval feudal tyranny. However, this pointed emphasis remained a minority opinion, even among Scottish MPs. Margaret Ewing, the member for Moray, considered the stone not as a symbol for the rule of kings, but as a symbol for the political sovereignty of the Scottish people that had already been proclaimed in 1320 with the declaration of Arbroath. The Scottish Labour MP, Thomas Graham, spoke in favour of the re-establishment of a Scottish parliament, the members of which would respect the citizens and pay attention to their wishes. However, with the return of the stone the Government was only pursuing a policy of symbols: "not a token artefact; real stones for building houses – that is what our people want."[31] John Major had probably expected more enthusiasm in the House of Commons. But it became apparent that the Scottish members did welcome the return of the stone, however would not allow themselves to be distracted from their real political objectives. This Commons debate is an example of selective dealing with the past. There were several cultural and political traditions into which the stone as a memory box, that so to speak represented these pasts, could be

30 According to The Independent (04.07.1996), Steel said in the Commons that most people in Scotland "want not just the symbol but the substance of the return of democratic control".

31 See footnote 28.

classified. In the Commons, the political memory makers in each case interpreted these traditions with regard to their current political objectives.[32]

Apart from the varied interpretation of the stone as a representation of historic traditions at the highest political level, very practical questions were negotiated. John Major had, it is true, proposed the Castle or St. Giles' Cathedral in Edinburgh as the place of display, however, the stone had never before been there, but in 1296 had been transported away by Edward I from Scone (by Perth), the place of the coronation of Scottish kings. Therefore it was no surprise that Bill Walker, in whose constituency Scone lays, demanded the stone be brought back there. He reinforced this opinion once again on 16 July 1996 during a debate in the Commons.[33] The old abbey, in which the stone used to be kept, did not exist anymore, but a suitable building should be erected in its place for the stone, he felt. This building should be large enough to accommodate the stone and to receive the expected masses of visitors. Walker then expounded on the history of the stone in detail, emphasising above all that it had already been stipulated in the Treaty of Northampton in 1328 that the stone should return thither, whence it had been transferred to London, namely to Scone.[34] With a concerted action, the Perthshire Tourist Board, the local Chamber of Commerce as well as the owner of Scone Palace wanted to file a petition in order to support the stone's return to Scone. At all events, the stone should be kept in a building on consecrated ground. And the Scottish regalia (crown, sceptre and sword)[35] could also be exhibited, together with the stone in Scone. Such a centre was the only realistic possibility of giving the stone a prestigious home. This argumentation, with the reference to the religious significance of the place, as well as the planned joint display of the secular symbols of political independence envisaged there, appealed to fundamental aspects of Scottish nationalism.[36]

The minister responsible for Scottish matters, Lord James Douglas-Hamilton, finally declared that during a hearing all the local authorities, such

32 GREEN, 2008, p. 105.

33 House of Commons Debate Stone of Destiny 16.07.1996, Column 1051.

34 The Rt. Hon. Member made a mistake here, the stone is not mentioned in the treaty; see STONES, 1965, pp. 329-341; in addition STEVENSON, 2007, pp. 1-15.

35 After the Union with England in 1707, these so-called Honours of Scotland were placed in a chest and immured in Edinburgh Castle. In 1818, Sir Walter Scott received permission to open the chest. He found the regalia allegedly just as they had been laid there, see BURNET/TABRAHAM, 2001, p 47.

36 Even if one may also assume the intention among the supporters of this solution o also promoting tourism in the region.

as Edinburgh, Scone or Arbroath, which had an interest in the stone should explain how they wanted to meet the important criteria of accessibility, security, close connection with the past as well as the promotion of the historical significance of the stone on the spot in each case. The decision was then taken between Scone, where a centre for the Scottish kingdom was intended to be built with the stone as the main attraction, and Edinburgh, which could argue with its large numbers of visitors and the guarantee of security in the case of the display of the stone in the Castle.[37] The security aspect was decisive and it therefore was announced on 21 October 1996 that the stone would be displayed in Edinburgh Castle after its return to Scotland. On 30 November 1996, on St. Andrew's Day, the ceremonial transfer took place. On this occasion, the Scotland Minister, Michael Forsyth, made it clear once again what memory the Government in London associated with the stone. He thanked the Queen for the fact that the stone could return to its old home, where it would stand as a powerful memory of Scotland's heritage and as a symbol for the Scottish nation within the United Kingdom.[38]

But precisely the question of the terms under which Scotland would remain part of the United Kingdom was not resolved with the stone's return. Scottish politicians' demand for greater scope for political action (*devolution*) was no longer to be fulfilled by symbolic politics. In Scotland, on the contrary, concrete changes in political structures and more independence in government matters were expected – the stone should be followed by the establishment of a separate parliament. However, the Conservative government refused this during its 17-year rule. Thus there was speculation about the motives of John Major and his ministers for returning the stone to Edinburgh. In the press it was presumed that it was an electoral manoeuvre in order to win over Scottish electors for the Conservative Party in the elections due in 1997. In *The Independent* one could read: "The Scots asked for a parliament and John Major gave them a Stone."[39] For Alex Salmond of the Scottish National Party (SNP) the return of the stone was a transparent manoeuvre in order to placate Scottish national feelings.[40] Ian Hamilton did not take part in the ceremony for the

37 WELANDER, 2003, p. 238.

38 AITCHISON, 2000, p. 150.

39 The Independent, 04.07.1996.

40 Alex Salmond in HAMILTON, 2008, p. viii: "The final return of the stone by a Tory Government in 1996 was meant to placate Scottish feelings". DEVINE, 2012, p. 615 argues that the return of the stone of Destiny from Westminster Abbey "must rank as an especially fine example of the invention of tradition". However, this was not

stone's return to Scotland in November 1996. He was disappointed that the stone was *quasi* just being lent and in fact remained in the possession of the royal family. Thus, despite the transfer of the stone to Edinburgh, an example was not set for Scottish independence. Rather, even in Edinburgh Castle the stone remained a memory box for the Unionist history of Scotland and England.[41]

The Labour Party under Tony Blair gained their electoral victory in 1997 among other things because they had given high priority to devolution. [42] His government had a referendum held in September 1997 in which over 74 percent of voters spoke in favour of a Scottish parliament. The *Scotland Act* was passed in November 1998 and the establishment of a Scottish parliament approved. The first elections took place in May 1999, and in July the newly elected members assembled for the first time.[43] It was then even possible to produce a connection between the stone's return to Scotland and the constitution of a parliament, for the Gaelic prophecy seemed to have come true: "Unless the fates shall faithless prove, And prophets voice be vain. Where'er this sacred Stone is found, the Scottish race shall reign".[44]

In 2006, on the tenth anniversary of the stone's return to Scotland, a discussion flared up again where it should have its best place in Scotland. Murdo Fraser (deputy head of the Conservatives) made the proposal in the Scottish parliament that the stone should be taken to Scone because there were no historical, political, constitutional or economic reasons for the display of the stone in Edinburgh. The stone had always been in Scone and it was now time to return it to its rightful place. This would also give the region an impetus to tourism because people would make their way to Scone to see the stone. The SNP member, John Swinney, supported the move: "It is an iconic image; it is part of the great distinguished history of our country".[45] However, this proposal to bring the stone back to its medieval abode was not taken up, either.

an invention of tradition but rather the use of cultural memory in a current political debate.

41 HAMILTON, 2008, p. 210: "That stone belongs not to any royal family but to the people of Scotland".

42 JEFFERY, 2010, pp. 33-40. In retrospect Tony Blair assessed the devolution policy as a tricky game, because one could not be certain "where nationalist sentiment ends and separatist sentiment begins". Tony Blair's quotation in The Daily Telegraph, 01.09.2010.

43 DEVINE, 2012, p. 617.

44 Quotation in HAMILTON, 2008, p. 7.

45 Stone's destiny is to sit in castle, 2006.

The stone filmed in 2008

In 2007, the Scottish National Party won 31 percent of the votes in the elections to the Scottish Parliament and Alex Salmond became First Minister of a government led by the SNP. According to the Scotland Act of 1999, the Scottish Parliament has legislative powers in the fields of education, agriculture, justice, health and in fixing rates of taxation. In these fields of politics the Scots have been able to act for the most part independently since then and thus fundamental demands for greater political self-determination were fulfilled. Consequently, the political and constitutional position of Scotland within the UK was quite satisfying for the majority of Scots at this time.

In this situation, a film entitled *Stone of Destiny* opened in the cinemas in autumn 2008 in which the history of the robbery (or abduction, respectively) of the stone by the students under the leadership of Ian Hamilton was recounted.[46] One can regard this film as an attempt by memory makers to create an – as they probably thought – important episode in the Scottish struggle for self-government and national pride accessible to audiences at the beginning of the twenty-first century. Just like Ian Hamilton in 1950, the film team also wanted to make audiences proud of being Scottish. But the reactions to this form of presentation of history were not uniform. There were cultural authorities who spoke up for an official memory, such as e.g. film critics who did not find this form of reminiscence work on the collective memory particularly interesting or successful.[47] But there were also very positive reactions from members of audiences,[48] so that the students' "heroic feat" in 1950 apparently had a place

46 Ian Hamilton had first published his report of the events under the title *No Stone Unturned* in 1952; the text then appeared in 1991 with the title *The Taking of the Stone of Destiny* and finally an expanded version was published in 2008 as *Stone of Destiny* in connection with the filming.

47 "Nationalist sentiment is tricky to put into words and the painting-by-numbers script too often comes across as awkward and hollow", EDG, 2008. The review in The Scotsman: "There really isn't much you can do with a script full of patronizing platitudes that spell out the film's themes in 72-point bold capital letters", Film review, 2008.

48 13 of 18 comments in the Internet Movie Database assess the film as very well worth seeing and as a contribution towards strengthening Scottish national pride, Stone of Destiny (2008).

in the "vernacular memory".[49] Perhaps the film did touch the Scottish souls of some members of audiences, and when watching the film they felt the way Ian Hamilton had done when he was able to touch the stone in 1950. In an interview shortly after the film's premiere, he recalled: "I felt I was holding Scotland's soul when I touched it for the first time".[50]

In connection with the release of the film, the question of the genuineness of the stone, which is to be seen in Edinburgh Castle, was raised again. The First Minister, Alex Salmond, again took up the opinion that had often been advocated before, namely that Edward I had already received a fake from the Abbot of Scone in 1296.[51] This view is based on the assumption that the Scots would not have simply handed over their most important symbol of political independence. However, even if a fake stone did not come to England already in 1296, then perhaps a false stone was deposited in Arbroath Abbey on Easter 1951 and the original was hidden somewhere up in the North. In the general memory, the idea that the stone, as the symbol and memory box for Scottish self-government and independence, had never left the country remained very attractive. However, this played a subordinate role in the political debates and in the interpretation of the significance of the stone for Anglo-Scottish relations in the twentieth century. The artefact now displayed in Edinburgh fulfils its function as a memory aid and interpretation aid for the past, regardless of whether or not it is the genuine coronation stone from the thirteenth century.

Conclusion

The coronation stone of the Scottish kings was used in the twentieth century as a vehicle for the selection and interpretation of the political relationship between England and Scotland in past centuries. Like a prism, it has captured various epochs in the history of political-cultural memory.[52] It served the actors in the debates about Scotland's political independence to put historical arguments into concrete terms. Of the various possibilities of interpretation,

49 For the differentiation of "official memory" and "vernacular memory", see GREEN, 2008, p. 113.

50 CRAIG, 2008.

51 Salmond: 'Stone of Destiny is fake', 2008.

52 ASSMANN, 2011, p. 117.

the actors have, above all, brought forward two concepts for recalling Scottish or Anglo-Scottish history on the basis of the stone into the debate and then advocated them in an active and committed manner in each case: The interpretation that the stone had symbolised Scottish freedom and political independence over the centuries competed with the interpretation that, since 1707 at the latest, the stone had been a memory box for the union of Scotland and England and for Scotland within the United Kingdom. The stone is thus one of the artefacts which assume important functions in the choice of what it is intended to recall. It was a carrier of political and institutional ideas over the centuries and therefore a means for cultural transfer in a diachronic mode.

For the young nationalists around Ian Hamilton at the beginning of the 1950s, the stone embodied the cultural memory of a free and politically independent Scotland; it was a witness to that past in which the Scots had defended a special political culture different from the English.[53]

In 1996, it was used by the government under John Major in an attempt to reconcile the two dominant but also diverging memory traditions linked with the stone as a memory box by the transfer back to its country of origin. The acknowledgement of an independent Scottish history was thus expressed, however, without drawing the consequence from this of also granting the Scots self-determination. The memory in Scotland preferred independence, and therefore the transfer of the stone was disputed. As a symbolic measure to placate the Scottish wish for independence and to ward off demands for devolution, thus self-government, it did not work. By comparison with the situation in 1950/51 it becomes clear that the living memory is being interpreted for the political interests of the present. For this reason, the meaning of the coronation stone as a bearer of the memory of Scottish independence and political self-determination has changed. When the students abducted the stone from Westminster Abbey, they wanted thus to arouse or revive their compatriots' national awareness. They were decidedly concerned about a symbol policy with the help of the stone. In the mid-1990s, however, a symbol policy with the help of the transfer of the stone could no longer distract from the demands for self-government. For nationally minded Scots a concrete change in structure was decisive – a parliament, in which Scottish members decide on Scottish matters. The handling of the coronation stone as a memory

53 In this respect the stone is a store in which knowledge of political culture can be transferred over long periods of time regardless of person; ASSMANN, 2008, pp. 111-118; LANDWEHR, 2009, pp. 52-54.

box is an example for the fact that memory in modern societies can no longer be controlled by an elite. There are various memory cultures which compete with each other over the interpretation of the past. That is then a process in which artefacts, such as the coronation stone, are of great significance, because they circulate and influence their surroundings.[54]

Since May 2011, the SNP has absolute majority (69 out of 129 seats) in the Scottish parliament.[55] It had campaigned with the promise, in the event of an electoral success, to hold a referendum in the following legislative period on Scotland's withdrawal from the United Kingdom. In October 2012, Alex Salmond and the English premier David Cameron signed an agreement that envisages the Scots' referendum on independence within a period of two years.[56] The vote will take place on 18 September 2014 and Scottish electors may then answer the question: "Should Scotland be an independent country: yes/no?"[57]

List of References

Sources

Bis die Engländer froh sind, in: Der Spiegel 7 (1950), pp. 18-20, http://www.spiegel.de/spiegel/print/d-44447390.html, 10.02.2014.

CARRELL, SEVERIN, Scottish government changes wording of independence referendum question, in: The Guardian 30.01.2013a, http://www.theguardian.com/politics/2013/jan/30/scottish-government-wording-independence-referendum-question, 10.02.2014.

CARRELL, SEVERIN, Alex Salmond announces Scottish independence referendum date, in: The Guardian 21.03.2013b, http://www.theguardian.com/politics/2013/mar/21/scottish-independence-referendum-date 10.02.2014.

54 NEUMANN/ZIEROLD, 2012, pp. 225-248.

55 SPARROW, 2011.

56 WATT/CARRELL, 2012.

57 CARRELL, 2013a. The electoral commission pushed through this wording against the proposal by Alex Salmond who had phrased it: "Do you agree that Scotland should be an independent country?" In this it was criticised that electors would be unduly influenced by "agree" to vote with "Yes". Alex Salmond publicly announced the date for the referendum at the end of March 2013; see CARRELL, 2013b.

CRAIG, OLGA, Ian Hamilton on Stone of Destiny: I felt I was holding Scotland's soul, in: The Telegraph 14.12.2008, http://www.telegraph.co.uk/culture/film/3743946/Ian-Hamilton-on-Stone-of-Destiny-I-felt-I-was-holding-Scotlands-soul.html, 10.02.2014.

EDG, Stone of Destiny Film Review, in: EdinburghGuide.com 19.06.2008, http://www.edinburghguide.com/festival/2008/edinburghfilmfestival/stoneofdestinyfilmreview, 27.11.2013.

Film review: Stone of Destiny, in: The Scotsman 26.06.2008, http://www.scotsman.com/news/film-review-stone-of-destiny-1-1173907, 26.11.2013.

House of Commons Debate Stone of Destiny 16.07.1996, in: Hansard, Column 1050-1058, http://www.publications.parliament.uk/pa/cm199596/cmhansrd/vo960716/debtext/60716-34.htm, 20.03.2013.

House of Commons Debate Stone of Destiny 03.07.1996, in: Hansard, Column 973-977, http://www.publications.parliament.uk/pa/cm199596/cmhansrd/vo960703/debtext/60703-23.htm, 20.03.2013.

No trace of missing Stone of Destiny – already over the border?, in: The Guardian 27.12.1950, http://www.theguardian.com/news/1950/dec/27/mainsection.fromthearchive, 10.02.2014.

Return of the Stone, in: The Guardian 12.04.1951, http://century.theguardian.com/1950-1959/Story/0107888,00.html, 10.02.2014

Salmond: 'Stone of Destiny is fake', in: The Scotsman 14.06.2008, http://www.scotsman.com/news/salmond-stone-of-destiny-is-fake-1-1433959, 10.02.2014.

SPARROW, ANDREW, AV referendum result – Friday 6 May 2011, in: The Guardian 06.05.2011, http://www.theguardian.com/politics/blog/2011/may/06/av-referendum-result-live-blog, 10.02.2014.

Stone of Destiny (2008), in: IMDb, http://www.imdb.com/title/tt1037156/?ref_=fn_al_tt_1, 27.11.2013.

Stone's destiny is to sit in castle, in: The Scotsman 14.12.2006, http://www.scotsman.com/news/politics/top-stories/stone-s-destiny-is-to-sit-in-castle-1-734277, 10.02.2014.

STONES, E.L.G. (Ed.), Anglo-Scottish Relations, 1174-1328. Some Selected Documents, Oxford 1965, pp. 329-341.

[Unknown Author], [Unknown Title], in: The Independent 04.07.1996.

WATT, NICHOLAS/CARRELL, SEVERIN, Scottish referendum countdown begins with Cameron visit to Salmond, in: The Guardian 15.10.2012, http://www.theguardian.com/politics/2012/oct/15/scottish-referendum-countdown-begins-cameron-salmond, 10.02.2014.

Secondary Literature

AITCHISON, NICK, Scotland's Stone of Destiny, Myth, History and Nationhood, Stroud 2000.

ASSMANN, ALEIDA, Cultural Memory and Western Civilization. Functions, Media, Archives, Cambridge 2011.

ASSMANN, JAN, Communicative and Cultural Memory, in: Cultural Memory Studies. An international and interdisciplinary Handbook, ed. by ASTRID ERLL/ANSGAR NÜNNING, Berlin 2008, pp. 111-118.

BARROW, G.W.S., Robert Bruce and the community of the Realm of Scotland, 4th ed., Edinburgh 2005.

ID., The Removal of the Stone and Attempts at Recovery, to 1328, in: The Stone of Destiny. Artefact and Icon, ed. by RICHARD WELANDER et al., Edinburgh 2003a, pp. 199-205.

ID. (Ed.), The Declaration of Arbroath, Edinburgh 2003b.

BROWN, MICHAEL, The Wars of Scotland, 1214-1371, Edinburgh 2004.

BURNET, CHARLES G./TRABAHAM, CHRISTOPHER G.: The Honours of Scotland. The Story of the Scottish Crown Jewels, Edinburgh 2001.

DEVINE, THOMAS M., The Scottish Nation. A Modern History, London 2012.

GREEN, ANNA, Cultural History, Houndmills 2008.

HAMILTON, IAN: On Identity, 15.02.2012, http://www.ianhamiltonqc.com/blog/?p=507, 26.11.2013.

ID., Stone of Destiny, Edinburgh 2008.

ID., No Stone Unturned. The story of the Stone of Destiny, London 1952.

HARVIE, CHRISTOPHER, Scotland and Nationalism. Scottish Society and Politics, 1707-1994, London 1998.

HILL, PETER, The Stone of Destiny examined: an overview and Discussion, in: The Stone of Destiny. Artefact and Icon, ed. by RICHARD WELANDER et al., Edinburgh 2003, pp. 11-31.

JEFFERY, CHARLIE, Devolution: Auflösung des Vereinigen Königreichs?, in: Aus Politik und Zeitgeschichte 49 (2010), pp. 33-40.

Diebesgut in Ihrer Kirche, in: Der Spiegel 17 (1951), p. [illegible]2, http://www.spiegel.de/spiegel/print/d-29193764.html, 10.02.2014.

LANDWEHR, ACHIM, Kulturgeschichte, Stuttgart 2009.

LEVITT, IAN, Britain, the Scottish Covenant Movement and Devolution, 1945-1950, in: Scottish Affairs 22 (1998), pp. 33-58.

MUNRO, GRAEME, The Stone of Destiny in Modern Times, in: The Stone of Destiny. Artefact and Icon, ed. by RICHARD WELANDER et al., Edinburgh 2003, pp. 225-233.

NEUMANN, BIRGIT/ZIEROLD, MARTIN, Cultural Memory and Memory Cultures, in: Travelling Concepts for the Study of Culture, ed. by BIRGIT NEUMANN/ANSGAR NÜNNING Berlin 2012, pp. 225-248.

NORA, PIERRE, Zwischen Geschichte und Gedächtnis, Berlin 1990.

ROGGE, JÖRG, Kämpfen, Verhandeln, Verträge schließen. Zu den Praktiken der Konfliktführung und Konfliktbewältigung in den englisch-schottischen Auseinandersetzungen um 1300, in: Konfliktbewältigung und Friedensstiftung im Mittelalter, ed. by ROMAN CZAJA et al., Toruń 2012, pp. 101-116.

STEVENSON, WENDY B., The Treaty of Northampton (1290). A Scottish Charter of Liberties? In: Scottish Historical Review (2007), pp. 1-15.

WELANDER, RICHARD, The Events of 1996, in: The Stone of Destiny. Artefact and Icon, ed. by RICHARD WELANDER et al., Edinburgh 2003, pp. 235-259.

An Epilogue

Reflections on Working with the Concept of Memory Box

CATHLEEN SARTI, ALEXANDRA SCHÄFER

Dealing with the concept of memory box was more than a theoretical approach to cultural exchange, as in practice, cultural exchange has also been going on between the two parts of the project group. Our Finnish-German discussions about the concept and every article in this volume revealed some differences in our academic cultures, even though all of our discussions were in the third language English, and thus oriented on a different approach to academic culture. Aside from such different practices, the meetings and constant online-discussion, we showed that most accordance was achieved between researchers focusing on similar time periods: the similarities of the research subjects were more important than the differences of the scholars' culture. The surplus of working in a binational group was certainly to have our own assumptions questioned and ideas, which were taken-for-granted, challenged.

When we first started discussing different ways of cultural transfer and cultural exchange, we soon discovered Roeck's concept of memory box. Since it resonated with all of us, we chose it to explore cultural transfer in more depth. Keeping the concept in mind, we nonetheless tried to adapt our research interests to this concept – and sometimes, this just did not work. The concept of memory box turned out to be one possible approach to cultural transfer. One which was especially strong when processes of transfer and aspects of collective memory came together, because the approach allowed to combine those two in focusing on one element (the box). When either transfer or memory was not in the centre of research, or when there was not one thing to focus on, the approach did not work. We do think it important to mention this inaptitude of the concept as well as our positive experiences with it.

We see the surplus mostly in the possibility to combine synchronic and diachronic transfer processes, in its concreteness by focusing on one element as an anchor for memories (*Erinnerungsanker*). This focus on one element, its *isolation* by the researcher, could be criticised as achronistic, since nothing is ever really isolated from its context. However, using exactly this method of identifying an element, thereby isolating it, and looking at it in its original context and/or several other contexts when it was later displaced, made cultural transfer tangible. This (artificial) isolation made it also possible to concentrate on the different ways, people made sense of these boxes or elements.

After two years of working on our articles as well as on and with the concept, we judge our approach to be especially apt for combining different aspects of cultural transfer as well as for dealing with collective memory.

By comparing our articles on an abstract level and having more case studies, it will be possible to learn more about general aspects e.g. of characteristics of memory boxes, of the way actors use these memory boxes, of similarities and differences in opening moments, and of the relationship between memory box and public. The concept of memory box should be used further, e.g. to answer these questions on the meta-level. Nonetheless, the memory box-approach should not be confused with an entire theoretical system that opens up new questions or changes the way scholars see the past. It allows for an in-depth-look at certain elements in their context and provides a specific approach within the concept of cultural transfer.

LIST OF CONTRIBUTORS

HETA AALI is a doctoral candidate in Cultural History at the University of Turku, Finland. Her research interests are cultural history of France, nineteenth-century French historiography, gender history and history of French queenship.
Contact: heta.aali@utu.fi

KRISTINA MÜLLER-BONGARD is a research assistant in the Research Unit Historical Cultural Sciences at the University of Mainz, Germany. Her research interests are art, art literature and theory in the early modern period, the history of art collections, and the political-religious staging of violence as well as its socio-cultural perception.
Contact: muellkr@uni-mainz.de

ASKO NIVALA is a doctoral candidate in Cultural History, University of Turku. His research focuses on German early Romanticism and especially on Friedrich Schlegel. His other interests include Heinrich von Kleist and the recent theoretical discussion on posthumanism and political theology.
Contact: aeniva@utu.fi

ANNA-LEENA PERÄMÄKI is a doctoral candidate in Cultural History, University of Turku. Her research interests include cultural history of writing, autobiographical sources, women and children in the Holocaust and daily life in World War II.
Contact: alpera@utu.fi

JÖRG ROGGE is Professor of History, Middle Ages, at the University of Mainz. He is also Spokesperson of the Special Research Group Historical Cultural Sciences, Mainz. His main research interests are methods and theory of historical cultural sciences and politics and culture in Late Medieval Europe.
Contact: rogge@uni-mainz.de

JUHANA SAARELAINEN is a doctoral candidate in Cultural History, University of Turku. His research interests include cultural history of knowledge and art, early nineteenth century and theory of history.
Contact: jksaar@utu.fi

HANNU SALMI is Professor of Cultural History, University of Turku. He is a historian of the nineteenth century, especially music history, and has written on the history of media and popular culture. He is currently leading a research project Travelling Notions of Culture: Itineraries of Bildung and Civilisation in Early Nineteenth-Century Europe (Academy of Finland, 2012-2015). He is also a member of The Romantic Era Research Group (RERG) and a founding member of the International Society for Cultural History.
Contact: hannu.salmi@utu.fi

CATHLEEN SARTI is a doctoral candidate in Early Modern European History at the University of Mainz. Her research focuses on political culture in Northern Europe, including the British Isles.
Contact: cathleen.sarti@gmail.com

ALEXANDRA SCHÄFER is a doctoral candidate in Early Modern History at the University of Mainz. Her current research focuses on media and communication history as well as religious conflicts in early modern Europe, especially France and the Holy Roman Empire.
Contact: alexandra_schaefer@yahoo.de

MATTHIAS SCHNETTGER is Professor of Early Modern History at the University of Mainz. His research interests cover the Holy Roman Empire, especially the so-called "Reichs-Italien", the situation of the small principalities and republics in Germany and Italy as well as transfer processes in early modern Europe.
Contact: schnettger@uni-mainz.de